Undocumented Storytellers

Undocumented Storytellers

Narrating the Immigrant Rights Movement

SARAH C. BISHOP

OXFORD
UNIVERSITY PRESS

Oxford University Press is a department of the University of Oxford. It furthers
the University's objective of excellence in research, scholarship, and education
by publishing worldwide. Oxford is a registered trade mark of Oxford University
Press in the UK and certain other countries.

Published in the United States of America by Oxford University Press
198 Madison Avenue, New York, NY 10016, United States of America.

Library of Congress Cataloging-in-Publication Data
Names: Bishop, Sarah C., 1984– author.
Title: Undocumented storytellers : narrating the immigrant rights movement /
Sarah C. Bishop.
Description: New York, NY : Oxford University Press, [2019] |
Includes bibliographical references and index.
Identifiers: LCCN 2018016073 (print) | LCCN 2018038982 (ebook) |
ISBN 9780190917173 (updf) | ISBN 9780190917180 (epub) |
ISBN 9780190917197 (online content) | ISBN 9780190917159 (cloth :alk. paper) |
ISBN 9780190917166 (paperback :alk. paper)
Subjects: LCSH: Illegal aliens—United States. | Storytelling.
Classification: LCC JV6475 (ebook) | LCC JV6475.B57 2018 (print) |
DDC 304.8/73—dc23
LC record available at https://lccn.loc.gov/2018016073

A NOTE ON THE COVER

The cover image was photographed by artist and designer Lizania Cruz. Her project, Flowers for Immigration, features the personal stories of undocumented flower workers in New York. With the intention of fostering self-expression, Cruz invites undocumented immigrants working in bodegas to make flower arrangements in response to US immigration policies during Donald Trump's presidency. Flowers for Immigration welcomes empathy for undocumented workers and provides them with a means for visualizing their stories without revealing their faces.

CONTENTS

ACKNOWLEDGMENTS

The Eugene M. Lang Foundation, a James W. Carey Urban Communication Grant, the Weissman School of Arts & Sciences at Baruch, the City University of New York's Diversity Projects Development Fund, the Faculty Fellowship Publication Program, and a CUNY Book Completion Grant generously funded this project. I owe a debt of gratitude to Stephen Steinberg, Elizabeth Nisbet, Sophie Marinez, Eduardo Contreras, Trevor Milton, and Christian Gonzales for reading my work and sharing their fantastic recommendations.

My research assistants were invaluable. Greta Kastner's cheery disposition and determination made me look forward to the long days we spent together on the project. I have rarely met someone with the kind of unwavering attention to detail that Lauren Reeves possesses—thanks for always giving your very best. Nora Lambrecht's guidance in argument articulation and narrative writing was vital to the text. Kristi Ensminger, thank you for swooping in at the eleventh hour to lend your expertise.

To all the narrators who shared their stories: Your work stands alone, but I'm glad it has also found a home with this academic audience. I am grateful that you trusted me with your words, and for the chance to talk with you about how to better support immigrants and be an ally in the immigrant rights movement.

Thanks to my colleagues at Baruch and to my students in the Department of Communication Studies, the Macaulay Honors College, and the Marxe School of Public and International Affairs whose tenacity and intellectual curiosity inspire me.

To Bo, who so blinds me with admiration that I managed to accidentally thank him twice in my last book, thanks for setting an example of meticulous writing, being generous with your wisdom about the power of stories, and for letting me talk in circles while I sorted this book out.

I am thrilled to have the opportunity to feature a work of art on the cover of this book from Lizania Cruz, an artist and designer whose work centers the stories of undocumented New Yorkers in such an evocative and beautiful way. Lizania, thank you for your encouragement and generosity.

Thanks to those who invited me to present this work at various stages of its development: Christine Lohmeier, Andreas Hepp, Kent Ono, Alison Griffiths, Aldemaro Romero Jr., David Birdsell, and Tamar Rabinowitz. It was a pleasure to have opportunities to share the work with colleagues, students, and advocates whose feedback helped to shape it from its infancy.

I am grateful for the expert guidance of the anonymous reviewers, and especially to Hallie Stebbins and Hannah Doyle at Oxford University Press. Chapter 2 of this book is derived in part from an article published in a special issue of *Communication & Society* 31, no. 3, in 2018. Thanks to the other attendees of the 2017 Congreso Internacional de Comunicación, the journal's anonymous reviewers, and to Marta Rebolledo de la Calle for feedback on that piece. Chapter 4 of this book is derived in part from an article published in *Critical Studies in Media Communication* 34, no. 5, in 2017. Thanks to the journal's anonymous reviewers and to Robert Alan Brookey for the attention you gave to that piece.

To everyone at Mixteca, Make the Road, the New York State Youth Leadership Counsel, the New York Immigrant Coalition, Families for Freedom, the MinKwon Center, the New Sanctuary Coalition, the CUNY Sanctuary Group, and all those who work to protect the rights of immigrants and their families in New York City, thank you.

Undocumented Storytellers

| Introduction

You may have heard the world is made up of atoms and molecules,
but it's really made up of stories.

—William Turner, 1538[1]

MIGRATION IS A story—a series of stories, really. Some overlap and intertwine; many unfold in obscurity. Even though attempts at distillation have been made, there is no grand narrative, no simple explanation that can encapsulate the experience of migration. In fact, most migration stories are inaccessible: lost to history, forgotten, and sometimes—often—never recorded at all. The stories that remain are disjointed, partial. The migrant herself has a story, filled with hopes and uncertainties and ambitions. There is the story of her place of origin, left reluctantly or boldly abandoned. There is a version told to children, with the more frightening bits left out, and the version written in her diary—secret, confessional, the writing itself an act of healing.

These stories have many names and iterations. They are told around tables, at rallies, through artwork and poetry. They are scrawled onto protest signs, photographed, and filmed. Governmental representatives tell stories of immigration to encourage a particular political outcome; undocumented immigrants tell their own stories in search of understanding and empathy. Fear-mongering news media tell the story of criminals pouring across borders, while immigrant parents tell their children about a journey toward hope and a brighter future. The way the story is told has everything to do with its impact, which is why so many fight to tell it.

In this sense, all migration can be read through the lens of storytelling. I do not mean to suggest that migration lacks connection to fact or reality—on the contrary, migration is sometimes one of the most determining factors in one's lived experience. Reading migration as a series of narratives does not negate the push and pull factors that lead individuals to resettle away from their places of birth, but rather it opens a discursive space in which to consider how these material realities are constituted, reified, and remembered by way of political, cultural, and personal narratives about who does and does not belong. Migrations are stories in the sense that they are always being told and retold, constructed and interpreted, offered to audiences as arguments for the inclusion or exclusion of traveling bodies. Narratives mold a sojourner's new home in her mind before she arrives; a narrative guides a neighbor's response to discovering a newcomer's arrival next door. These stories hold the power to fashion the world around migrants—fostering some possibilities for movement and relocation while removing others.

The stories that follow in these pages do not represent all migrants but only a particular group: young adult undocumented immigrants growing up in New York City. The story of this group is one many are fighting to tell, and each party has a stake in the outcome of the telling—a "dog in the fight," to use a violent metaphor. More than 11.3 million undocumented immigrants live in the United States, and current immigration policy does not offer this group a path to citizenship. While at the time of this writing around 700,000 undocumented youth (less than 7 percent of the undocumented population) have temporary protection from deportation through former president Barack Obama's Deferred Action for Childhood Arrivals (DACA) program, the future of the program remains uncertain.[2] Therefore, thousands of immigrant and non-immigrant activists and allies have come forward in recent years to campaign for comprehensive immigration reform that would provide undocumented immigrants the ability to sustain their livelihoods in the United States and rectify their current lack of legal status.

Because the story of undocumented immigration is impossible to tell in full, it is told in fragments. This book is about who tells that story to whom and why, and about the audiences who listen and respond. Drawing from a mixed methodology—forty interviews with undocumented immigrants from eighteen unique nations of origin across five continents, critical-rhetorical ethnography of immigrant rights events, and narrative analysis of immigrant-produced media—this work interrogates the centrality of storytelling to the immigrant rights movement, offering broad insights about the power of framing and strategy in activism and social movements.

Though the United States is often exalted in political and popular discourse as a so-called nation of immigrants, even a rudimentary analysis reveals the penchant of US media for nativist portrayals of immigrants. Undocumented immigrants carry a double burden with respect to anti-immigrant portrayals. In addition to the general anti-immigrant sentiment at work in much of the media that engages with immigration, immigrants without legal status must bear the often misleading, even violent portrayals of "illegal" immigrants flooding the borders in uncontrollable waves. These pervasive narratives, combined with a constant threat of exposure and deportation, drive many undocumented immigrants to retreat behind a wall of silence. Despite the risks, a young generation of activists and media makers, anxious for their futures and emboldened by DACA and the proposal of the Development, Relief, and Education for Alien Minors (DREAM) Act, have been making the difficult decision to talk publicly about their immigration status and counter prevailing stereotypes through photography, writing, music, art, and film. By projecting their stories into the public arena, these undocumented activists attempt to refute blanket characterizations, trading anonymous narratives for individuality and revealing the determination of those who elsewhere have been vilified by presupposition.

To understand why those who lack legal status would willingly take this risk, one must keep in mind that many undocumented immigrants have no memory of, do not speak the languages of, and/or have no family in the nations in which they were born. The United States is the only home many of these individuals know; returning to an unfamiliar country—possibly alone—is an unfathomable option. Still, this group has limited opportunities for success in the United States. For many, the only option for survival may be working illegally without health insurance or other benefits for less than minimum wage while hoping for a change in US immigration policy. The ambiguity of an uncertain future pervades immigrants' lives on multiple fronts, leaving them—as Roberto Gonzales illustrated in his seminal twelve-year study of undocumented youth—in a perpetual state of liminality and limbo.[3]

It is from this context that this book explores the decisions of young people to tell the stories of their lives publicly in order to advocate for immigration reform. The individuals interviewed in these pages are determined because their futures depend on it; the risks to safety and security that many willingly take to become public supporters of the movement underscore the perceived power of self-representation and narrative activism. In this book, I argue that the future of immigration reform hinges on the power of storytelling and that the political impact of these stories depends on narrative strategy and framing. I advance this argument by talking with undocumented artists and activists who explain how they have grappled with and negotiated telling their stories in public, and have put these storytellers into conversation with foundational scholars of narrative's persuasive potential and limitations. In this way, I aim to recover underrepresented perspectives—to enfranchise voices that have historically been left out of academic research. My goal, while being mindful of narrative's limitations, is to demonstrate the power of storytelling to both construct and negotiate the material realities of undocumented immigration in the United States.

This work foregrounds particular instances in which undocumented storytellers have confronted prevailing myths and opened possibilities for conversation and exchange by sharing their own autobiographies in attempts to motivate audiences to action. By focusing my analysis not just on these stories themselves but also on how the storytellers strategize about their narratives—and restrategize when things go wrong—this study reveals immigrant rights storytelling as a dynamic and responsive process. Centering the perspectives of immigrant narrators avoids the danger of presumption about what motivates their stories and for whom they are intended.

In the following chapters, the narrators offer clear evidence of the power of stories to (1) counteract some of the isolation of living undocumented, (2) offer a kind of cultural citizenship in the face of their lack of legal citizenship, (3) provide a means of civic engagement despite the fact that undocumented immigrants cannot vote or hold political office, and (4) engage their audiences' analytical and emotional faculties as they share their experiences within the context of the immigrant rights movement. It would be a mistake to measure the efficacy of undocumented storytelling only by its ability to advance changes in policy and legislation. When one pulls back from the potential future of comprehensive immigration reform, one can see more clearly what these stories have the power to accomplish personally and culturally, in addition to what they can do politically.

Because I regard the unique power of narrative as unassailable, I do not shy away from illuminating the ways stories may falter and fail. Analyzing narrative's shortcomings may help to articulate some of the hazards to which stories are prone and fortify the potential of narrative in activism and social movements.

While much has been said about the impact of the ways immigrants without legal status are portrayed in political, popular, and news discourse, more work bringing into focus how immigrants themselves confront these representations and strategize about using their own stories is necessary. By revealing the role of personal and biographical storytelling in undocumented immigrants' precarious social status in the United States, I intend to demonstrate how, for these immigrants—to borrow a phrase from feminist activism—the personal becomes political.[4] Migration narratives exist in spaces simultaneously corporal (related to and affecting particular bodies) and corporate (shared and systemic). Individuals migrate, but the narrative arc of migration becomes illuminated only when set against the backdrop of the sociopolitical realities that fuel and frame it.

This study is driven by four overarching questions: How and why are young undocumented activists in New York choosing to use their stories as activism? What are the prospects and limitations of storytelling for developing a public and political voice? How do immigrant-produced mediated narratives abate the effects of isolation for undocumented immigrants and facilitate communal coping? By what means do immigrant activists confront foundational notions that predispose many US citizens to believe that the United States is simultaneously a result of the labors and dreams of an ideal class of immigrants and the victim of a new class of unworthy and illegal job stealers who refuse to "get in line" for citizenship? I address these questions using an intersectional and sustained analysis of the role of storytelling in the US immigrant rights movement.

I take as a starting point for this analysis Walter Fisher's *narrative paradigm*. Fisher's paradigm provides a means for considering how communicators manipulate the tools of storytelling as they send and receive messages—messages which themselves affect the lived experiences of the storytellers. Fisher's paradigm understands individuals "as storytellers, as authors and co-authors who creatively read and evaluate the texts of life."[5] Within this paradigm, individuals come to recognize themselves as both consumers and producers of the stories that shape the world they live in.[6]

In much of the existing discourse about immigrants, those considered fit to speak in the public sphere are the governments and media that frame immigration for their audiences, rather than immigrants themselves. In recent years, immigrant-led organizations such as United We Dream and the New York State Youth Leadership Council have fought to contest this trend by prioritizing immigrant self-representation in news media. But by virtue of undocumented immigrants' lack of representation in government and their inability to legally work in fields such as media, law, or education, self-representation still comprises only a fraction of the total mediated content about undocumented immigration.[7] In political and news discourse especially, American institutions appear to possess all the faculties of authority and rationality necessary for determining policy with regard to borders, rights, punishment, and citizenship, but immigrants do not. In Fisher's words, "the sort of hierarchy to which the narrative paradigm is inimical is hierarchy based on the assumption that some people are qualified to be rational and others are not." Employing Fisher's narrative paradigm allows one to recover the validity and rationality of immigrant narratives and position them alongside the narratives of those who speak about immigrants from positions of privilege, offering due consideration to each.

This egalitarian possibility is complicated by the reality that the debate over immigration does not, by any stretch of the imagination, constitute what Jürgen Habermas calls an *ideal speech situation*.[8] In an ideal speech situation, all involved parties are given equal time to participate and their opinions receive equitable public consideration based solely on reason, without the influence of power or hierarchy. The immigration debate, however, is deluged with power imbalances that affect both speaker and listener at every turn. The conflict exists *because* of these imbalances and is constituted by the ability of one party to speak on behalf of and presume authority over the other.

Consider the following five discrepancies. (1) Positive immigration rhetoric was a hallmark of the Obama administration, yet more undocumented immigrants were deported during Barack Obama's tenure in office than at any prior point in US history.[9] (2) Both conservative and liberal economic reports repeatedly demonstrate the positive economic effects of immigration, but undocumented immigrants continue to face accusations of stealing American jobs and draining the economy.[10] (3) US media disproportionately represent undocumented immigrants as Mexicans who crossed the border illegally, but in fact Mexican undocumented immigration has been slowly declining since 2007, and the increasing numbers of Asian undocumented immigrants are much more likely to overstay legal tourist or student visas than to cross a border into the United States without permission.[11] (4) There have been repeated calls in popular and governmental discourse for undocumented immigrants to "get in line" to become citizens, but in fact there is no legal path to citizenship—and thus no line to join—for the vast majority of undocumented immigrants in the United States.[12] (5) Much existing scholarship has noted the penchant of US media to conflate undocumented immigration with criminal activity.[13] The myth of immigrants' disproportionate likelihood to engage in criminal activity is pervasive in political, news, and popular discourse and survives even widespread evidence drawn from the US Bureau of Crime Statistics that has led social science researchers to conclude that "the problem of crime in the United States is not 'caused' or even aggravated by immigrants, regardless of their legal status."[14]

These myths are able to survive even direct evidence to the contrary because not everyone in the United States possesses equal power to tell their stories.[15] While Americans born in the United States may be called upon to express their opinions toward immigration with votes, by participating in government, or through public statement in media outlets, undocumented immigrants usually cannot. Evidence used in public discourse about undocumented immigrants originates primarily from individuals who possess legal status in the United States. Citizens, legal residents, and elected representatives quite often speak about immigration, while immigrants *are represented*—the former group maintains active voice, the latter group listens as it is constituted, portrayed, and implicated through secondhand narrative. It is by way of this public telling and retelling of secondhand narratives that myths about immigration manage to survive even when built on precarious foundations.

In his systemic analysis of the ways news and other media constructed, over time, the idea that Latino immigrants in the United States are a threat to US culture and the US economy, Leo Chavez writes, "Such myths have organic-like lives of their own. Once given birth, they grow and take on ever more elaborate and refined characteristics until they are able to stand on their own as taken-for-granted 'truths.'"[16] Mythical "truths" about immigrants require less and less evidence for support as they become more and more normalized and naturalized within a culture.[17] Repetition stands in for proof; myths are reified and reinforced each time they are communicated.

In his *Mythologies*, Roland Barthes posits that myths always appear in and are sustained by communicative contexts. He writes that "what must be firmly established at the start is that myth is a system of communication, that it is a message . . . a mode of signification."[18] For Barthes, communication both creates and sustains myth. Stuart Hall continues this logic, showing how language serves as a medium for signifying practices that create shared cultural understanding. "Representation through language," Hall writes, is "central to the processes by which meaning is produced."[19] If we follow these accounts, it becomes clear that the power to produce meaning and sustain myths about undocumented immigrants is directly related to the power to control representative communication of the immigration narrative in public contexts.

One comes to hold such power through access to what Karl Marx calls the "means of production"—that is, the tangible and intangible resources required for the creation and dissemination of a product.[20] In mediated narratives of immigration, the means of production include both the resources and technology necessary to send messages through a public channel and the skills and education necessary for creating and implementing content. Because undocumented immigrants traditionally have not had access to the means of mainstream media production, much of the power of the representation of immigrants has historically belonged to others. But as the means of media production are becoming more accessible through digital technologies, and as immigrant rights organizations raise up immigrant leaders who promote the importance of the public telling of firsthand narratives of undocumented life, undocumented immigrants' stories are appearing in ever-growing numbers in American public discourse.

Situation in the Scholarship

Scholars in anthropology, sociology, and communication studies have considered the interaction of storytelling and migration; however, undocumented immigrants are often underrepresented in scholarship and popular discourse because they are an isolated and largely inconspicuous population that often avoids practices that could reveal their immigration status.[21] The studies that have provided scholarly accounts of undocumented immigration in the United States tend to focus on the Latino population rather than incorporating immigrants of different nationalities and ethnicities, resulting in few academic works that feature ethnically diverse undocumented voices and leaving many scholarly stones unturned.[22]

This project draws on and seeks to continue the work begun in pivotal existing research of the undocumented population in New York, including Alyshia Galvez's *Guadalupe in New York: Devotion and the Struggle for Citizenship Rights among Mexican Immigrants*, Sarah Mahler's *American Dreaming: Immigrant Life on the Margins*, Jason Pribilsky's *La Chulla Vida: Gender, Migration, and the Family in Andean Ecuador and New York City*, and Robert Smith's *Mexican New York: Transnational Lives of New Immigrants*.[23] While this research has been instrumental in providing scholarly insight into undocumented life across New York City, each of the aforementioned studies focuses exclusively on Latino immigrants, and all but Mahler's text focus on populations born in only a single Latino country. Extending this work by incorporating the voices of individuals across the spectrum of New York's ethnic diversity opens space in the current project to interrogate the ways undocumented status intersects with other identity markers such as race, socioeconomic class, and accent.

Welcoming non-Latino undocumented perspectives into contemporary research is especially timely given estimates from a Pew Research Center report showing that almost a million fewer undocumented immigrants lived in the United States in 2016 than in 2007. While undocumented Mexican immigration to the United States has been on the decline in recent years, undocumented immigration from Asia, Central America, and Africa is on the rise.[24] The individuals who narrate this project—born in Thailand, the Philippines, Colombia, Mexico, Spain, Albania, South Korea, El Salvador, Ecuador, the Dominican Republic, Peru, Bangladesh, Bahrain, Uzbekistan, Mali, Jamaica, Hungary, and Russia—reveal the myriad ways individuals encounter, interpret, and create public narratives of immigration in the United States.

This book is unique in its focus on the way undocumented immigrant activism is advanced through activists' autobiographical storytelling. To address the intersection of undocumentedness and narrative, I draw heavily from the field of communication studies. Traditionally, academic analysis of migration in the United States has been the purview of anthropologists, political scientists, and sociologists. But, as I will demonstrate, assessing the relationship of storytelling to migration through the lens of communication studies brings a tradition rich with insight to this area of inquiry. Scholars from this field have already made significant contributions that lay the groundwork for the current project. Specifically, communication scholarship has highlighted the power of discourse in the rhetorical construction of borders and belonging, demonstrated the relationship of representation of immigrant others to conceptions of and anxieties about nationalism and citizenship, and established the centrality of vernacular storytelling to community building and community exclusion.

Scholars in the field of communication studies have provided invaluable accounts of the contested narrative means in which immigrants are portrayed in media, law, and political discourse, and their resulting work advances broad understanding about the power of language and visual rhetoric to fashion the borders and boundaries that constrain immigrants and shape public understanding of the importance of border security.[25] Kent Ono and John Sloop scour the discourse surrounding California's Proposition 187—which would have prohibited undocumented immigrants from using basic social services—to reveal how anxious nationalisms manifest in a dynamic process of border negotiation. As they argue, "rhetoric *shifts* borders, changing what [borders] mean publicly, influencing public policy, altering the ways borders affect people, and circumscribing political responses to such legislation."[26] Lisa Flores applies and extends Ono and Sloop's argument in her own analysis of how the rhetorical construction of the US-Mexico border fueled the deportation drives of the 1920s and '30s.[27] Flores's research shows not only how communication surrounded these events but also how rhetoric about Mexican immigrants was foundational and central to establishing the public's understanding of the need for mass deportations. This scholarship demonstrates clearly the ways public communication about borders has direct and tangible implications for the individuals who are excluded or rendered "illegal" because of their movement from one side of a border to the other, and it serves my own project by illuminating what undocumented storytellers are up against and what is at stake. The narrators in this study extend the existing scholarship in this area by revealing how the stories they tell confront and contest dominant imaginations of borders. If borders can be discursively constructed and shifted, it follows that discourse may prove instrumental to the critique and dismantling of both the physical and ideological borders that constrain immigrants' lived experiences.

Beyond highlighting the discursive construction of borders, communication scholarship has elucidated the relationship of representation of immigrant others to conceptions of Americanness and anxieties surrounding nationalism. Radha Hegde asserts that "without documents or status, [immigrants'] claims for inclusion and very presence within the nation-state have precipitated public reengagement with discourses of belonging and unleashed widespread anxiety about the nation coming apart at its cultural seams."[28] The presence of undocumented immigrants draws nationalism out from a place of unexamined existence and into a realm where it can be challenged and questioned, in some cases causing anxiety in those who benefit from citizenship privilege. In *The Border Crossed Us,* J. David Cisneros offers an extensive historical analysis of case studies ranging from the Mexican American war in the 1840s to multi-city immigrant rights marches in the early 2000s to show how undocumented immigrants are rendered according to anxieties regarding the immutability and security of the nation.[29] These anxieties often result in discursive attempts by those who oppose immigration to advance the differences between Americans and immigrants. Tatyana Thweatt's critical discourse analysis of a local Midwestern newspaper over a ten-year span found that deleterious descriptions of immigrants are often accompanied by positive, ideological statements about America. Thweatt refers to proud, national-istic statements that exist throughout discourse surrounding immigrants as the "general strategy of positive Self-presentation and negative Other-presentation."[30] When immigrants are villainized, an opportunity arises for citizens to characterize themselves in contrast to outsiders, thereby reaffirming their own sense of belonging and reifying the importance of national borders. This finding is not specific to the United States and has been confirmed in other works of international communication scholar-ship. For example, Joachim Trebbe and Philomen Schoenhagen conducted a qualitative study of portrayals of immigrants in Switzerland and found that "perception of the other [always] includes the perception of one's own group and the feeling of being a part of this group."[31] This existing research suggests the promising potential of the strategy of immigrant activists whose stories challenge the perceived differences between citizens and immigrants. In many cases immigrants use stories to assert the similarities of their experiences to the experiences of other ordinary Americans, re-vealing their lack of documentation as the only barrier excluding them from full participation in American life.

Finally, existing research from the field of communication studies has advanced understanding about the role of personal narratives in interper-sonal exchange and community building. While most of this work does not relate directly to migration, there are a few notable exceptions. Karma Chávez offers a critique of the role of personal narratives in immigrant rights debates that I explore in detail in the next chapter. Likewise, Hegde demonstrates the ways politicians and journalists have strategically chosen and amplified preferred types of DREAMers' stories in emotional appeals to voters. In Chapter 3, the narrators in this project illustrate the effects of this selective choosing of narratives deemed as "fit" for public consump-tion at the expense of others that are not.

Even when studies of the power of storytelling focus on topics other than migration, they nonetheless provide productive insight into the une-qualed facility of storytelling as a unique communicative act. As Kristin M. Langellier writes, "Personal narrative performance is situated not just within locally occasioned talk . . . but also with the forces of discourse that shape language, identity, and experience."[32] For Langellier, understanding the capacity of storytelling requires considering not only what is said but also the forces that inspire and act on storytelling on all sides. Like Fisher, she considers how audience members become narrators of the narratives they hear, revealing storytelling as a dynamic and ever-evolving com-munication event that adapts according to context and goal. Langellier's approach lends theoretical support to this project; as I extend what is already known about what Langellier calls "storytelling in everyday life" to storytelling in the immigrant rights debate, I illuminate the challenges and limitations narratives face when those who tell them exist in precarious social and legal positions. In contrast to Langellier's work, the storytellers in this project resort to narrative in the face of exclusion from political engagement such as holding public office and voting. In the context of these constraints, the stakes of storytelling become formidable; examining these stories' function extends what is already known about this genre of communication and opens up new areas of theoretical exploration.

There is much to gain by welcoming these communication-centric approaches into the interdisciplinary realm of migration studies, and I lean on contributions from the field throughout this book. Exhaustive histories of US immigration policy and its corresponding rhetoric can be found elsewhere. My purpose is to invite undocumented activists into the academic conversation about the power and shortcomings of storytelling and to thereby extend understanding about the function of public narratives in the immigrant rights movement. Walter Nicholls contended in 2015 that "research still falls short of providing an account of how a legitimate and public voice for undocumented immigrants is produced."[33] Existing studies, Nicholls argues, "do not address the core issue of how undocumented immigrants overcome barriers, construct a powerful and legitimate choice, and assert this voice in the public sphere."[34] I set out to address this lack by foregrounding the voices of undocumented artists and activists who confront personal, social, and sometimes legal risks to tell their stories and assert themselves as deserving stakeholders in need of more rights than the nation currently affords them. The resulting work reveals these undocumented storytellers as powerful but constrained agents of change in the debate around immigration in the United States.

Method

This book employs methods of oral history, critical-rhetorical ethnography, and narrative analysis of immigrant-produced media. From May 2015 to November 2016, I conducted forty oral history interviews with individuals in New York City who have, for varying amounts of time, lived as undocumented immigrants. Immigrants may be undocumented because they entered the Unites States illegally, often via the Mexican border, or because they arrived legally in the United States with visas that later expired.

Oral history involves conducting in-depth, semi-structured, autobiographical interviews with open-ended questions that are designed to avoid anticipating particular findings. The interviews are long-form, conversational, and nongeneralizable since they tell involved histories of individuals in highly particular contexts. Oral history creates unique environments for the sharing, recording, and archiving of embodied historical narratives and allows for an intersectional approach that is not limited by the constraints of more structured styles of interviewing. In this method, qualitative, personal description takes precedence over accurate representation of past events.

Oral accounts of the past exist ubiquitously as means to pass down family traditions, knowledge of ancestry, or familial folklore. In these instances, individuals tell personal histories not in formal interviews, but by way of informal moments around the dinner table, gatherings of families during holidays or funerals, or upon welcoming a newcomer into a community. Oral history recognizes the significance of these personal histories and seeks to gather collections of them through interviews for the sake of analysis, comparison, and historical archiving. In oral history, unlike other historical methodologies, the unit of study is not a particular historical fact or event but rather the ways personal histories are preserved within individuals' memory and shared in communicative contexts.

The decision to employ oral history for this project had both pragmatic and symbolic implications. Pragmatically, oral history allowed me to "radically contextualiz[e]" the narrators' experiences rather than to consider them in isolation.[35] I draw on a model suggested by Stuart Hall for analyzing events in terms of their impact on individuals. Hall describes how any message, experience, event, or encounter is "decoded" according to individuals' "structures of understanding," or personal tendencies to react in highly specific ways based on previous knowledge, level of involvement in the experience, values, beliefs, or desires.[36] Oral history works to draw these structures of understanding into view by providing opportunities for narrators to talk at length about their lives and experiences rather than limiting the focus to a certain prescribed hypothesis.

Symbolically, collecting and archiving oral history accounts promotes the validity of multiple histories rather than only a few authorized accounts from a dominant cultural group. It contests the monopolization of history by individuals in privileged social positions and preserves for future individuals, students, and scholars accounts that may otherwise be inaccessible or prone to neglect.

As is often the case in research involving undocumented populations, I used multiple means for recruiting and had several trust-building conversations with some participants before conducting recorded interviews. Because I was especially interested in the ways individuals without legal status develop a public and political voice, I first began to identify participants through a review of New York–based digital immigrant rights activism. Reaching out to immigrant artists and activists via email, Facebook, or LinkedIn, I provided a brief description of the project and an invitation for a meeting and interview. Because of my focus on political advocacy, undocumented activists who have told their immigration stories publicly are purposefully overrepresented in this study. In order to understand what is at stake in the decision about whether or not to cultivate a public voice, and to incorporate the stories of individuals who have not gone public about their status, I supplemented the aforementioned recruiting technique with announcements about the project throughout the City University of New York, which currently enrolls around 6,000 undocumented students.[37] Recruitment became easier and more natural as I began investing myself more in the undocumented community in New York through attendance at pro-immigrant rallies, performances, and events; volunteering with local immigrant rights associations; and developing more immigration-related courses. At this point, snowball sampling helped to round out the number of interviewees and to increase the diversity of the immigrant-produced media I encountered. For example, a family member who works with Sonia introduced her to me; Sonia referred me to Esther; during her interview, Esther pointed me to her own digital work and some protest art from the organization CultureStrike, whose members I met later at the National Immigrant Integration Conference in Brooklyn and whom I invited to come speak in one of my classes.

My priorities during recruitment were diversity of ethnic background and of current status. The participants were born in eighteen unique nations of origin across five continents and currently hold a range of statuses—some have been granted asylum; others gained permanent residency and later qualified for citizenship through their own or a parent's marriage to a US citizen. Still others hold temporary protected status through DACA, which allowed some immigrants who entered the country before their sixteenth birthday and before June 2007 to receive a two-year work permit and temporary exemption from deportation.[38] Other narrators in this project continue to lack any legal protection because they were too old to qualify for DACA, lacked the monetary means to pay the fee, or refrained from applying for fear that their applications would be used to find and deport them after their two-year protection expired.

The average length of each interview was approximately one hour. To avoid the risk of perpetuating the pervasive underpayment of immigrant labor, after completing five pilot interviews I was able to secure funding so that each of the remaining narrators received a $60.00 gift card in exchange for their time. Table I.1 provides the name, date of interview, and nation of origin for each narrator. I invited the narrators to come to my office in Midtown Manhattan for the interviews and offered to meet them elsewhere if it was more convenient. In the end, likely because of local familiarity with Baruch College and the sensitivity of sharing a home address while undocumented, all but three of the interviews took place in my office at Baruch; I conducted Esther and Katherine's interviews at their respective workplaces at their request, and because Jin is away at school pursuing an undergraduate degree, we conducted our interview over Skype. Following the Oral History Association's recommendations, I prepared an interview guide of some questions that I asked each narrator; other questions were developed mid-interview and guided by the narrator's responses. The narrators range in age from nineteen to forty-two; all of them arrived in the United States before the age of twenty-seven. Though some knew about their immigration status growing up, many did not find out they were un-documented until their late teenage years.

I recorded the audio from each interview and had the recordings pro-fessionally transcribed. I worked with my research assistants to index the transcripts by arranging their content thematically to identify issues that were of concern to more than one narrator. In keeping with the Oral History Association's view that interviewee and interviewer are co-creators of a narrative, and because the barriers to education and work that undocu-mented immigrants face has led to their gross underrepresentation in aca-demic research, I have attempted wherever possible in this work to include the narrators' perspectives in their own words instead of paraphrasing. In the interview quotes that appear in the following pages, I have removed filler words ("um," "uh," and "like") and false starts.

Oral historian Kate Willink advises that interviewers maintain a crit-ical self-reflexivity throughout oral history projects that leaves space for reflections on the limitations of storytelling and the danger of generali-zation.[39] Though I appreciate and follow this recommendation, power is never absent in any methodology, and I ask the reader to consider the par-tial and constructed nature of any embodied account.[40] Oral history offers a public performance rather than a private or "hidden transcript."[41] That

TABLE I.I. Narrators by Name, Date of Interview, and Nation of Origin

NAME	DATE	NATION OF ORIGIN
Pang	6-May-15	Thailand
Chris (Pseudonym)	9-Jun-15	Philippines
Angy Rivera	6-Jul-15	Colombia
Sonia Espinosa	18-Aug-15	Mexico
Esther Meroño Baro	24-Sep-15	Spain
Praq Rado	19-Jan-16	Albania
Ricardo Aca	3-Mar-16	Mexico
Jin Park	14-Mar-16	South Korea
Gabriela Quintanilla	14-Mar-16	El Salvador
Freddy	15-Mar-16	Ecuador
Ximena	16-Mar-16	Colombia
Javier Zamora	21-Mar-16	El Salvador
Jon (Pseudonym)	21-Mar-16	Dominican Republic
Piash Ahamed	24-Mar-16	Bangladesh
Katherine Chua Almirañez	24-Mar-16	Philippines
Mitasha Palha	14-Apr-16	Bahrain
Francisco Barros	14-Apr-16	Ecuador
Josue Guerrero	19-Apr-16	Mexico
Ben (Pseudonym)	21-Apr-16	Uzbekistan
Jolie Walde	21-Apr-16	Mali
Felix Rivera	5-May-16	El Salvador
Ahram Kim	5-May-16	South Korea
Maria Luisa (Pseudonym)	10-May-16	Peru
Erik Romero	10-May-16	Mexico
Gloria (Pseudonym)	11-May-16	Mexico
Gaby (Pseudonym)	12-May-16	Mexico
James Jeong	26-May-16	South Korea
Omrie	15-Jun-16	Jamaica
Jenny (Pseudonym)	15-Jun-16	Hungary
Adam	15-Jun-16	Hungary
Jung Rae	15-Jun-16	South Korea
Natalia	27-Jun-16	Russia
Daniel	27-Jun-16	Philippines
David Chung	29-Jul-16	South Korea
Sam (Pseudonym)	16-Sep-16	Colombia
Kattia	21-Oct-16	Peru
Selene Muñoz	7-Nov-16	Mexico
Estefany Gonzaga	7-Nov-16	Mexico
Elainie Lendebol	7-Nov-16	Dominican Republic
Oscar	7-Nov-16	Mexico

is, narrators always chronicle partial accounts of their lived experiences rather than offering an exhaustive or complete view.

Authorities on the methodology of oral history have often cautioned interviewers to take precautions if, during the course of an interview, a narrator admits to engaging in some illegal activity.[42] Renowned oral historian Valarie Yow recommends that the interviewer stop the recording momentarily whenever a narrator ventures into discussing illegal activity to ensure the narrator's understanding of the risks involved in revealing this material.[43] From time to time in my previous oral history work, I have encountered narrators who reveal some past involvement in illegal actions, such as recreational drug use, and I have observed Yow's suggestion. However, all of the interviews in this project are predicated on each narrator's experience of living without legal status and, therefore, without exception, all of them discuss their participation in activity that is not legal in the eyes of US law.

Because oral history does not seek to produce generalizable knowledge, the Internal Review Board at my institution determined that review of this project was not necessary. In lieu of these protections, the project abided by the principles and best practices of the Oral History Association, which acts as the governing organization for the method,[44] and I employed the following five safeguards to mitigate potential risks. (1) The implications of participation were discussed prior to every interview in a conversation about the "deed of gift" that secured informed consent for each interview. Instead of including narrators' home addresses, as is typical in deeds of gift, I asked the narrators only to indicate the borough of New York where they live(d). (2) All participants were given the opportunity to use pseudonyms or first names only; several elected to do so. In these cases, the titles, locations, and specifics of the narrators' work that would compromise their anonymity have also been omitted. (3) Every narrator was assured that any question s/he preferred not to answer could be skipped or rephrased without inquiry. (4) After each interview, the narrator was offered an opportunity to create restrictions on what s/he shared. These restrictions included, in some instances, requests to withhold details that would reveal the immigration status of friends or family members, statements expressing the desire for the interview not be archived in a public library, and clarifications about or the suggested removal of one's opinion about certain public figures or members of government. (5) Finally, because the political precariousness of immigration to the United States intensified between the time of the first interview and the writing of this manuscript following Donald Trump's election as president of the United States, it was imperative for me to ensure the narrators' knowledge of and comfort with how their words would appear in this work. To accomplish this, prior to publication I circulated each chapter to all of the quoted interviewees and made changes in cases where the narrators desired to refine, add, remove, or clarify their perspectives.

With these protections in place, I honor the decisions of some of the narrators who still live without legal protection to use their real names and speak openly and boldly about the implications of their lack of status. These narrators' words are a performance of activism. I respectfully ask my readers to self-reflexively deny the tendency to make determinations about this group until you have considered critically the attributes that render some bodies legal while denying the legitimacy of others.

The findings discussed throughout this work are informed by my participant-observation at a range of immigration-related events, including pro-immigrant rallies and protests in Manhattan and Brooklyn, a strategic yearly planning meeting at the immigrant-led New York State Youth Leadership Council (NYSYLC), a deep listening event organized by immigrant youth, an undocumented storytelling gala, immigrant naturalization oath ceremonies at the Brooklyn Federal Court, the annual National Immigrant Integration Conference, and an immigration teach-in I planned and hosted with other faculty at Baruch College. These events provided insights into the ways stories about immigration adapt to and evolve within diverse venues, and they supplemented my digital media analysis of sites where conversations about immigration take place online. In addition to these episodic events, I also volunteer at an immigrant-serving nonprofit organization in Sunset Park, Brooklyn, where I teach weekly English classes to newly arriving Spanish-speaking immigrants and help to facilitate programming that offers legal support services, women's health resources, and educational initiatives. Because throughout the duration of this project I was simultaneously researching the immigrant rights movement and working in support of immigrant rights, the methodology for the ethnographic parts of this work can be understood within the framework of Aaron Hess's *critical-rhetorical ethnography*.[45] Hess describes this ethnographic method as one that "is not mere observation of advocacy but rather an embodiment and enactment of advocacy through direct participation."[46] Critical-rhetorical ethnography carries with it the benefit of allowing the analysis of emergent forms and manifestations of advocacy—in this case, storytelling. As Hess writes, "Rather than seeing deliberation as it *occurred*, rhetorical ethnographers see deliberation as it *occurs*."[47] Taking up this method has allowed me to engage in concurrent and analytical assessment and participation in instances of advocacy as they take place rather than offering only post hoc interpretation of events that occurred in the past. For instance, around the 2017 New Year, at the NYSYLC, I participated in a meeting designed to plan the organization's goals for the coming year. At this event, immigrant activists and citizen allies brainstormed and strategized about the kinds of messages and actions on which they would focus their efforts in the coming year. I listened as the leaders discussed emergent, not-yet-realized plans for the future, providing insight about the meta-messaging of immigrant storytelling and guiding my analysis of how activists conceive of the role of storytelling and how to maximize its effectiveness.

Like oral history, the method of critical-rhetorical ethnography requires a self-reflexive approach that does not ignore the privilege of my academic position and my American citizenship. After Donald Trump announced in early 2017 two executive orders that sanctioned the construction of a wall on the US-Mexico border and would work to significantly restrict immigration to the United States, I stood alongside undocumented activists in a protest in Battery Park, Manhattan. We carried similar signs and joined in the same chants, but my participation induced in me no fear of the legal repercussions of my attendance. For immigrants without legal status, the physical act of standing in the presence of police to advocate immigrant rights carries with it a risk of exposure, because if they are detained by law enforcement personnel, undocumented immigrants do not have the same rights and protections as citizens, including due process and government-paid lawyers. My role as a critical-rhetorical ethnographer allows to me advocate alongside the immigrants whose stories I study but not to place myself in their shoes or to hold the same stake in immigration reform as someone whose livelihood depends on it.

Narrative analysis of media is a method for analyzing how stories are told within artifacts, such as works of art, photographs, blogs, and essays. I follow Sonja Foss's guidelines for this method, which include identifying the *dimensions of the narrative*—that is, the setting, characters, causal relations, and so on—and discovering an *explanation for the narrative*—in other words, to illuminate the "explanatory value" of the artifact through a series of pointed questions.[48] The pursuit of explanatory value investigates the fidelity of the narrative, the cultural tropes it employs, its omissions, and the potential counternarratives it condones or represses.

Throughout this work, I incorporate narrative analysis of media through close readings of mediated texts that acknowledge how power, images, and language are inextricably linked. In each instance in which I provide some narrative analysis, it is with the understanding that meaning exists in people rather than in media. While narrative media analysis may reveal how style, format, framing, and other mediated cues suggest or encourage particular readings, only through encounters with media audiences can one determine the impact or effect of any message. It is because of this reality that this project forgoes the neatness and simplicity of a single method in favor of a strategic combination of the three described here.

All of the fieldwork for this project was completed in New York City. The city has a rich and varied relationship to immigration. About 42 percent of New York City's workforce was born outside the United States, and New York has a reputation for being a "sanctuary city" for immigrants because of its progressive policies like Executive Order 41, which forbids city services to ask clients or customers about their immigration status "unless it is necessary to determine eligibility for a benefit or service."[49] For reasons that may already be clear, precise data about the undocumented population in the United States is notoriously lacking. What data do exist are built from estimates and generalizations based on samples determined to be representative. New York State houses the fourth largest undocumented population in the United States, behind California, Texas, and Florida,[50] but almost 75 percent of New York State's immigrant population—approximately 301,000 individuals—lives in the five boroughs of New York City.[51]

New York City and Los Angeles house more foreign-born individuals than any other US city, and New York is unique: whereas the foreign-born population in Los Angeles is primarily comprised of immigrants from Central America and Asia, New York's foreign-born population is more global. The Migration Policy Institute estimates that that 37 percent of the undocumented population in New York is from Central America, 22 percent from Asia, 17 percent from South America, 11 percent from the Caribbean, 7 percent from Europe, Canada, and Oceania, and 5 percent from Africa.[52] The most common country of birth for undocumented immigrants in New York State is Mexico (20 percent), followed by El Salvador (10 percent) and Ecuador (9 percent). While the forty narrators in this project do not make up a representational sample of undocumented immigrants in New York City, they do exemplify the great ethnic and racial diversity of this group.

Because New York offers in-state college tuition to undocumented students at state-funded schools, because I recruited some of the participants in college settings, and because of this book's emphasis on activism, the population whose voices appear in this text represent a particular cross-section rather than a representative whole of the undocumented population in the United States. This focus should not obscure more wide-ranging realities of the US undocumented population overall, such as the fact that only 5 percent to 10 percent of undocumented immigrants in the United States attend college.[53] Existing work has focused on other important cross-sections of the undocumented population—such as migrant farm workers in Arizona,[54] Mexican college students and "early-exiters" in Los Angeles,[55] Latinos living in an immigrant enclave on Long Island,[56] recent border crossers living in San Diego County,[57] and undocumented parents of young children in New Jersey and Ohio,[58] to name a few. The narrators in this project—aspirational young adults in New York City who experienced the personal and social hardships of living without legal status—have much to add to the existing conversation.[59] They experienced the implementation of DACA and the failure of the DREAM Act; they watched as Barack Obama's pro-immigrant rhetoric obscured an unprecedented number of deportations; many of them stood in view of the Statue of Liberty during one of the largest immigrant rights demonstrations in United States history to raise their voices against Donald Trump's exclusionary executive orders.[60] This group has shown significant potential for political engagement in the US city that exists at the center of both historical immigration to the United States and contemporary immigrant rights activism.[61]

One must keep in mind when approaching studies of undocumented immigration that individuals are only rendered "undocumented" in contexts where documentation is required. Because legal documentation was not required for the vast majority of migrants throughout the history of the world, as Mae Ngai famously points out, undocumented immigration did not exist in the United States before the 1920s, when the federal government introduced widespread restrictions on particular migrants for the first time.[62] Alternatively, one could say that all immigrants before the 1920s were undocumented, and only after this period did documentation begin to matter. While power may exist in the extraordinary, it is more often evident in the mundane. In other words, discourses and techniques of power may be so normalized in one's life that they appear as naturally occurring realities rather than constructed techniques of control. When ideological constructs become domesticated—such as when the American public comes to accept that some immigrants belong and are legal and others do not and are not—one may fail to notice when power is at work. With this in mind, my purpose is not to establish undocumented immigration as unproblematic but rather to defamiliarize what is known about it on all sides while privileging the insights of storytellers with firsthand experience of life without legal status. I follow Lisa Marie Cacho, who demonstrates the importance of "taking what we know about criminalized statuses and making this knowledge unfamiliar."[63] The objective is both an interrogation of the norm and an analysis of this interrogation. I take a critical approach to the forms and manifestations of power that appear throughout the narratives in the immigrant rights movement.

A Note on Intersectionality and Interactionality

I maintain the approach throughout this book that power affects individuals' lives in ways that demand an intersectional view.[64] In the words of Audre Lorde, "There is no such thing as a single-issue struggle because we do not live single-issue lives."[65] Kimberlé Williams Crenshaw introduced the importance of intersectionality in law scholarship to demonstrate that neither power nor oppression is singular in its effect but rather intersects with multiple aspects of an individual's life, including race, gender, geography, age, education, sexual orientation, and occupation.

Karma Chávez builds on Crenshaw's notion of intersectionality in two respects by offering a theory of interactionality. Interactionality both resists the notion that oppression, identity, and social location are fixed realities in order to show the dynamic nature of these entities, and promotes a focus on "possibilities for creative and complicated responses to oppression."[66] An intersectional approach is paramount to a study of undocumented immigration because one's immigration status is but a single facet on a prism of identities, and members of this group also hold membership in multiple overlapping groups that may either increase the likelihood of oppression or alleviate it. Pairing this approach with Chávez's notion of interactionality allows for an illumination of the ways immigrants' social positions morph and evolve according to personal and political shifts in context, and also reveals the necessity of more work that focuses not only on immigrant oppression but also on immigrants' creative responses to this oppression.

One example of the centrality of intersectionality and interactionality to immigrant rights activism is the impossibility of having anything more than a superficial conversation about immigration without considering the impact of race. In *The New Jim Crow,* Michelle Alexander argues that "the dirty little secret of policing is that the Supreme Court has actually granted police license to discriminate" on the basis of race when immigration is in question.[67] She points out that in *United*

States v. Brignoni-Ponce, the Supreme Court ruled that police officers may take a driver's appearance into consideration when determining whether a car being driven near the Mexican border contains undocumented immigrants.[68] In such cases, racial exclusion and legal exclusion overlap.[69] Waters and Kasinitz suggest that race can even trump immigration status in American perceptions of outsiders; they remind readers that "two-thirds of the Japanese Americans interned after the attack on Pearl Harbor were U.S. citizens—in this case, clearly race mattered far more than legal status."[70] Some of the narrators I interviewed confirmed this perspective. Angy told me, "I'm not undocumented anymore, but I still get [people saying to me,] 'Go back you your home country. You're illegal.' That's something that a lot of my friends who are citizens, who are just brown people, get told. I think there's just a mixture of racism and ignorance."[71] For undocumented immigrants, race and status are constantly working in tandem. Piash suggested that part of the struggle of being undocumented is that "we're different. We don't look like regular white people."[72] Piash's use of the word "regular" here to describe white people testifies to the ways whiteness works as an unmarked norm in the United States.

Of course, there are undocumented immigrants who benefit from racial privilege. Esther, an immigrant from Spain who speaks English fluently with an American accent and identifies as white, suggested to me that her racial identity works to confer privilege upon her even as she simultaneously struggles with the lack of rights of citizenship and legality. Esther is consistently aware of this advantage and spoke with me about it plainly. "I look and I sound like a white American woman," she explained. "I blend in and no one ever question[s] me on my documents. Most people would assume I have dual citizenship when they found out I was born in Spain. There's no reason why they should associate me with being undocumented, because most people who are undocumented—people always think Latinos."[73] Whereas some immigrants exist at the mercy of a lack of racial privilege, others are able to harness the power of white privilege and even use it as leverage to downplay their lack of legal status.

Beyond looking at how the layers of an individual's identity affect one another, an intersectional/interactional approach also allows for a consideration of the context in which undocumented activism takes place among other kinds of activism. The immigrant rights movement does not appear in a vacuum but is influenced by other social and political movements. As undocumented activist David Chung explained to me,

I think that if you are against racism, if you are against people being discriminated against [because of] the color of their skin, then immigration should be a matter that matters to you, because that's really what these policies are. . . . If you are against racism you are for immigration. That's where I'm coming from. We're building across movements. We recognize that black people are getting killed everyday and that connects directly to our movement. People are killed crossing the border and we can't just say this is just an immigration issue anymore but this is an entire issue that is based on race.[74]

Race is only one of the other identities that intersects with immigration status. Immigrant artists have been diligent to highlight the interactions between the immigrant rights movement and related initiatives.

Favianna Rodriguez created the work shown in Figure I.1 after learning that three-fourths of migrants are women and children. "The print is a call out to feminists to embrace migration as a women's issue," Favianna wrote

FIGURE I.1. © Favianna Rodriguez 2018 (favianna.com)

when she posted the image to Facebook. Building connections across movements helps immigrant rights activists to garner wider audiences and enables those audiences to understand the connections between immigrant rights and other kinds of rights.

Readers should keep in mind that while this book highlights immigration and undocumentedness in particular, being an immigrant is only one aspect of the dynamic makeup of these narrators. They are also New Yorkers. They are brothers, sisters, parents, and children. Some struggle with life-threatening physical and mental health concerns. Others have ambitions and goals that have little to do with immigrant activism. Consequently, reading their stories exclusively through the lens of immigration would result in a reductive view. With this in mind, I have attempted to contextualize my intersectional/interactional view wherever possible, but I have not managed with so many narrators to rid this book of all essentialism. The reader must remember that what appears in the following pages is only a partial view, bound in both space and time.

Chapter Outline

This book is divided into five thematic chapters that trace the paths of undocumented storytelling as it appears throughout varied contexts in immigrant rights discourse. In Chapter 1, I introduce the role of narrative in the lived experiences of undocumented immigrants in the United States. Drawing on both existing scholarship and the narrators' observations, I work to theorize *reclaimant narratives* by illuminating the experiential, partial, public, oppositional, and incondensable nature of the narratives that appear throughout this book. In this chapter, I establish how the role of narrative in the immigrant rights context puts both storytellers and stories at risk.

Chapter 2 chronicles how young undocumented immigrants uncover their own immigration stories experientially—through interactions with parents and others, by attempts at pursuing rites of passage reserved for citizens, and as audiences of governmental rhetoric. The narrators recount their families' immigration narratives and reveal the personal and social effects of learning about their own status. I explain the power of public representations of immigration and why immigrants themselves are sometimes prevented from participation in crafting these representations. Finally, the narrators reflect on the processes of determining whether to cultivate a public voice and narrate their experiences in the context of activism.

In Chapter 3 I offer both theoretical and pragmatic contextualization as activist narrators describe the diverse ways they conceive of and negotiate narrative frames and strategies toward the goal of immigration reform. The chapter chronicles the public work of undocumented immigrants who use their own stories as persuasive evidence that immigrants deserve a path to citizenship, and the narrators discuss the power and limitations of different ways of framing immigrant rights narratives. I illuminate the strategies the narrators describe by way of textual analysis of some exemplars of each, demonstrate the ways members of the movement have campaigned for necessary shifts in the framing of their messages, and explore how these negotiations are promoted and implemented in grassroots activism.

Chapter 4 takes a closer look at immigrant activism online. Because many undocumented immigrants are prohibited from higher education and professional employment, much of their narrative activism has found its home on the internet, where production costs are low, amateur professionalism is the norm, and the option for anonymity is still vaguely present. Sharing their personal stories in digital spaces both enables and restrains immigrants in negotiating the effects of stigma affiliated with being undocumented, abating isolation through communal coping, and advocating for reform.

Unless stories of living undocumented extend beyond the immigrant community and have an effect on the audiences who hold the power to vote and advance changes in policy using the full rights of democratic citizenship, they have limited potential to inspire reform. In Chapter 5, I turn from undocumented creators to documented audiences to illuminate how undocumented storytellers conceive of and characterize their audience, and to demonstrate the ways that spreading information about immigration advances both knowledge and ignorance in American audiences. The narrators describe the challenges they confront when trying to engage American audiences and the implications of these challenges for the movement at large.

CHAPTER 1 | Inside Story

KATHERINE CHUA ALMIRAÑEZ remembers learning that she was *tago nang tago*. "I didn't understand what that meant as a kid," she recalls. "The label was there and I would hear the words, but . . . I didn't really understand."[1] Katherine was born in Manila, Philippines, in 1979. Her grandparents, survivors of World War II, brought her to the United States when she was eight years old and told her she was tago nang tago—a Tagalog phrase that translates as "always running or hiding" and a common moniker for undocumented Filipinos. Though she did not understand the implications as a child, Katherine would soon discover that these three words would change everything.

Katherine was ambitious in her youth. When she started high school in Queens, New York, she remembers, "I really started to discover this sense of leadership and desire for leadership in me." She helped to start a school newspaper and was nominated as a freshman to participate in a prestigious leadership training experience in Europe with one of her classmates. She was thrilled when the nomination arrived, but her hopes were soon dashed. "It came in the mail, and I showed it to my grandmother, and she just very matter-of-factly said 'That's not going to be possible.'" Katherine was devastated. "That was really the first time where I suddenly was hit with something where I go—Oh, this is actually going to *prevent me from doing things.*" Katherine remembers that day as a turning point in her life. "I think that was the first time where I started to dream small. I started to think small and I started to realize the shame in it. I started to see how I was different. I already felt a sense of apart-ness because I was a teenager and also because of what I looked like, and this was another layer of that. That was really the first time."

Since Katherine did not want her friends at school to know about her status, she was not sure where to turn for help. She recalls, "When I really needed it, the only access to information that I knew about legal status was the church across the street used to have a sign saying they were providing immigration support and it was in the basement, but it was for adults. I remember thinking, 'What about kids? What do they do?'" When she got to college, she started to write papers for her classes about immigration, but was careful not to implicate herself: "I would do assignments in the periphery. I would be interested in immigration, but I never talked about undocumented folks." She did sometimes use the library computers at the university to look up information about her status, and remembers, "I went online at the university, because I thought if I looked it up on my computer—[I was] paranoid that the government would track down my laptop and deport me." It was during one of these searches at the library that Katherine found out about the New York State Youth Leadership Council (NYSYLC)—the first undocumented-led immigrant rights association in New York. Soon after, she began to attend their events, and started "coming out very slowly."[2] But the process of becoming vocal about her status, as she had seen people at the NYSYLC do, left her anxiety-ridden. Katherine did meditation to try to keep her unease at bay.

Like many undocumented immigrants, Katherine's fear was not for herself: "I had this fear that if I was found out . . . I always thought the government would then try to find out about my past and it would then eventually lead to my grandmother. My grandmother was in her eighties and I was, like, terrified of that." Once her grandmother passed away, Katherine felt she had nothing to lose by sharing her story. "I just remember thinking, all I want is just to be able to go to work, have friends, feed my dog, and be of service in some capacity. I'm not asking for applause every time I walk out of my apartment. I'm not expecting anybody to revere my story any time I walk into a room. I just wanted to be acknowledged as a human being. . . . I want to be able to dream big and I want to be able to not have to lie."

She began with painting. "I just kept painting, until I found the strength or the permission to use words," Katherine remembers. In 2011, she wrote and directed a stage play called *Undocumented* that ran from August to October and toured around New York City. "Where do you go when you get tired of hiding, but [are] too scared to run? What do you do when you're not sure if you're a victim or a criminal?" the play's description asks.[3] In 2013, Katherine was featured in a short film called *Out of the Shadows,* where she tells her story candidly.[4] Today, she describes herself as a multidiscipline storyteller. As the program director for the Creative Arts Team at the City University of New York, she spends a good deal of time working with undocumented students who are learning to tell their own stories. Every year, on the anniversary of her arrival in the United States, she goes out for Filipino food to reflect on her journey and honor her heritage.

For Katherine, storytelling is inseparable from the undocumented experience, because, she explained, "The thing that nobody can take from us is our story." Still, she gets frustrated when narratives are oversimplified into binaries. "I don't like the way immigrants are portrayed because it's always in extremes. I'm either seeing the celebration of immigrants or the degradation of immigrants," Katherine explained with some exasperation. "Either they're [about how] undocumented immigrants are stealing our jobs and raping our people, or they're sad, sad stories and the families are being broken apart. . . . I just find it frustrating that in order to get attention, it has to be the worst story or the greatest story." These extremes overshadow the idea that immigrants are real people with lives that do not easily fit into a prescribed mold. "That's why I really appreciate stories that are just stories of young people who are undocumented who are *living*—just living their lives," Katherine stressed.[5]

To contest the dominant representations of their lives, the "celebration" or "degradation" of generic portrayals of immigrants, young undocumented people like Katherine have been making the difficult decision to go public about their status in conversation, online, and in marches and protests in favor of immigration reform. But while DREAMers have made a good deal of progress in instigating local conversations about immigration, their central goal of comprehensive immigration reform and a path to citizenship has yet to be realized. The DREAM Act has been proposed multiple times at the federal level and never passed. In June 2016, a tie in the Supreme Court stalled Obama's Deferred Action for Parents of Americans and Lawful Permanent Residents (DAPA) program.[6] In September 2017, President Trump announced an end to the DACA program and tasked Congress with determining a viable solution to the problem of the almost 800,000 young people that this decision would leave without protection or work authorization. At the time of this writing, Congress has yet to quell the uncertainty surrounding the end of the program, and DREAMers are left to speculate about what their futures might hold. These setbacks raise the question: What explains the discrepancy between the demonstrable social/political activation that immigrant activists have achieved on the local level and the elusive promise of comprehensive immigrant reform? Katherine's journey and creative work hold one answer.

Katherine's frustration the over polarized, extreme narratives that dominate the immigration debate clarifies the contested role of storytelling within the conversation about undocumented immigration in the United States. Stories—whether held tight, expressed creatively, or told secondhand in ways that feel foreign to those they portray—hold power both within and beyond the undocumented community. In this chapter, I argue for a perspective that recognizes the centrality of storytelling in the lived experiences of undocumented immigrants by theorizing a particular kind of story: I call these *reclaimant narratives*.

Reclaimant narratives are the experiential, partial, public, oppositional, and incondensable stories that marginalized individuals use to assert their right to speak and reframe audience understanding. As is clear from the narrators' perspectives guiding my project, this kind of storytelling is an act of *re*claiming the power to speak for oneself; although these autobiographical stories belong to those who have lived them, they have been usurped by others, with motives of their own, who hold the social and legal power and privilege to speak for or about undocumented immigrants to public audiences. Feminist poet Gloria Anzaldúa describes the necessity of a reclaimant practice when she asserts, "I speak, to rewrite the stories others have miswritten about me. . . . To achieve self-autonomy."[7] Like Anzaldúa, the narrators in this work are reclaimants who speak in order to rewrite stories that others have told about them. Undocumented immigrants who have appeared merely as characters in others' stories use reclaimant narratives to reposition themselves as storytellers and reframe public narratives according to autobiographical lived experience. These narratives do not exist merely to entertain or even to explain but to reinterpret and redefine who immigrants are, demonstrate the effects of a lack of documentation, and advocate for immigration reform.

Theorizing Storytelling

Stories draw their audiences in and encourage them to engage with both their analytical and emotional faculties. They can illuminate in moments of uncertainty, engage imaginations, and inspire action. For Katherine, the goal of storytelling goes beyond mere recognition. When she clarifies, "I'm not asking for applause every time I walk out of my apartment. I'm not expecting anybody to revere my story any time I walk into a room," she points to another goal: "I just wanted to be acknowledged as a human being. . . . I want to be able to dream big and I want to be able to not have to lie." Katherine's storytelling is a means to an end—an opportunity to shape the narrative of her life so that it is not shaped for her. But the power storytellers hold over their stories is limited; once told, narratives take on lives of their own, sometimes failing to persuade, often evading intended interpretation or impact. Sorting through the variables that determine a story's creation, telling, and outcome requires close reading and contextualized analysis.

Walter Fisher argues that humans are inherently storytelling creatures. They critically evaluate the ways stories are told—like Katherine's determination that immigration discourse disproportionately advances the "worst story or the greatest story"—and see themselves as storytellers capable of shifting these narratives. Fisher's work on narrative throughout the 1980s and '90s was foundational in establishing a communication studies approach to analyzing stories, and it has guided and been in conversation with the work of many of the scholars whose work I make reference to throughout this book. I take Fisher's paradigm as a starting point for this work because it blurs the boundary between speaker and audience, revealing how individuals become "teller[s] of stories that aspire to truth"[8] and allowing one to consider how every individual and group who encounters a narrative about immigration might bend and filter the narrative through the knowledge they have gained from stories that have come before. As Fisher writes, "Audiences do not ordinarily assess isolated arguments but respond to them as an integrated message, a supported thesis."[9] Certainly, immigration narratives weave throughout audiences' lives, supporting or contradicting one another and fostering both knowledge and ignorance.

While Fisher's narrative paradigm is quite useful for recovering a view of the ways traditionally marginalized populations participate in their communities as storytellers, and for considering the potential of reclaimant narratives to work effectively as arguments, it risks painting a utopian view of the role of storytelling in society. Fisher positions narratives as an antidote to societies ruled by experts who are presumed to be more rational than others. An expert-led "rational world paradigm," Fisher argues, is "a hierarchical system, a community in which some are qualified to judge and to lead and other persons are to follow."[10] This type of system fails its members by making the assumption that only elites with access to the tools of rational argument have the ability to contribute effectively to public argument. Enacting a narrative paradigm in place of the rational world paradigm, can, in Fisher's view, dismantle such a problematic hierarchy.

The applicability of Fisher's critique of the rational paradigm to the immigrant rights movement in this respect is clear—undocumented immigrants have been rendered unfit for public argument not only through the classist elitism Fisher describes but also through the illegality of the presence of their very bodies in the space where deliberation over their futures occurs. Their participation as storytellers who recount personal histories in service of immigration reform works to recover their right to speak and resists homogeneous and stereotypical portrayals— Katherine's decision to contest oversimplified and binary portrayals of immigrants exemplifies Fisher's rejection of the idea that "reasoned discourse . . . presents uncontested truths."[11] But stories cannot solve every problem, and sometimes they cause some of their own. As Robert Rowland has remarked in response to Fisher's paradigm, "Narrative modes of argument are not necessarily democratic."[12] In other words, reading communication through a narrative lens does not immediately dismantle hierarchies of reasoning or grant equal power to all speakers. Further, though Fisher suggests that people have a "natural tendency" to be drawn to stories that are "true and just,"[13] Barbara Warnick resists this logic by pointing out instances when stories have argued in favor of and been the direct instigators of violations of human rights, leading her to conclude that people still sometimes choose "bad stories" because of rationalizations or delusions.[14] Likewise, Gerard Hauser criticizes Fisher for being too "thoroughly committed to valorizing as rational 'the people's' storied reasonings."[15] Rowland, Warnick, and Hauser's responses to Fisher point to the necessity of opening to critique any instance of storytelling, whether hierarchical or democratizing, in order to temper the danger that its narrative might be considered infallible. To know the potential and limitations of stories within this modified iteration of the narrative paradigm, we must subject them to a critique that recognizes not only the ways they may attain primacy but also the ways they may fail.

My goal in problematizing Fisher's paradigm and explicating the ways narratives may falter is certainly not to dismantle storytelling's promise as a strategy for activism. On the contrary, it is to draw attention to and evaluate the strategies of specific actors who have harnessed this power successfully from the fringes of US society. By interrogating the limitations and risks of storytelling in the immigrant rights context within the framework of the critical-rhetorical ethnographic method I described in the introduction, I hope to uncover areas where negotiations in rhetorical strategy and framing may serve to protect storytelling from unintended consequences and work in service of amplifying the voices of those who hold little legal power to participate in policy and lawmaking.

Academics who discuss storytelling are not always clear about how they define the term; the word "story" is used to describe all kinds of discourses. I use "narrative" and "story" interchangeably throughout this work. Fisher sees stories as a series of "symbolic actions—words, and/or deeds—that have sequence and meaning for those who live, creative, or interpret them."[16] Fisher's definition has been criticized for its breadth— Rowland asserts that Fisher's work defines narrative "so broadly that the term loses much of its explanatory power"[17]—but I advocate a preservation of this breadth. Taking a wide lens view of storytelling equips a critical reader to detect the narrative structures embedded in all kinds of messages, to consider how emotion, drama, style, and language all weave together in narratives designed for particular audiences and are remade each time they appear.

Still, it is imperative for narrative critics to clarify and characterize the form and functions of the messages they assess. Not all storytelling has the same characteristics or potential. While Fisher argues that narratives are not specific to a genre, in this book, I do not set out to write about all genres of stories but rather a particular type: reclaimant narratives that are (1) experiential and (2) partial accounts offered as (3) public performances to (4) counternarrate prevailing discourses by revealing the (5) incondensable nature of the perspectives of individuals living without legal status. While the stories that undocumented immigrants tell in service of advancing immigration reform differ a good deal from each other, they hold these characteristics in common. This definition of story is unique, and so I will unpack it in sequence.

Stories as Experiential

Sharing autobiographical experiences both builds and dismantles the case against undocumented rights. As a central storytelling strategy employed on all sides of the immigration debate, both immigrants and those who oppose them claim personal experience as proof of their validity of their argument. The reasons for appealing to experience are clear—as the data surrounding immigration policy are complex and dynamic, experience offers a more tangible, and in some cases simpler, view. Moreover, citizenship and nationality are experiential phenomena; their importance is reified when both citizens and those who lack citizenship internalize and attest to the value or meaning of the nation. When Katherine remarks at the beginning of this chapter that "the thing that nobody can take from us is our story," she points to the reality that the stories that appear in immigrant rights activism are autobiographical—that is, they appear as embodied testimonies of the lived experiences of individuals rather than as broad or generalizable information. Katherine appreciates "stories that are just stories of young people who are undocumented who are *living*— just living their lives" because they counteract prevailing myths of faceless waves of immigrants pouring across the border with ill intent. But to know the implications of appealing to experience in storytelling, one must consider how experience is *used*. What counts as experience? And what authority is granted on the premise of experience?

A consensus definition of "experience" does not exist. In the conclusion of his historical account of the evolution of experience, Martin Jay recognizes the "warrant for wondering if the term means anything coherent at all."[18] Philosopher Michael Oakeshott declares, " 'Experience,' of all the words in the philosophic vocabulary . . . [is] the most difficult to manage."[19] But others are more assured. For James Carey, experience is closely linked to communication. He writes, "Our minds and lives are shaped by our total experience—or, better, by representations of experience," and he invokes Raymond Williams by asserting, "a name for this experience is communication."[20] This view reinforces the centrality of sending and receiving messages to one's ability to interpret events or encounters. In the context of immigrant activist storytelling, experience and communication are certainly inextricably linked. But Carey's equation of experience and communication does not reveal how individuals piece through their histories, choosing to communicate some and leaving out others altogether. Autobiographical storytelling is not the telling of all of one's experiences exactly as they have occurred but rather a strategic selection and framing of particular happenings that may change according to both audience and purpose.

Experience is a sticky subject because its ability to supersede other forms of knowledge and truth seems almost ubiquitously accepted. Raymond Williams argued in 1976 that "the general usefulness of experience past is so widely recognized that it is difficult to know who would want to challenge it."[21] He asserts that audiences often regard experience not only as evidence but as "the most authentic kind of truth."[22] But historian Joan Scott takes issue with the power that Williams grants experience because it fails to take into account the social locations of those who employ it—in other words, to suggest that all experiences are equally useful or persuasive ignores the hierarchies of power that would attribute a higher truth-value to some claimants of experience than to others. For this reason, Scott contends, "Experience is at once always already an interpretation and is in need of interpretation."[23] If we follow Scott's logic here and apply a critique of experience to the role of storytelling in the immigrant rights movement, it becomes clear that the subjugated and marginalized social locations of undocumented immigrants have a direct effect on their potential to employ experience effectively in acts of storytelling. This imbalance in power becomes particularly visible when immigrants' experiences must compete against citizens' experiences in confrontations about truth. To demonstrate, I will offer an example of competing experiences.

At the 2016 Republican National Convention, Fox News' Megyn Kelly interviewed Jose Antonio Vargas, an undocumented journalist and activist, and Laura Wilkerson, the mother of a man who was killed by an undocumented immigrant in 2010.[24] Addressing Wilkerson, Kelly begins, "You're in this arena where I think most of the folks here see this issue as you do, you know, you want a harder stance on illegal immigration. And you're sitting next to Jose, who is himself an admitted undocumented immigrant." In this opening statement, both Wilkerson and Vargas's lived experiences become more than personal; they serve Kelly as opposing representatives of two sides of a debate. On one side sits a frustrated and traumatized American mother who has experienced direct loss at the hands of an undocumented immigrant, and on the other, a man who is assigned to speak for and in defense of undocumented immigrants—a population that, Vargas reminds viewers, is roughly the size of Ohio's. Any counterpoint Vargas has to offer is already subordinated by the imbalance of civic power in the conversation.

"It's up to you to get in line and become an American citizen," Wilkerson tells Vargas. He responds, "Actually ma'am, there is no line for me to get in the back of." The following exchange represents a common point of contention in the debate around immigrant rights.

WILKERSON: You've had plenty of time.
VARGAS: Well, there is no process.
WILKERSON: Yes, there is.
VARGAS: I mean, if there was a process, I would have already done it.

At this point in the conversation Kelly interjects and remarks, "Jose, I understand your problem that you're identifying, but what about Laura's problem? Sympathy is nice, but they want it to stop. And they see the best way of stopping future murders by illegal immigrants is to keep them out of the country—and throw them out of the country." Here, Kelly indicates both her presumed full knowledge of Jose's position and an indication that Wilkerson's experiences demand more attention because of the validity of her experience. At the end of the conversation, Wilkerson repeats, "You've had long enough to get in line." Vargas raises his hand to speak but Kelly moves on to the next interviewee. Vargas's participation is over.

These kinds of appeals to experience—in this case, recounted personally by a mother whose son was killed by an undocumented immigrant—seem to suggest that when a speaker tells of some experience from a position of power, even a single encounter has the capacity to provide an uncontestable, complete perspective. To be clear, the issue in this scenario is not that the experience is false; it *is* the case that an undocumented man was charged with the murder of Wilkerson's son. But when singular instances of anecdotal experience are called upon as general truth-claims about the danger of "future murders by illegal immigrants" as a group, the speakers fail to conceptualize experience as what it is—a partial, autobiographical encounter that may or may not speak to broader trends and realities. Here, a privileged social position stands in for empirical evidence of a truth-claim.

In light of the power of privileged experience, I read the ways undocumented immigrants utilize experience in activist storytelling from subjugated positions as a defensive technique. Making a case for one's humanity through experiential storytelling is not required of all persons equally but especially of those whose rights to personhood are doubted. In her book *Social Death,* Lisa Marie Cacho demonstrates how undocumented immigrants have been rendered *"ineligible for personhood . . .* subjected to laws but refused the legal means to contest these laws as well as denied both the political legitimacy and moral credibility necessary to question them."[25] Read through this lens, the public telling of narratives of experience by immigrants appears as an attempt to recover the right to personhood in a nation where this right has been compromised. The gathering, recording, and sharing of experiences is a declaration that these experiences matter, that they should be preserved, that they belong within the canon of United States histories.

But undocumented immigrants' sharing of their experiences is not solely in response to or for the benefit of those who express anti-immigrant sentiment. Javier, a poet who was born in El Salvador and crossed the border into the United States when he was nine, told me, "People who are undocumented just sharing their story or having artwork that is about this experience—I think the more and more we have of those, the more a young person would see that it's okay to be undocumented and be a writer, to be undocumented and a lawyer, to be undocumented and be a doctor or whatever."[26] Daniel, who was born in the Philippines, agreed. "I think the more I kind of started studying why my life is the way it is and kind of understanding it on more structural terms, and I'm working with people who share similar experiences, it has helped me to kind of really understand that people are very dynamic people and are very different in their own ways," he explained. "For me, it's really a growth of more listening than talking, and seeing where people are at, and really who they are rather than me kind of already placing my preconceived notions about them."[27]

Reflections such as these reveal that public sharing of undocumented experiences serves a dual purpose—on one hand, to change the misconceptions of individuals outside the undocumented community, and on the other, to aid immigrants in relating to each other while simultaneously recognizing their differences. Javier's and Daniel's reflections testify to the fact that firsthand undocumented perspectives regularly highlight the specificity and singularity of experience. Experience reveals the humanity of those who have elsewhere been objectified and dehumanized, and, in storytelling, operates as a strategy to highlight differences between narratives in an effort to contest homogeny and stereotype. Experience as a rhetorical device, though sometimes presented as a complete view, is in fact always embodied and therefore only reveals the perspectives that are available from the storyteller's social location. To chart the successes and setbacks of experiential knowledge claims in immigrant storytelling, one must maintain a critical view of experience that considers both the indeterminacy of communicated experience and the position within a society's power hierarchy of the teller. Only by maintaining awareness of these limitations can one begin a clear-sighted analysis of experience as a narrative strategy.

Stories as Partial

Autobiographical reclaimant narratives refute dominant and totalizing portrayals of immigration that advance what Donna Haraway calls a "conquering gaze from nowhere."[28] Such a gaze is unlocatable, has the ability to see without being seen, holds the power to characterize without being characterized, and, Haraway argues, presents a "serious danger of romanticizing and/or appropriating the vision of the less powerful while claiming to see from their positions."[29] This gaze from nowhere is evident in generalized prescriptive claims about the harms of immigration, but it is also present in pro-immigrant advocacy that presumes to know what immigrants are like and what value they add to the United States. According to Haraway, any individual's experience of truth is acquired from the knowledge gained by existing within a specific position in society; any "parables about objectivity" or proof become subservient to a recognition that because each person's position is unique from any other, his or her perception of truth will also remain unique.[30]

In March 2016, I met Jin Park, a twenty-year-old who was born in South Korea, grew up in Queens, and is now a student at Harvard. I had come across his story on Jose Antonio Vargas's DefineAmerican.com. Jin had stayed quiet about his immigration status growing up, but an article that Vargas wrote in *Time* magazine where he talks openly about his undocumented status gave Jin the courage to go public himself. "I read that and I connected so much to it," Jin told me. "I felt that this is something that's much bigger than me, and I could possibly contribute to this movement or add my voice to this wide array of perspectives. That's when I realized that I could possibly have an impact." Jin uploaded his own story to the site and has since become an activist for immigrant rights. He believes firmly that sharing immigrants' experiences will be the antidote to the oversimplification of the issue in mainstream media. He explained,

> It's important that we diversify the issue—I know from my experience and from reading and all that stuff that it's not complicated enough yet in the media, and maybe the goal is that the media wants to simplify and have the public be focused on this issue from one side, but I feel like that's one of the biggest failings of immigration policy. . . . If there wasn't print media or online media about undocumented people and their stories, I think it would be completely bare, because it would just be reporting, and it would be completely impersonal and nothing would be about experiences of undocumented people.

In Jin's mind, partial perspectives that are unique from each other have the potential to make all the difference because distinct narratives expand the possibility that someone may be able to relate to an immigrant. While a listener who is a citizen may not be able to understand or empathize with what it is like to live without legal status, they may be able to find a point of commonality with a narrator who speaks, for example, about the weight of carrying a secret into a job interview, or the hardship of the inability to pay one's bills with an inadequate income. "Making this issue more diverse, I think, in my view, it expands the number of people that have to take a stake in it," Jin emphasized. "If it's just one type of person, one type of worker, one type of anything, it decreases the number of people that have to have an interest in this issue."[31]

Gabriela, who arrived in New York from El Salvador when she was thirteen, agreed with Jin's perspective:

> The stories themselves are important because they're real. They come from real people, like my personal story and for people in my network that might not have known that I was undocumented. It might be shocking or it might be like, "Wow. I never knew that Gabriela had these struggles." It will make it real because my story is real, so it will be more powerful and more touching I think. It's important because the more stories out there, the better the understanding, the better that it will move us towards change and changes people's minds.[32]

This insight characterizes immigrants' stories as pieces of a bigger picture, similar to a jigsaw puzzle. No individual piece can tell a whole or complete story, but instead they work in tandem with each other so that, when placed side-by-side, they reveal a reality larger and more telling than any singular experience.

Stories as Public Performances

The function of storytelling performances becomes most clear in light of a body of work known as performance theory. As defined in the work of John L. Austin, Erving Goffman, Jacques Derrida, and Judith Butler in particular, performance theory aims to describe how public acts of communication enacted by embodied actors advance desired truths while disallowing others.[33] Performance theory corresponds to Carey's definition of communication as "a symbolic process whereby reality is produced, maintained, repaired, and transformed,"[34] and it allows for an interrogation not just of language but of the purpose and effect of certain types of language enacted in particular, power-laden contexts. Performance theory likewise extends Fisher's narrative paradigm by emphasizing not only the ubiquity of storytelling but also the ways culture is negotiated and maintained through the public performance of narratives. Performances put narratives on display for others to watch. It follows then, that these performances will vary depending on who is watching as their narrators include and exclude language, affect, and style to suit their goals.

There are many stories that never get told, and the ones that do make it into mainstream consciousness do not arrive there without reason. Rather, they are tended to and maintained for a specific purpose. The stories of immigration that appear throughout this book are limited to those that undocumented activists, US citizens, and media content creators have deemed acceptable to share in public. Therefore, they offer an incomplete view into the thoughts, opinions, beliefs, and values that make up the immigration debate on all sides.

In *Domination and the Art of Resistance,* James Scott delineates this kind of "public transcript" from one that is held privately, or "hidden." Scott asserts that marginalized groups who are subject to the authority of others "ordinarily dare not contest the terms of their subordination openly. Behind the scenes, though, they are likely to create and defend a social space in which offstage dissent to the official transcript of power relations may be voiced."[35] The following chapters hold the narratives of many activists who have in fact "dare[d] to contest the terms of their subordination openly" and therefore offer some counter evidence to Scott's claim. But his argument remains crucial to recognizing that any publicly delivered narrative is likely full of strategic omission. Because reclaimant narratives are inherently performative, they will necessarily leave out the "hidden transcript," or private messages told only within a community and guarded from outsiders.

The division between public and private transcripts is clearly evident in immigrant rights discourse. A close look at the progress immigrant activists have made toward changes in legislation—namely, the success of DACA and the proposal of the DREAM Act—suggests that undocumented activists are more likely to be successful when they perform normative American citizenship despite lacking legal status.

Writing about immigrant activism in the early 2000s, Walter Nicholls describes how advocates "stressed assimilation over distinction and conformity over difference. American flags were now widely disseminated at public demonstrations and flags from other countries were pushed out of sight." This "move to embrace American symbols and silence displays of foreignness and otherness" reveals the strategic framing of a public transcript most likely to find support with American audiences.[36] It continues to be the case that through alignment with the nation, rather than divergence from it, immigrants hold the potential to frame themselves as deserving individuals rather than as threats. The performance of Americanness serves as a precursor to claims of humanity in displays of activism; and humanity, in turn, acts as a precursor to a path to citizenship. By aligning themselves with the nation and demonstrating their identification with US culture, reclaimant narrators minimize the threat to conservative hegemony that immigrants pose and publicly reify the nation's sovereignty and legitimacy.

On first glance, one might assume that such performances exact a price—immigrants perform their Americanness at the expense of their other cultural ties. But if we recall Scott's notion of hidden transcripts, it becomes clear that one's public self can be but a strategic presentation—a limited view of a more complex reality that exists behind the scenes. This perspective challenges the assumption that narrative performances, like that of Americanness, tell the whole story of immigrants' allegiances, desires, and opinions, and recognizes the agency that immigrant activists carefully employ. To state it more plainly, what is found in the pages of this book and in public immigration activism more generally is only what the involved parties are willing to state publicly; it is best to assume there are gaps in every reclaimant narrative that are purposefully left unbridged.

Stories as Counternarratives

The stories that the narrators share throughout this book provide a window into undocumented experience that runs counter to dominant discourses that appear in political and popular discourse.[37] This is not to say that reclaimant narratives always contradict all manifestations of dominant representations and portrayals of immigrants; rather, they function as opportunities for individuals without legal status to speak for themselves and participate in the creation of what Ono and Sloop call "outlaw discourses," or public messages that refute stereotypes by foregrounding individuality and that originate from a perspective that is distinct from prevailing representations.[38] The stories that appear in this project are outlaw discourses in the sense that those who tell them refuse the logic that governs the status quo; they are "heterogeneous with regard to one another and with regard to dominant logics."[39] But because they are always experiential and autobiographical, reclaimant narratives are only one particular type of outlaw discourse. We might say, then, that all reclaimant narratives can be read as outlaw discourses, but not all outlaw discourses are reclaimant narratives.

To understand how these narratives appear and function within US public discourse, it is possible to divide reclaimant narratives into two broad categories: some of the narratives directly address and respond to prevailing stereotypes and presuppositions; others seek to gain traction of their own accord and may contest existing narratives only implicitly, choosing an offensive, rather than defensive, posture. Both of these strategies contest and complicate oversimplified and generic accounts of living undocumented and thus appear in opposition to other accounts.

The kinds of messages that choose to directly address and respond to fallacies and myths in public discourse match Michael Warner's notion of a counterpublic in that they come into being "in relation to texts and their circulation."[40] Jose Antonio Vargas provides an example of one such message during a key moment in a Twitter conversation with another user who Tweets under the handle "LatinoPATRIOTS2016" (see Figure 1.1).

In this case, Vargas responds to a single manifestation of the trope of immigrants as "illegal," as it appears in the Tweet from LatinoPATRIOTS2016. By pointing out the difference between a civil and criminal offense, Vargas directly contests an existing narrative that gathers all undocumented immigrants under one name. Butler argues that that "being called a name is . . . one of the conditions by which a subject is constituted in language."[41] Vargas's attempt to contest a name he sees as inaccurate works here as a means for *re*constituting himself in opposition to this name.

Vargas's tweet illustrates how a reclaimant narrative's ability to directly contest both popular and official governmental discourse sets it apart from

FIGURE 1.1. Jose Antonio Vargas Responds to a Tweet Calling Immigrants "Illegal"

other types of human rights rhetoric. For instance, Hauser advances a theory of human rights rhetoric that he calls a "moral vernacular."[42] This type of rhetoric holds some similarities to reclaimant narratives as it enables disenfranchised groups to "contest for rights withheld under conditions of oppression"[43] and shows how individuals may participate in activism even when relegated to the margins of society. According to Hauser, those who practice a moral vernacular rhetoric often lack opportunities to participate in official deliberations over their rights, and so they participate in "nonofficial" spheres where they engage in performative acts of asserting personal dignity.

But Hauser's characterization of this human rights rhetoric diverges from reclaimant narratives in two fundamental ways. He contends that instances of moral vernacular do "not engage [their] opponent in debate . . . and overtly dismiss the state as irrelevant to their liberatory goals while addressing the people as the only relevant audience to affect them."[44] The reclaimant narratives that appear in the immigrant rights movement in the United States both frequently engage their opponents directly—as in Vargas's tweet above—and figure the state as *directly* relevant to their goals. Because the laws of the state are the apparatus that keep undocumented immigrants from the rights they seek, and because these immigrants lack the legal power to vote or become elected members of government, the central goal of many of the reclaimant narrators featured in this project is to encourage their audiences to take direct action to change the nature of the laws that govern immigration.

Still, it is clear that not all reclaimant narratives are overt about what they counternarrate. Some stories appear to stand on their own, without directly confronting some existing representation of immigrants. Sonia, a musician and filmmaker who was born in Mexico and now lives in Brooklyn, tells stories of this kind. Sonia's song about being undocumented, "Cielo" (Heaven), was posted on Buzzfeed. Sonia and I had the following conversation about the song:

SB: I noticed on Buzzfeed that "Cielo" garnered several comments from readers. Did you read all those comments?
SONIA: Nope.
SB: You didn't on purpose?
SONIA: Yep.
SB: Why not?
SONIA: Because they don't know, and I don't care, and they're just never going to know. All I can do is know who I am and put what I am

out there. I understand the limits. I understand that there's going to be things that I don't understand about people and that I also make judgments, so I don't care. Unless I'm meeting you face to face and I'm developing a relationship with you, I don't care.

SB: Even the positive responses, the ones that felt they could relate and saw something of themselves in you, you wouldn't seek those out?

SONIA: No. It's nice that people feel that way after listening to "Cielo" or seeing *Nenas* [Unknown, a short film Sonia produced], but I'm not seeking them because I'm not doing things to gain people's approval anymore. I do things to love myself and to love who I am.

SB: Why post it online at all if it's just to serve you and to help on this journey of self-discovery? What is the purpose of making it public?

SONIA: Because I want people to know, but I don't care what people think. I just want them to know.

SB: Whom do you want to know, other immigrants?

SONIA: Other undocumented youth, other undocumented parents, American people, everyone.[45]

In this instance, Sonia emphasizes that while she wants a wide audience to encounter her messages, she does not care to hear or reply to their responses; she has no wish to engage those who might respond.

Even when apparently autonomous narratives like Sonia's avoid responding to others directly, they do not operate outside the milieu of US law and culture—these realities have crafted the material conditions from which Sonia speaks. Regardless of whether they express it explicitly, reclaimant narratives appear at an intersection of their political, social, geographic, and temporal surroundings so that the form and content of any public narrative reflects or suggests the attributes of the surrounding culture. Creative works like Sonia's do not appear as stagnant texts relating generic experience; instead they relate the shifting desires and anxieties of a specific group of people.

Because oversimplified narratives about undocumented immigration pervade US public discourse, even analyses of counternarratives that do not directly address these oversimplifications should not ignore the importance of cultural context. This is not to say that anti-immigrant public opinion or media have the power to determine what immigrants produce in response; such an assumption would afford very little agency to a group that has demonstrated a substantial amount of creativity and difference within its own ranks. But this recognition does demand that critics acknowledge how existing mainstream discourse about immigration affects the ways firsthand immigrant narratives are both constructed by storytellers and interpreted by audiences.

Stories as Incondensable

One of the primary goals of this work is to move beyond migration scholarship that casts undocumented immigrants as only threats, victims, or heroes. There is much more to the story of undocumented immigration, but uncovering it requires a purposeful suspension of the desire for a simple explanation. Existing analyses of news discourse about immigration reveal the continued efforts to generalize (1) the reasons undocumented immigrants came to the United States, (2) immigrants' intentions, and (3) the effect immigrants have on US culture, crime, economy, and political stability. As Barbie Zelizer explains, "Organized in mediated systems, news delivery works by parameters that favor the broad over the narrow, the simple over the complex, the uniform over the differentiated."[46] This penchant for simplification has a direct impact on the lives of undocumented immigrants in the United States because it fosters a sense of mastery and understanding even in audiences who know very little about undocumented immigration. Zelizer uses a metaphor of cannibalism to describe the effects of oversimplified news on those it portrays, suggesting that such representational media "devours its victims, leaving no evidence to contest what went wrong."[47] Certainly the effort to distill, simplify, and essentialize is not specific to media about migration—it pervades public discourse in general. But because undocumented immigrants rely on US sentiment and community support for their very livelihoods, more robust knowledge about their precarious status in the United States is essential to their well-being.

The desire to distill undocumented immigration to a single narrative or grand odyssey is essentially a desire for domination; claiming to understand the risks or benefits of undocumented immigration fully suggests that subsequent claims in support of or opposition to it come from a position of knowledge and authority that resists counterarguments and silences critique. Such presumed authority was evident the evening Donald Trump announced his bid for president:

> When do we beat Mexico at the border? They're laughing at us, at our stupidity. And now they are beating us economically. They are not our friend, believe me. But they're killing us economically. The U.S. has become a dumping ground for everybody else's problems. Thank you. It's true, and

these aren't the best and the finest. When Mexico sends its people, they're not sending their best. They're not sending you. They're not sending you. They're sending people that have lots of problems, and they're bringing those problems with us. They're bringing drugs. They're bringing crime. They're rapists. And some, I assume, are good people.[48]

Here, Trump advances a simplistic and alarmist narrative of undocumented immigration from Mexico that he claims to comprehend in its entirety. Not only does Trump employ a violent metaphor to describe the totalizing effect of immigration on the economy ("they're killing us"), but he also promotes his knowledge of Mexicans' general disposition toward Americans ("they're laughing at us, at our stupidity"). The final claim—"They're bringing drugs. They're bringing crime. They're rapists. And some, I assume, are good people"—reifies the unsubstantiated likelihood of immigrant criminality. Though this picture of immigrants from Mexico employs hyperbole and fear mongering, it offers a simple and straightforward narrative that requires little from the audience and provides a clear takeaway. The power of such oversimplification should not be underestimated.

Such a desire for a simplistic immigration narrative is evident both in explicitly anti-immigrant discourse and in pro-immigrant rhetoric. Hints of a claim to authorial knowledge appear in heart-tugging stories of undocumented youths' pursuit of the "American Dream" and in pro-immigrant messaging that DREAMers arrived in the United States "through no fault of their own."[49] While these messages attempt to establish some common ground and work toward legal reform, many unintentionally reinforce stereotypical perceptions of undocumented immigrants by claiming to know the entire group's intentions, desires, and goals. In anti-immigrant narratives, this tendency is even more pronounced. As Cacho contends, "When simply 'being' is criminalized, there is little to no room for discussion of a person's reasons, motivation, or premeditated intent—all these details are assumed always already known, universal, and unchanging."[50] Motivations for painting immigration with a broad brush vary, but generalizations from any side diminish the reality that immigrants are a diverse group whose experiences differ according to a whole host of internal and external factors.

In her 2016 account of the mediation of immigrant activism in the United States, Radha Hegde suggests that DREAMers "use their private stories as a pivotal focus of attention, a point of entry to talk about the commonalities in the larger shared script of the undocumented."[51] But beyond the surface-level commonality of a shared lack of legal status and desire for change, a close reading of DREAMer narratives reveals much more difference than similarity. Undocumented storytellers contest generic representations of their lives by highlighting the ways their stories differ from each other.

Jose Antonio Vargas's *Define American* website provides one exemplary instance in which several immigrants' stories are placed side by side, resulting in an amplification of the differences between them. The website functions as a digital archive of short films that immigrants upload to share stories of experiences from their lives. Users are offered a series of instructions that read in part, "Your own personal life story is needed to encourage a mature, reasoned conversation about immigrants and citizenship in America today."[52]

The videos currently available on the site vary widely in terms of length, tone, quality, and topic.[53] Some narrators cry as they speak; others laugh as they describe embarrassing memories. Some are strictly personal while others tell the story of a family or community group. Visitors to the site are able to sort the pages of videos by topics ranging from "sports" to "activism" to "healthcare." Certainly, these stories hold some pragmatic matters in common—many narrators discuss the frustration of the inability to get a driver's license, to work legally, or to travel internationally. But hearing these stories side by side, it becomes clear that in many cases, similarities between experiences cease where topics other than migration begin. Likewise, in my conversations with undocumented activists and my close reading of immigrant-produced media, it became clear that in addition to differences in storytelling style, reclaimant narrators hold divergent goals for their stories. At the beginning of this chapter, Katherine remarked, "I'm not asking for applause every time I walk out of my apartment. I'm not expecting anybody to revere my story any time I walk into a room. I just wanted to be acknowledged as a human being." But in a recent piece of art he created and posted on Instagram, undocumented activist Julio Salgado states, "No Longer Interested in Convincing You of My Humanity" (see Figure 1.2). This piece of art, punctuated by a graduation cap lying crumpled on the ground in disdain for the ways high-achieving DREAMers have been more successful at convincing audiences of their humanity than others, reveals a contrast to the work of other activists, like Katherine's, that exists in order to encourage audiences to see immigrants as human.[54]

In every way that does not have to do with lack of legal status, members of the undocumented community in the United States are as different from each other as are members of any multi-origin group. Their stories reveal these differences and function as an activist collective of perspectives

FIGURE 1.2. © Julio Salgado 2017 (juliosalgadoart.com)

that fight back against oversimplification and the domination of presumed knowledge.

While rich and varied first-person stories offer insight into the multidimensional and sometimes conflicting experiences of life without legal status, the impossibility of distilling a simple, archetypal narrative from that experience presents a challenge for undocumented activists hoping to gain broad public support. Prevailing mainstream portrayals offer easy conclusions without nuance: immigrants are flooding across the border from Mexico to steal American jobs and drain the economy through an abuse of social services. The realities—immigrants' reasons for arriving in the United States and their struggles to succeed in spite of their lack of status—are in fact much more complex than such a simple myth suggests.

As Daniel explained to me during his interview, "We are not part of the dominant major narrative because it's not a popular story. *It's a complicated story*. No one wants to tell something that's too complicated to understand."[55] Firsthand accounts of living undocumented do not always hold together in meaningful ways. Some immigrants live with the advantage of white privilege; others confront racial prejudice frequently. Some are terrified of being found out or detained; others speak boldly against the US government without fear. Some dramatically recount dangerous journeys across the Mexican border in conditions of extreme poverty; others tell the story of wealthy cosmopolitans who overstayed tourist visas. Some narratives appeal to emotion and pull at one's heartstrings; others reveal aberrant behavior with candor.

No single DREAMer encapsulates the narrative. As the succeeding chapters will reveal, young undocumented activists work assiduously to contest portrayals that reduce undocumentedness down to a single archetype. But the refusal to give in to the simple story has its own consequences. Because their stories do not offer an easy takeaway or simplistic conclusion, they are not always easy for activists to package and promote. In her rigorous historical analysis of US immigration laws, political scientist Lina Newton suggests that mainstream immigration discourses "offer dramatic tales with heroes and villains but they also condense information, reduce uncertainty, and provide heuristics for decision-making in a field for which conflicting or incomplete evidence may provide no definitive course of action."[56] While incomplete narratives or conflicting experiences may serve the purpose of revealing the diversity within the undocumented population, they may also have the adverse effect of prohibiting definitive action in favor of immigrants because they disallow the possibility of simple answers to simple problems.

Immigration is one of the most central plot points in the well-worn patriotic US narrative. From the poetry inscribed on the base of the Statue of Liberty ("Bring me your poor, your huddled masses")[57] to the reassurances offered by presidents past ("We are, and always will be, a nation of immigrants"),[58] the tale of the United States as a Promised Land for those seeking a better life permeates national consciousness. But a close inspection makes clear that the branding of the United States as a nation of immigrants only makes space for a particular kind of immigrant—and a particular narrative—and leaves others out of the story altogether. Because the contemporary immigrant rights movement does not fit the constraints of this timeworn archetype, both reclaimant narratives and those who tell them remain at risk.

Stories at Risk

Stories have a unique power to lure audiences, engender empathy, and make complex problems personal and relatable. In light of their inability to vote, run for political office, or lobby with great financial force, undocumented storytellers harness the power of storytelling instead, and stories become the capital used to spur immigration reform. But the power of storytelling is limited and leaves undocumented narrators in a precarious state where they must navigate the potential of storytelling without falling prey to its hazards. The limitations of narrative affect both content and medium. In Chapter 4, I discuss the limitation of medium in detail. Here, I take up content—that is, the subject matter of the stories themselves and the implications of this content for the storytellers.

The reclaimant narratives that undocumented immigrants tell in efforts to advance reform hold a great deal of potential, but the current state of immigrant rights in the United States reveals that both storyteller and story are at risk. Storytellers, in many cases, occupy a precarious position; they are quite literally in social and political danger for recounting their lived experiences publicly. And less visible but just as sure is the reality that reclaimant narratives' content puts them at risk of obscuring the economic and political realities that would need to change for comprehensive immigration reform to become a reality. One storyteller I spoke with illustrates both of these risks clearly.

Praq Rado, a former student of mine, grew up as a shepherd in Albania and moved to the United States alone when he was twenty years old in hopes of earning money that he could send back to his family. "My childhood was kind of challenging because I was very poor," Praq recounted. "Growing up with six siblings, sometimes there was no food on the table. I didn't have that childhood like some kids might have in America—they can eat ten types of cereal, like any kind of milk you wanted." After his arrival in New York, Praq enrolled in college and started taking acting classes. As the students brainstormed about material for their performances, Praq began to share his story with some of his classmates. "They were like, 'Oh my God, you can make a film of this. This can totally relate to people,'" Praq recalls. "I took their ideas and I started writing my journey." The result was a screenplay for a short film called *Dreaming American*. Praq shopped the project relentlessly. He remembers:

> I brought it to film festivals where you can pitch your story. I got turned down so many times because people don't really know what it's like to be undocumented, and I understand why, because if you don't experience something, it's hard to be in somebody else's shoes. They just look at you— "You want to have a movie about your life?" It's not just about my life; it's about millions of others! [I am] trying to raise an issue about something!

Praq saw his story as bigger than a single experience; the reclaimant narrative that appeared in his film's script was an attempt to assert immigrants' right to speak for themselves and reframe audience understanding. The script was turned down over and over until finally, it caught the attention of some seasoned producers who agreed to make the short film with Praq in the starring role.

He remembers, "The first day we were shooting the film, I was crying because I remember how many times I pitched that story to hundreds of people and no one really cares to listen to it." Once it was finished, Praq was thrilled to learn that *Dreaming American* would be screened at film festivals on both coasts of the United States. Because he did not have the legal identification required for flying, Praq would take cross-country Amtrak trains to attend the festivals. He traveled to Los Angeles from New York this way eight times, each trip longer than seventy hours. Praq has a Twitter following of almost 18,000 users, and he would alert his followers via Twitter about which festivals were screening the short film to let them know where he would be and when. On September 27, 2012, Praq tweeted, "I'm looking forward to Hamptons International Film Festival Dreaming American Film will screen there Oct 8th."

On October 7th, immigration officials boarded the train that Praq was taking to the festival and arrested him. He is convinced the arrest was directly related to his digital media presence: "Someone called immigration. Because I was really out there raising awareness about undocumented people, and someone called immigration because I was Tweeting a lot, Facebooking a lot, reaching out to people." Praq spent six nights in jail after the arrest.

When I asked him why he risked exposing his status to make the film and promote it on social media, he told me:

> I [was] honestly tired of being scared; there are so many other students in the same situation. It's like being able to raise an issue about something that is so important to so many others. I know what it's like to be afraid because I was one of them. . . . If I can raise an issue about something that is so important, maybe others can do it. We all can stand together and eventually people can hear about this, and maybe do something.

Praq's arrest did not deter him from telling his story; he continues to advocate publicly for reform and hopes to make a feature-length film about his life. But his arrest illuminates one of the multifaceted risks of undocumented storytelling and offers a reminder that the dangers of stepping out of the shadows are not imagined. More than 600,000 immigrants are deported from the United States each year. For undocumented storytellers—and most especially for those without temporary protected status through DACA—the risks are ever present, but rarely clear.

The United States government retains the right to monitor digital activity through the National Security Administration (NSA) under its mandate to prevent terrorism. The NSA is authorized by Executive Order 12333 to "Collect, process, analyze, produce, and disseminate geospatial intelligence information and data for foreign intelligence and counterintelligence purposes to support national and departmental missions."[59] But even if, like Praq, immigrants are detained after revealing their status online, they are unlikely to find out whether the two events are related or coincidental. Undocumented storytellers must weigh the necessity of telling their stories against the threat of detention.

Praq's story also points to a less tangible but perpetual risk related to the power and limitations of immigrant storytelling. Above, he describes his frustration when trying to pitch his film to individuals who viewed the film merely as an autobiographical work ("You want to have a movie about your life?") rather than a testament to a larger systematic issue ("It's not just about my life; it's about millions of others!"). Reclaimant narratives regularly maintain an intent focus on the personal; as I have argued earlier in this chapter, this focus works to humanize the problems affiliated with immigration and show the range and scope of experiences. But because this focus is so specific to the storyteller—taking up his or her unique emotions, hardships, and encounters from within the particular context of a single life—they risk obscuring *both* the historical, economic, and political realities that created the circumstances from which they speak *and* the local and national changes that would be necessary to alter those circumstances.

Reclaimant narratives like Praq's often place individuals rather than issues at their center so that listeners go away familiar with a life but not necessarily with the laws, policy, or discrimination that relegated that life to the margins. By prioritizing selfhood and emotion, these narratives risk obfuscating the structural sociopolitical changes that would be necessary for advancing comprehensive immigration reform. Using Fisher's language, we could say that highly personalized stories that illuminate the day-to-day realities of living undocumented but leave audiences unsure of both cause and solution lack "coherence." That is, they lack an internal "completeness" through the "omission of relevant arguments."[60] Those without legal status are walking testimonies to the failures of the political immigration system. But when storytellers stop short of drawing an explicit connection between a problem and the political realities that made it inevitable, their audiences may be left without a clear indication of what needs to change.

The decision to focus on the personal instead of the changes that would be required to instigate reform may neglect to offer actionable conclusions, but this is not to say that such an individualized strategy is ineffectual. As immigrant activist stories trend toward the personal and intersectional—that is, they portray not only undocumented life but also focus on interacting aspects of one's identity and experience—they emphasize the relatability of their narrators, allowing listeners from diverse social locations to find and connect to some point of commonality.

As Jin noted earlier in this chapter, "Making this issue more diverse, I think, in my view, it expands the number of people that have to take a stake in it." Undocumented storytellers sometimes share successes and hopeful stories, but common themes in reclaimant narratives are the hardships and heartaches that work to incite audience empathy. The narrators are aware that if they can get audiences to empathetically relate to and feel troubled by some facet of their stories, they may try to assuage this bad feeling by taking some action that replaces it with a sense of accomplishment. Psychologists David Schroeder, John Dovidio, Mark Sibicky, Linda Matthews, and Judith Allen call this type of response "egoistic" (as opposed to altruistic) action because while a helping response may appear to be motivated by the hardships of another, it is often in fact "motivated by a desire to enhance one's own emotional state rather than a desire to enhance the welfare of the person in need."[61]

This possibility incurs a risk of its own. While an audience taking action in favor of immigration reform after hearing a story is the exact goal of many immigrant storytellers, Karma Chávez points out the hidden danger of these egoistic, empathy-based motivations. She posits that " 'feeling good' about helping an individual in a bad situation [can] stand in place of a critique of the labor conditions and capitalist expansion that have created the bad conditions in the first place."[62] Experiencing egoistic sympathy because one relates to a storyteller is much easier than pushing for systemic change. Chávez argues that avoiding this danger requires "retool[ing] narrative and emotion in productive ways," but she suggests that this retooling is only possible through a serious consideration of what conditions motivate people to activism.[63] Chapter 2 takes up this question by foregrounding the voices of undocumented immigrants in New York who must reckon with their own immigration stories before determining the means through which to craft their experiences into compelling narratives that spur audience action.

My critique of undocumented storytelling on the basis of both its potential and its limitations results in a view of storytelling that is less celebratory than either Fisher's narrative paradigm or the body of immigrant rights discourse that uncritically suggests that telling more and more stories will automatically lead to a better chance at immigration reform. But this approach is far from denying the merit of stories. Considering both the unique power and the potential dangers of storytelling in activism may serve to sharpen and clarify the powers of narrative in ways that can directly serve the immigrant rights movement.

In this chapter, I attempted to reveal the centrality of narrative and storytelling to the sociopolitical status of undocumented immigrants living in the United States. The narrators in this project draw on personal experience to tell partial, performative, oppositional, and incondensable reclaimant narratives of life without legal status. Despite attempts to essentialize and distill this narrative, the reality of undocumented immigration is a complicated story with no easy one-size-fits all tagline. This reality complicates the process of public education about immigration and works both for and against immigrants who use their stories as activism. Though immigrant rights organizations and platforms call for ever more stories to join the existing corpus, I argue that the proliferation of highly personalized narratives puts both storytellers and stories at risk. The emergence of voices of undocumented storytellers in the immigrant rights movement has the capacity to engender empathy, motivate listeners, and even advance reforms in laws and policy. But these narratives also have the capacity to stunt the movement by detracting from systematic problems and viable actions to advance reform. From here, I trace reclaimant narratives back to their inception by demonstrating the ways young undocumented people learn the story of their immigration status for themselves and the kinds of experiences that may either incite or inhibit their decision to cultivate a public voice within the immigrant rights movement.

CHAPTER 2 | Learning the Story for Myself
Growing Up Undocumented

LATE IN THE evening of November 4, 2008, Ximena sat anxiously in front of the living room television. When it became clear that Barack Obama was pulling ahead in the election results, Ximena told me, laughing, "Literally I started running around the house screaming, 'I'm going to be a citizen!' . . . My parents were sleeping, and I was like, 'Obama won! We're going to be legal!'" Ximena had good reason to hope. As a presidential candidate, Barack Obama had been outspoken about his desire to implement meaningful immigration reform. Undocumented immigrants across the country anticipated that this could be a crucial turning point for immigration policy. But when the DREAM Act—which would have created a path to citizenship for millions of young immigrants—failed to pass in the Senate in 2010, hope gave way to despair, and Ximena was awakened again to reality: "Undocumented people have no power. They have no voice. They are not [considered] human."[1] For Ximena, being undocumented meant being inexorably tethered to feelings of inefficacy, anonymity, and fear.

Ximena, whose preferred third-person pronouns are "they" and "them" in order to avoid binary gender identification, was born in Colombia and arrived in New Jersey with their parents at the age of five on a tourist visa. Growing up, they excelled academically and were placed into a prestigious honors high school. "It was a big deal," Ximena recalled during an interview in early 2016. The high school emphasized college preparation—it was a foregone conclusion that graduates would go on for higher education—but, for Ximena, this was not financially realistic. After graduation, while many of their friends left for dorm rooms and lecture halls, they continued to live at home and took a job doing manual labor in a warehouse. "Worst experience of my life," they confessed. "Just absolute, like—it was just terrible. I was verbally abused, bullied." During breaks, Ximena would check Instagram and see photos of friends. "Anywhere I would go—any social media—it's just, 'Freshman year! Pledging! Blah, blah, blah,' and I'm like, 'Okay, cool. I'm here hiding between boxes because I hate my life because it's horrifying.' "[2]

But Ximena did not stop envisioning a better future. After working in the warehouse for a year, they applied for DACA, obtained a work permit, and accepted a job with an airline that allowed them to attend two courses per semester at a local community college. While the promise of higher education was becoming a tentative reality, Ximena still felt embarrassed about not going to a more prestigious college like many of their former classmates. These feelings intensified when they started dating a student at New York University and trying to establish new friendships. "It's like we meet cool people. Then they always end up going to all these cool-ass schools and then they're like, 'Where do you go to school?' " When these questions arise, Ximena feels like "I have to give them my whole life story because I don't want to sound like I'm not ambitious."

Ximena's emotions are consistent with Leisy Janey Abrego's findings that limitations to education "can often create disillusionment for undocumented students, many of whom have already internalized U.S. values that guarantee upward mobility for those who succeed academically."[3] But Ximena reminded me that schooling is only one of many intersecting challenges they must confront. They revealed, "I have barriers that are outside of the academic world. The fact that I'm smart enough to fund my own school and budget my own schooling and survive, I feel is a lot. Not to mention this entire time I'm still gay. Well—I'm queer." Navigating the terrain of an evolving gender and sexual identification is daunting for many, but these experiences are further complicated by Ximena's undocumented status and their family's cultural expectations. "It's like all the while I'm dealing with [these issues] not only [in] American society, but with the society I come from. Like my Colombian roots—my Catholic, Latino, machismo thing that runs in my family."[4] Attempting to push back against what felt like a repressive culture of masculinity and to connect with others who would understand, Ximena has discovered agency and solidarity online: "I find social media useful with the whole queer identity, because where would I be if I told my parents this and then they send me to reparative therapy and then I have to keep it all inside? . . . At least I know that people watch my story and that I contributed."

Ximena recently filmed their story and shared it online through *Define American*, Jose Antonio Vargas's digital campaign for undocumented storytellers. It was an opportunity for Ximena not only to find their voice, but also to raise it—personal narrative becoming social activism. "I really appreciate the fact that the campaign is about recognizing people as Americans, recognizing like a national identity," Ximena told me. "You can't strip that off of me. You can't take that away. You can't take away my American accent. You can't take away my American memories. I have just as many memories as any other American."

In the months following our interview, Ximena was accepted to Columbia University, came out as transgender, and began transitioning. We stay in touch via email, and they periodically stop by my office to talk. Although thrilled to be studying at Columbia, they have yet to meet any other undocumented transgender students. "It's a very lonely feeling," Ximena wrote to me in a recent email. "But being an immigrant is married with being lonely, to be honest."[5] I found that this sentiment reverberated throughout my conversations with other undocumented narrators. While their individual stories are unique, the loneliness they express is pervasive.

This chapter chronicles the ways young undocumented immigrants like Ximena uncover their lack of legal status experientially—through interactions with parents and others, in attempts to pursue rites of passage reserved for citizens, and as audiences of political and popular media. It examines the questions that often confront undocumented youth. What, for instance, do you do when you are not sure if you are a victim or a criminal?[6] The narrators featured in this chapter recount their immigration stories and explore the personal and social ramifications of discovering their status, including feelings of isolation and anomie like those Ximena described above. I explain how these experiences influence one's decision about whether to cultivate a public voice, and the narrators reflect on the processes of determining how to narrate their experiences in the context of activism.

In his development of the narrative paradigm, Walter Fisher draws on the work of philosopher Alasdair MacIntyre. Of finding one's way in life, MacIntyre suggests, "I can only answer the question 'What am I to do?' if I can answer the prior question 'Of what story or stories do I find myself a part?'"[7] After undocumented youth learn and grow to understand the implications of their undocumented status, they come to a crossroads: Will they come to see themselves as part of the story of immigrant activism, or does this story belong to others?

Learning My Own Story

Piash arrived in the United States from Bangladesh when he was ten years old. "We came on a tourist visa," he remembers. "I didn't know at the time, [but] within three months it was expired." For the next six years, Piash lived without any knowledge of his undocumented status; the subject simply never came up. His experience is not unusual. Before they are old enough to apply for a driver's license or a job, children who do not attempt to travel by plane are rarely required to show legal identification or present social security numbers. In 2006, Piash abruptly discovered one consequence of not having legal status when his father was deported back to Bangladesh. "I guess in the back of my mind I knew something was wrong," he remembers, "[but] I never really questioned it, because as a kid, you know, papers and stuff like that doesn't come up in conversation until you need to get a driver's license or you need to join a sports team and they ask you for your social security number, stuff like that." Even after his father was deported, Piash explained, "I knew that we didn't have the right status but I did not know the extent of what it meant."[8] His experience testifies to the reality that many undocumented youth discover the full implications of their status experientially, over months or even years, often through a series of events and interactions involving family members.

In the most extensive existing academic project about undocumented young people coming of age, Roberto Gonzales observed 150 Latino youth in Los Angeles over twelve years and concluded in a study published in 2011 that adapting to the knowledge of one's undocumented status requires "a transformation that involves the almost complete retooling of daily routines, survival skills, aspirations, and social patterns."[9] Gonzalez's longitudinal research provides invaluable insight into the ways undocumented young people "learn to be illegal" by coming to terms with the limitations their status imposes on them.[10] While the process is highly dependent on contextual circumstances, Gonzales's work shows, the realization of one's undocumented status is often one of the most determining factors in an undocumented person's lived experience.

Among the greatest contributions of Gonzales's work is his characterization of social stigma as a "secondary border"[11] that undocumented youth face. As is clear from Ximena's reflection about the dread they experienced when they had to tell their "life story" to explain why their achievements appeared less impressive than their friends', the consequences of social stigma go beyond what can be understood from studying the effects of immigration law and policy alone. However, while Gonzalez's work details these consequences at length, he stops short of considering the ways undocumented individuals may attempt to negotiate the limitations of their status by crafting their experiences into narratives designed to overcome the social and legal challenges they face. This chapter extends the conversation on crossing the secondary border begun by Gonzales, detailing the evolution the narrators in this project underwent from grappling with their undocumentedness to choosing whether to take some narrative action.

I met Sam in September 2016. She and her twin sister were born in Colombia, where their family was wealthy and outspoken against the government.[12] They fled the country after the family received written threats from the Revolutionary Armed Forces of Colombia (FARC); members of FARC took photographs of Sam and her sister and sent them to the girls' parents to prove FARC's ability to get close enough to the family to cause harm.

Sam and her family arrived in New York just a few days before September 11, 2001, and applied for asylum. When the family's application was denied, Sam's parents disagreed over whether or not to tell the girls about their undocumented status.[13] "When [my mom] wanted us to know, my dad didn't want us to know. As we got older, my dad wanted to tell us that we were undocumented in case something ever happened, but at that time my mom no longer wanted us to know," Sam remembers. When her uncle's family, who also lived in the United States without status, was deported, Sam's parents lied and told her that his family had "randomly decided that they were going back to Ecuador," where Sam's father had been born, and that it was "for the best." Sam remembers, "When we got older and asked that same question, we were told the truth—that they got deported. Little by little we started learning about what that meant." She went on:

> In high school my mom started to tell us details little by little as to why we came [to the U.S.], but not that we were undocumented—just seeking asylum. When we applied to colleges we were asked our status in the country, and I didn't know how to answer that question. . . . When we had to fill out scholarship forms or even the FAFSA [Free Application for Federal Student Aid] paper, I didn't know whether we were permanent residents or what I would put under "Details" once I checked "Other." My sister and I would talk late at night, and we questioned whether we were eligible to go to college. We were frustrated—not at our parents, but rather the situation. Knowing that our family was undocumented became clear to us days before Christmas on our last college year when

my parents received the deportation notice [for my father]. My parents told us every detail, and we knew that my father would have to present himself in court, be arrested, and we would then meet him in Ecuador soon. My sister and I spent nights reading about what would happen to my dad.[14]

Sam's experiences illustrate the uncertainty that plagues the lives of many undocumented young people. In her case, this uncertainty permeated both big questions, such as the circumstances that would surround her father's deportation, and more mundane ones, such as which box to check on the FAFSA paperwork. Sam's experience also exemplifies the ways one's status may be discovered over time instead of all at once. The memories she shares about learning "little by little" about what it meant to be undocumented reveal the complexity and ambiguity that mark this process and demonstrate how youth may supplement intergenerational messages about the family's status with mediated messages—like the ones Sam and her sister spent nights reading—to determine the implications of their lack of documentation.

After learning the story of their family's decision to immigrate to the United States, some undocumented youth who arrived in the country when they were young feel an immediate sense of gratitude. "I'm very thankful that my parents made the decision for me [to come to the U.S. from Ecuador],"[15] a young man named Francisco told me. Several of the narrators expressed their admiration of the bravery their parents showed throughout the process.[16] But in some cases, when young people learn about their undocumented status, it can create a rift in family relationships.

Kattia, who was born in Peru and arrived in the United States with her mother and brother when she was nine years old, realized she was undocumented when an employer asked her for some documents after a job interview. "I asked my mom for them, but she told me that I didn't have them because I'm not a legal immigrant. I felt very frustrated," she remembers. I asked Kattia to tell me more about her attitude toward her mother in that moment. "It made me think that she was selfish and that she kind of made rushed decisions without thinking about my and my brother's future. I think I hold a little bit of a grudge against her because of the decisions that she made, and that still affects me." Since I had spoken with several others who also felt this initial sense of resentment, but later came to respect their parents' decision to come to the United States, I asked Kattia, "As you grow older, is it easier for you to understand why your mom made the decision to bring you and your brother?" She replied,

I understand a lot more this last year because I've started to see a therapist, and I've started to talk about my experiences, and the things that I went through as a child, and the things that I went through because I moved here. That helped me out—a lot—to understand where she was coming from, but it also makes that grudge a little bit *bigger* because it's hard . . . for your parent to be that selfish. Personally, I've had to kind of censor myself around my mother so that she doesn't feel guilty about the way I feel and how it affected me, but lately I've decided to not walk on eggshells around her because it invalidates my feelings and it doesn't help to *not* talk about what happened. It's just not healthy. That's just how I've grown up—you know, not talking about things or acting like it didn't happen.[17]

Here, Kattia delineates the essential role that communication—or lack thereof—plays in the discovery of one's status and in the decision about how to manage this status once it is known. Kattia has not translated her experiences into a reclaimant narrative to be shared publicly. Instead, as she described above, she participates in more private experience sharing. She works through the trauma she has endured and the grudge she holds toward her mother by sharing her experiences in therapy, and, though this was not the case growing up, she now talks with her mother about the past, having realized that "it doesn't help to *not* talk about what happened." These private storytelling contexts serve different goals from the other modes of storytelling I explore in this book, but their importance should not be underestimated. For Kattia, these practices work to validate the feelings she has about being undocumented and to help her process the resentment she feels about her mother's decisions.

Walter Nicholls and others have emphasized in their research how the immigrant rights movement works to honor immigrant parents. "Rather than framing parents as guilty," Nicholls suggests, the movement "now frame[s parents] as responsible and courageous in their struggle to provide a better life for their children."[18] But Kattia's experiences suggest that behind the public storytellers who proclaim their parents' courageousness is another, less vocal group, struggling to grapple with their parents' decision to bring their children to the United States where they are so likely to face hardship and uncertainty. Kattia's experiences indicate that parents' decisions to reveal or conceal a lack of legal status to their children—and the ways they communicate or do not communicate about it once their children are aware—may have a direct impact both on the ways young immigrants come to see their place in the United States and on how private or open they will be about sharing their status with others.[19]

Other narrators confirmed the importance of parental communication to their decision about whether to cultivate a public voice. Sonia is a twenty-two-year-old musician who was born in Mexico. She arrived in the United States when she was six but did not know that she was undocumented until she was sixteen, when her father prevented her from attempting to get a driver's license. "I wish my father would've told me more," Sonia told me. "Because I think in his process to protect me from my identity, he never told me I wasn't documented until I found out myself. By him not telling me, I think it made it very shameful."[20] But Francisco, who was born in Ecuador and arrived in the United States with his parents when he was two, had a nearly opposite experience. He remembers,

> In my household, we were open. We were always open. My parents never felt embarrassed to say [that we were undocumented]. That's why I don't feel very embarrassed. In other households, sometimes they try to not mention it. Some people pretend that they're not illegal immigrants just to hide that. Then when people find out, they feel very embarrassed. I guess it just depends on the environment you grew up in.[21]

Both Sonia and Francisco draw direct connections between how their parents communicated—or failed to communicate—about their lack of documentation and how one might orient themself toward being un-documented in light of this parental choice. Sonia's admission that her father's lack of communication made her status into something that felt "very shameful" and Francisco's straightforward logic that his parents' openness is why he "do[es]n't feel very embarrassed" testify to the importance of parental narratives in shaping children's perceptions. Though Roberto Gonzales and Leo Chavez have highlighted instances where the self-discovery of one's undocumented status is comparable to "awakening to a nightmare," the disparity among Kattia's, Sonia's, and Francisco's memories indicates that individual experiences vary a good deal according to the ways the story of undocumented migration is told at home.[22]

Whereas some parents attempt to reassure their children about their lack of status, others purposefully or inadvertently instill fear and uncertainty. Omrie's mother was furious when she learned that he had revealed his status to a few friends. "She's paranoid, as always,"[23] he told me. Omrie was born in Jamaica, but his mother brought him to live in New York when he was only one month old, and so he has lived his entire life without legal status for a civil offense he "committed" as an infant. His mother recently warned him, "Be careful who you talk to, you have to be careful who you're saying this to, wrong people might get you, they might catch up with you." These cautionary messages are likely an attempt to protect Omrie from the possibility of harm. But other parents choose to reinforce the likelihood that their undocumented children will *not* be detained or deported. Piash remembers that when he felt nervous after learning about his status, his parents would tell him he would be okay if he would just "do well in school and go to college."

M. Brinton Lykes, Kalina Brabeck, and Cristina Hunter demonstrate in their research about intergenerational communication within immigrant families that the decision of whether or not to reveal a youth's undocumented status was a "contested" issue for the undocumented parents they interviewed, and that gender, socioeconomic status, and pragmatic issues may contribute to parents' decisions about whether to discuss the threat of detention or deportation with their children.[24] In 2013, these authors published an extensive interview and survey-based research project they conducted with Latino American immigrant parents in the United States; they found that in cases where parents attempt to reassure undocumented children that they are safe, they may "reassure children with incorrect information that they will not be deported."[25] While these messages are comforting, the authors argue, they may leave children unprepared if their family does face deportation, which can happen quite suddenly, leaving families little time to process or plan for the future.

While the existing research elucidates parents' perspectives, the narrators who reflect on their experiences in this chapter demonstrate, from the other side of the generational divide, the ways parental communication affects not only children's knowledge but also their orientation toward undocumentedness more broadly. As these narratives suggest, parents play a large role both in the way young people discover their status and the negotiation about what to do with that knowledge once it has been made clear. Once undocumented youth are made aware of their status, they are left to navigate the personal, social, and legal implications of this knowledge—to confront the "secondary border." As the narrators attest in the following section, these processes are rife with feelings of isolation and a lack of certainty.

Growing Up Undocumented: Isolation and a Lack of Certainty

When I first met Chris, I asked him how many other undocumented people he knew growing up. He answered, "I'm sure there's a lot of undocumented people. . . . I hear about it all the time. But I don't know anyone." At the outset of this project, I had presumed that because of the large population of undocumented immigrants in New York compared to other parts of the country, the narrators would have experienced more face-to-face, interpersonal conversations with other undocumented immigrants than individuals in rural areas. In fact, this was often not the case; most of the narrators mentioned intense feelings of isolation growing up. Several reported long bouts of alienation and, like Ximena, described the ways "being an immigrant is married with being lonely." As a result of direct instructions from authority figures, fear of legal or social consequences, lack of emotional preparedness, or shame, some of the narrators grew up afraid to reveal their status in interpersonal settings—even when they crossed paths with other immigrants lacking documentation.

Esther is a videographer and digital content developer who was born in Spain in 1987 and arrived in the United States when she was three years old. She remembers, "I wanted to get a job at the local movie theater because it was, like, a cool place to work. I was about to turn sixteen. That's when my parents told me that it might not be possible for me—that it was going to be complicated. I was, like, really angry. I didn't really understand." Shortly after she learned about her status, Esther met a girl in high school who was also undocumented, but Esther decided to keep her own status a secret. She explained to me, "I was scared. I think that when you're young, you see people who have problems, and it's almost like you think it's contagious. . . . I didn't like to be seen with other [immigrants] when I was young. It's very wrong, but I wanted to fit in."[26]

Others shared similar experiences. Pang was born in Thailand in 1985, arrived in the United States when she was eight years old, and knew about her immigration status from a young age. She described an encounter she had with an undocumented coworker: "Walter told me about how he had crossed the border and he was very scared," Pang remembered. "At the time, I was still very uncomfortable with sharing my story, so I didn't say anything. I said, 'I'm really sorry, Walter, that must've been really tough for you.' . . . I really tried to want to talk about it, and try to share my own experiences, but I couldn't. That was really the only time that I had come across somebody who was undocumented, that I know of."[27] Esther's and Pang's experiences demonstrate that even when young undocumented people have a desire to empathize with others and build a community, fear and the pervasive threat of consequences may immobilize them.

During my interview with Ximena, I explained that I was somewhat surprised that more undocumented immigrants in New York did not know each other since the population is relatively large compared to other locales. Their reply helped me to understand more about why this is sometimes the case:

> It is such a large population—eleven million—but it's hard to find unity when everybody is scared to come out as undocumented and when there [are] raids going on and where the government can just snatch you and take everything away from you. It's hard to find unity and it's hard to find a presentation. It's hard to be considered valuable in America, or to be considered yourself as valuable, or consider yourself important when the government is working against you.[28]

Kattia confirmed this view. She told me she still experiences a perpetual feeling of isolation from other undocumented immigrants and explained, "I don't feel connected to the immigrant community. . . . It's not like we interact, and it's just not public."[29] This isolation often leaves young people with the feeling that they have nowhere to turn for help or acceptance. Piash explained, "It is kind of like a hidden thing. Kids would ask me—in my senior year, they would be asking me why I'm not getting my driver's license or stuff like that. I would just play it off [like] I didn't want to get a car. . . . [Y]ou don't talk about that because anyone who doesn't like you could call up the INS [Immigration and Naturalization Services] and be like, 'Oh, I know someone who is illegal.' "[30]

The fear that someone may report immigrants to the government for speaking publicly about their status was a common theme among the participants. Ricardo told me, "I think when you're undocumented, you want to not tell people. It's to prevent people from telling other people or to prevent yourself from getting in trouble, I guess, with the law and stuff like that. You don't know who might get this information and have bad intentions and maybe call ICE on you."[31] Ricardo's fear is not unfounded. The Customs and Borders Protection website states, "If you would like to report illegal aliens, please call Immigration and Customs Enforcement (ICE) at 1-866-DHS-2ICE (347-2423). They will need to know names, locations (either work place or residence) and any other specific information you can provide. Visit www.ice.gov for more information."[32] Young people who are forthcoming about their undocumented status regularly encounter threats of deportation encouraged by these digital exhortations to report "illegal aliens."

Each year, around 700,000 undocumented immigrants are apprehended by the government—roughly 6 percent of the entire undocumented population.[33] Several of the narrators I interviewed recounted having friends or family members who had been through deportation proceedings; others reported seeing news reports of ICE raids in their neighborhoods or frightening accounts of border patrol arrests. These memories are ever-present for many immigrants as they decide whether or not to step out of the shadows and reveal their status publicly.

Donald Trump's presidency and actions against immigrants have led to more uncertainty for undocumented immigrants concerned for their safety and, in some cases, have persuaded immigrants to stay quiet even when they are facing threats of violence. The *New York Times* reported a "sharp downturn" of reports of sexual abuse among Latinos across the nation since Trump's election.[34] In Colorado, four undocumented victims of violent physical assault who had begun to pursue action against their perpetrators decided to drop their cases for fear of deportation when they learned of Trump's first executive orders on immigration.[35] Prosecuting Attorney Kristin Bronson explained, "Without victims willing to testify, we've had to dismiss those charges and the violent offenders have seen no consequences for their violent acts."[36] Unfortunately, the fear of legal punishment for immigrants who report gender-based violence is not unfounded. In February 2017, an undocumented woman was arrested for lacking legal status while at a courthouse in El Paso, Texas, where she was filing a complaint against an abusive partner.[37]

I follow several of the narrators in this chapter on social media and have witnessed instances where other users have attempted to report them. When Ximena, who Tweets as @undocuqueer, posted a link in October 2016 to a GoFundMe page to raise money to cover their housing costs while at Columbia University, another Twitter user replied with the ominous tweet, "Pack your shit," and a screenshot from FBI.gov that read, "Thank you. Your tip has been submitted." Just fifteen days later, a different user replied to another one of Ximena's tweets with "This fag is getting deported and there's nothing he can do about it!" Ximena currently has deferred action through DACA and therefore is less likely to be at immediate risk for deportation, but for less vocal undocumented immigrants who follow Ximena's feed and are watching from the shadows of an unrevealed status, witnessing such exchanges can induce terror and encourage continued isolation.

Jenny, who was born in Hungary, told me she has recently seen "a lot of immigration news on TV about deportations, and there was a lot of ICE trucks actually in my area. It was people talking about people coming into your house at night and raiding the places that they knew that immigrants lived in. It just made me feel like, I guess I was scared all the time because we'd been here for a while and it was just like, okay, so now what?" Jenny's mention of feeling fear "all the time" is common among the narrators I interviewed, some of whom had internalized rhetoric they have heard used against immigrants. Even though Jenny was only twelve when her parents brought her to the United States, she explained, "I felt bad about it. It makes you feel like maybe I *am* a bad person for being here without any documents."[38] The effects of internalizing one's status, as Jenny did, are beyond psychological discomfort.

Roberto Gonzales and Leo Chavez found during their fieldwork with undocumented Latinos who arrived in the United States at a young age (sometimes called the "1.5 generation") several instances of physical manifestations of stress stemming from a lack of legal status, including ulcers and chronic fatigue.[39] Samantha Sabo and Alison Elizabeth Lee found in their study of undocumented Mexicans in Arizona that "the internalization of 'illegality' can manifest as a sense of 'undeservingness' of legal protection in the population and be detrimental on a biopsychological level," showing that coming to terms with one's status may have a direct and negative impact on one's health.[40] The negative mental and physical repercussions of living undocumented point to the importance of expeditious immigration reform for the health of immigrants currently plagued with uncertainty about their futures.

Some social services are available to US residents regardless of immigration status and determined on a state-by-state basis. Sadly, several narrators reported being so afraid to seek out this information before they went public about their status that they were unable to take advantage of these services. Esther told me, "It wasn't until after DACA that I even felt brave enough to Google immigration issues." Pang agreed. She wouldn't look up immigration-related content or events online "because of paranoia. I didn't want to make an Internet trail. . . . [W]hat if there was a way for us to be tracked?" Jon confirmed, "When your entire life is at risk, you're probably going to be a lot more paranoid, I suppose, [about] what you do, even if it might seem innocent." No matter how helpful or even essential these services may be, they will remain ineffectual if immigrants are too afraid to seek them out. Sadly, the immigrants most vulnerable and in need of support are often the least likely to seek assistance.[41]

In some instances, undocumented youth might attempt to reach out for help or even just for friendship, only to be scolded or reprimanded. It is important to remember that many of the activists whose stories appear in this book had to negotiate or go against their parents' wishes to begin to speak publicly about their lack of status. Javier spoke at length about his parents' anxiety about his involvement in activism. Javier was born in El Salvador and his journey to the United States across the Mexican border when he was nine years old took two harrowing months. As a young adult, he began reading poetry about his immigration journey at protests in San Francisco. But his parents would sometimes forbid this, fearing police intervention. "Their fear is twofold," Javier explained. "One is because of the status. And two is because, in their mind, the poets that they know in El Salvador, most of them were exiled or murdered during the civil war. They were really scared for me."[42]

Parental concern over their children's safety keeps many potential activists from speaking out. Katherine believes that the propensity for isolation among undocumented youth stems in many cases from "being raised by individuals who already carr[y] their own sense of a culture of silence."[43] The culture of silence Katherine describes was evident in Sonia's memories about her father. Sonia explained to me that she did not want to connect to others who were undocumented because "my dad made it seem like we should just always, never tell anyone that you're undocumented, never ever, it's the worst thing you can do. That gave me a lot of anxiety for a lot of years." Portrayals of immigrants in media reinforced her father's warnings. Sonia remembers, "Sometimes I would try to forget about it, pretend that it wasn't real. Because at first it just felt like a very shameful thing. It felt like it was something so dirty and wrong. The way that it had been portrayed in the media, I felt like I was criminal."[44] Likewise, when Pang started working on a film in which she discussed her status publicly for the first time, she approached some acquaintances at a Thai restaurant where she thought a few of the workers may be undocumented. She explained, "[I told them] how I wanted . . . to come out and how I wanted to share my experience with someone, and a lady took me back to school in her car. When she dropped me off, she said, 'You know, this is a really dark secret; we don't share with people who are outsiders.' "[45] As Pang and other narrators indicate, even when immigrants desire to speak with others and cultivate a public voice, both interpersonal and mediated messages may reinforce the need to keep one's undocumented status hidden from public view.

It is difficult to conceive of the power of undocumented storytelling without a prior understanding of the prevalence of isolation in young undocumented immigrants' lives. The lack of meaningful connections with others who could relate to them leaves many immigrants with a lingering feeling of perpetual in-between-ness; they may never feel completely settled in the nation that renders their presence illegal, but they have no other home to which to return. Piash explained,

> If I go back to Bangladesh now, I would not fit in. I would be lost there. I don't even speak the language that well anymore. I can barely read it. I don't feel it culturally. Religiously, I'm not religious. I really don't pray, [and] Bangladesh is a very Muslim country—even though it's a secular country—it is very Muslim. People pray there every Friday and this and that. I know for sure I would not fit in there. I'm not alone in that. So many people from all over South America, Central America, Africa, Europe would not fit in their country anymore because they have been living here for so long.[46]

Piash is stuck between two worlds, and he worries he will never fully belong in either. Because undocumented immigrants risk forfeiting the ability to return to the United States if they travel to the countries where they were born, there is no opportunity to visit the place of one's birth in order to compare their perceptions of that place to reality. Instead, like Piash, they must rely on stories from family members and mediated representations to learn about life in the place the United States government insists is their rightful home.[47]

An ever-present lack of certainty about the future weighs heavily on many immigrants and may, Roberto Gonzales argues, cause them to stall in a perpetual life stage of "liminality." Though the liminal stage originally appeared in research as a means of describing the journey an adolescent makes across the somewhat uncertain terrain between childhood and adulthood,[48] Gonzales demonstrates how the lack of certainty that plagues undocumented immigrants' lives denies them of the ability to move into more certain, healthy adulthoods and instead ensnares them in a perpetual limbo.[49] This feeling of in-between-ness, where one has no place in the world that offers the comforts of home, holds only marginal similarity with the esteemed notion of "hyphenated identities" popular within globalization discourse.[50] In much of this discourse, the idea of living a hyphenated existence is a result of a privileged cosmopolitanism in which a travelers have moved away from homes to which they might return at any time. Though cosmopolitans may indeed feel the lack of a singular home, many promising possibilities remain available to them.

For undocumented immigrants, neither their birth nations nor the United States offers an unproblematic existence. Gabriela, who was born in El

Salvador and arrived in the United States when she was thirteen, explained to me how stressful this limbo is: "You're afraid you don't know what your future is going to be like. It's always uncertain."[51] Undocumented youth as well as those who are "DACAmented" with temporary protection from deportation cannot know if the US government will act in ways that will sustain or compromise their well-being in the future, and so their lives remain impossible to plan with certainty. It is from within this perpetual uncertainty that undocumented immigrants must decide whether they will translate the experiences they have encountered into stories to use as evidence of the need for immigration reform. This decision requires potential activist storytellers to grapple with the power of representation—that is, to determine how their stories have been portrayed by others and to strategize about how to reclaim and reshape this narrative according to their own goals.

The Power of Representation

Though much of this book chronicles the ways undocumented immigrants are finding creative means for reclaiming the right to tell their own stories in public forums, historically, undocumented immigrants have been limited in their ability to represent themselves in both news media and political rhetoric.[52] Instead of speaking with undocumented immigrants, news and political media often rely on individuals and groups who are not undocumented to speak about them and/or on their behalf. This reality is a result of several intersecting factors. First, the majority of the 11.3 million undocumented immigrants in the United States live in just six of the fifty states.[53] The uneven geographic distribution of undocumented immigrants combined with the reality that they comprise only a small segment (around 3.5%) of the US population means that undocumented perspectives are not always immediately available in instances where their voices could lend insight. As Ximena suggested, "It's numbers versus numbers. At the end of the day, the undocumented community is so small and media can try as hard as possible. I just feel that it's an uphill battle even for media because of the demographics of the United States."[54] But higher concentrations of immigrants in particular locations do not always lead to more media inclusion. Irene Bloemraad, Els de Grauuw, and Rebecca Hamlin found in an analysis of US and Canadian local newspaper content that the quantity of immigrant populations within a locale was not positively correlated to increased "civic visibility" or coverage of that population, suggesting that a low quantity of available immigrants cannot fully account for a lack of self-representation.[55]

Jon was born in the Dominican Republic and arrived in the United States with his parents when he was six. He told me during a recent interview, "The media has such a narrow view on undocumented immigrants because they don't have that much of an opportunity to actually go and talk to them personally."[56] Instead, the media Jon encounters is usually "one sided"—"very rarely I will see someone who is undocumented putting their own two cents in there and I would love to see more of that." He thinks a lot of progress could be made if more media gave their audiences an opportunity to "see where these people are coming from instead of hearing it from a second voice."[57] Several others mentioned a similar dissatisfaction with the deficiency of undocumented self-representation in major media outlets. While discussing the good work that local immigrant organizations or "community DREAMers" are doing in and around New York, Freddy expressed his frustration that this work is not finding its way into mainstream press. "I don't really see them in media," he explained. "Why has no media interviewed the president of community DREAMers?" Likewise, Ximena told me with exasperation, "There's no undocumented character at any TV show, ever."[58] Josue believes self-representation could reassure audiences and wishes that when news media "speak about immigrants coming from a certain place, [that] they show one person [who is undocumented] saying, 'We left because of this. We're not coming here to hurt you guys. We're not coming to steal your jobs.'"[59] When I asked Omrie how media in the United States could do a better job portraying undocumented immigrants, he responded eagerly, "They should have all these DREAMers speak! They should have all these DREAMers talking . . . they should really record that and put that out there. There should be more of that."[60]

Self-representation of undocumented immigrants in mainstream US news and political discourse is also unlikely because almost half of the undocumented adults in this country have not completed high school. While 25 to 30 percent of sixteen- to twenty-four-year-olds overall enroll in college, only about 10 percent of undocumented immigrants enroll, and those who do are less likely than native-born students to graduate.[61] The majority of individuals without legal status have no authorization to work in the United States, so few are able to go on to pursue careers as journalists or political correspondents or work in other fields that would encourage increased media representation. Finally, as attested to by the narrators at the outset of this chapter, individuals without legal status may be reticent to even search online for information about their status, let alone be interviewed or identified in media, for fear of detention or deportation. As Josue stated simply during his interview, "A lot of us are scared and we don't want to come out."

While it is the case that many US-born citizens may experience few mediated or face-to-face encounters with undocumented immigrants because of the aforementioned factors, Josue reveals that even when citizens do interact with undocumented immigrants, they may not be aware of it. Natalia, who was born in Russia and become undocumented after she overstayed a temporary US visa, explained to me, "I wouldn't say I keep it a secret, but it's not something I'm talking [about] very comfortably."[62] In the silence that results from such discomfort, both immigrants and citizens must often rely on secondhand representation to provide them with the tools needed to understand the contested issue of immigration.

These intertwined barriers to self-representation have resulted in "a significant lack of counter definition to the main frame[s]" used to describe and characterize immigrant life.[63] Unless these barriers are overcome, individuals who are not undocumented themselves will continue to retain control of the means of production of immigrant narratives by producing the majority of portrayals of undocumented immigration in mainstream media and will thus remain central to mythmaking about undocumented immigrants. The telling of others' narratives is never a neutral act; as Linda Alcoff writes, "When one is speaking about others, or simply trying to describe their situation or some aspect of it, one may also be speaking in place of them, that is, speaking *for* them."[64] Speaking about others is always a matter of power.

Though secondhand portrayals continue to dominate, three factors in particular have led to more appearances of undocumented immigrants in media than ever before. First, several of the larger immigrant-rights organizations recognize the power of media self-representation and have made it a priority in recent years. The newsrooms and media web pages of organizations such as United We Dream and the New York Immigration Coalition depict both significant production of in-house media content and direct quotation of immigrant activists.[65] Second, as I discuss in greater detail in Chapter 4, digital social media has, to a certain extent, democratized production and made self-representation more possible. Third, DACA gave some individuals temporary protection from deportation and the courage to seek out opportunities to participate in media interviews despite the uncertainty of their futures. Angy, a blogger, YouTuber, and activist who was born in Colombia in 1990, arrived in the United States when she was three and now has temporary protection through DACA; she explained to me, "The media is a tool for us as community organizers. When we're able to be interviewed for the newspaper, or TV, or radio, we're able to message what we want the audience to hear. Working with media has worked for us to be able to outreach [to] the people to tell them about different updates or events we're having."[66] Angy's experience illustrates how some undocumented immigrants are able to overcome the obstacles to self-representation in media and that they retain some agency in spite of the obstacles that prevent them from full participation in US civic life. Of course, self-representation in media does not guarantee the delivery of a preferred message to an audience, as other entities often choose which immigrants to interview and which sound bites to use in particular contexts.[67] In the next section, the narrators reflect on their decision to confront the lack of self-representation in mediated contexts by narrating their own experiences for public audiences.

Finding a Part in the Story and Cultivating a Public Voice

I met David Chung on a hot afternoon at the end of July 2016. David was born in Seoul, South Korea, in 1990 and raised by his aunt and uncle—who he assumed were his parents—until his grandmother brought him to the United States at three years old. In Queens, New York, David reunited with his real mother and father, who had migrated to the United States when David was a baby. He learned that he was undocumented in high school and first remembers seeing some public discussion about undocumented immigration in 2010, when the DREAM act came within five Senate votes of passing. In the lead up to the vote, David began to take notice of television portrayals of DREAMer activists who would often appear in graduation regalia or draped in the American flag as they petitioned for the passing of the act. "I started seeing the cap and gowns. . . . I saw young people holding flags over their shoulders, and I think that's the first image that I had of 'This is what it means to be a DREAMer'—that you have to go to school, that you may even go to the military to get a green card and eventually citizenship," he remembers.

He noticed a clear dichotomy in these portrayals. On one side, he explained, there were college-bound, America-loving immigrants who showed themselves to be "hardworking students—the narrative was they come in through no fault of their own and that they should be provided a pathway to citizenship because they are the good immigrants." On the other, David explained, "There are the laborers that are always portrayed as the bad immigrants, the people that came through the borders. . . . [T]hey just came here just so that they could steal the jobs of Americans." It was clear to him that the promise of the path to citizenship that would be afforded by the proposed DREAM Act was geared exclusively toward the former group. David told me that at that moment he did not yet "associate" himself with the movement: "I still called myself 'illegal,' I still didn't associate myself with other DREAMers, and when I saw it on TV, I knew it was something that would affect me but I still didn't take the initiative to be like, 'Oh, I should look into what I should be doing to further the cause.'" When the DREAM Act failed to pass in 2010, DACA had not yet been announced, and David was so discouraged he decided to self-deport: "I was like, at least in Korea maybe I'll have an identification number [so] that I'll be part of the society."[68]

After deciding to leave the United States, David joined the MinKwon Center—an Asian American immigrant rights organization in New York City—because, he thought to himself, "If I'm going to go back to Korea I need to know Korean."[69] He knew MinKwon offered social services, including language classes, to the community. In 2012, soon after he joined MinKwon, President Obama announced the DACA program and David learned that the center could help him to apply. The other organizers at MinKown saw DACA as a clear sign of progress and encouraged David to join the immigrant rights movement. He recalls, "Where I evolved into the movement building was when DACA happened, when I realized I would be eligible for it. . . . [T]here was this immense guilt that all of these other young people had sacrificed school, had sacrificed work to push for DACA and I had done *nothing* and I'm still going to benefit from it. That's when I was like, 'Let me at least help other people apply.'" He gave up his plans of self-deportation and began advocating for a path to citizenship that would not distinguish deserving immigrants from undeserving but would instead allow all immigrants an equal opportunity to earn their place as citizens of the United States.

Today, David is an activist and community organizer at United We Dream (UWD), the largest immigrant-youth-led activist organization in the United States. At the end of their articles and press releases, UWD makes the organization's purpose explicit, stating that "UWD's current priority is to win citizenship for the entire undocumented community and end senseless abuses and deportations."[70] The prioritization of citizenship is common among immigrant rights associations. The managing director of UWD, Cristina Jiménez, explained why in a 2013 press release: "Citizenship is the only sure way to be protected from senseless raids, abuses, and deportations that tear our families and communities apart, and the only way to fully achieve our potential and contribute to this nation."[71] The decision to fight for citizenship rather than legal permanent residence alone uncovers an important distinction: UWD seeks not only the end of "illegality," but also the ability to engage in full civic participation as Americans. For many, only citizenship can solve the cognitive dissonance of feeling both at home and like a foreigner in one's own community.

There is no formula for predicting whether undocumented immigrants will choose to develop a public voice. David's personal evolution from hiding his status and planning to self-deport to being eager to tell his story and convince others to do the same is just one manifestation of the transformation young people undergo after learning that they are undocumented. For David, temporary protection from DACA, a sense of support from a local organization, and a feeling of guilt about being passive while others worked for his rights provided the necessary conditions for him to make the transition from feeling dissociated from the immigrant rights movement to becoming an outspoken community organizer campaigning for the right to citizenship.

But others in similar situations stay quiet. There are many reasons that immigrants may decide not to share their stories and lobby for reform. Some are fearful of the legal or social implications; others simply do not believe in their ability to effect change. When I asked Kattia if she had ever considered telling her story as a means of activism, she told me frankly, "I think I would like to be involved in it, but it seems like we're just not going to be heard, so it feels like I would not be able to make a difference if I got involved in something like that."[72] Others have little concern about what American audiences think about immigrants and are therefore not compelled to take part in the movement. Adam told me, "At this point personally, I don't care what anybody really says about the whole immigration thing. I'm here—what are you going to do?"[73] For every immigrant activist who steps out of the shadows to tell reclaimant narratives of living undocumented, there are many more who never do.

Both material and immaterial factors play into the ways prospective storytellers approach MacIntyre's question—"Of what story or stories do I find myself a part?"—and decide whether to share their stories. Among the material factors, safety of one's family is often of paramount concern. The implications of coming to terms with one's status are not merely personal. Undocumented youth are well aware that their decisions about how to negotiate their status—and whether to tell their stories publicly—could have direct effects on their families, especially those members who also lack legal status. This reality prevents even some impassioned potential activists from having full confidence in their decision to make their status public. Jin, who was born in South Korea and has temporary protection from deportation through DACA, told me,

> Sometimes I'm a little apprehensive about whether I should be saying this stuff because I'm protected legally, but my parents necessarily aren't. There's always an internal conflict that I feel because I have relief from deportation under President Obama's executive order [DACA], but that doesn't extend to my parents, so even though I want to be vocal and I want to talk about and deal with this, it always feels a little scary because I know what the realistic possibilities are. That's something that I always try to find a balance about. My parents, they always encourage me to do what I feel is right, but what I feel is right is sometimes to not say anything because of that fear.[74]

Likewise, Ricardo explained, "I've always been very secure about myself. For me, if it was just me, I wouldn't care about what will happen to me, but it's my family too, so I also have to think about them. For me, that was, I guess, the hardest part to think about if [coming out] was worth it or not, because when I come out of the shadows, they will come out of the shadows as well."

Ultimately, Ricardo did decide to take the risk to "come out of the shadows." He has gone on to gather acclaim as an activist photographer, and has been featured in a short film called *Meet the Undocumented Immigrant Who Works in a Trump Hotel*.[75] When some of my colleagues and I hosted an immigration teach-in to support students who were processing the implications of the 2016 presidential election, Ricardo, seated facing the audience with representatives from the New York Mayor's Office of Immigrant Affairs and the State Department, spoke boldly about his own story and screened his short film for a crowd of around two hundred people.

Ricardo's film has now been viewed almost 450,000 times on YouTube. Though he was initially concerned about how his mother would respond to it, "when she saw how big it blew up, she just was proud, I think." He remembered, "I think for a while she was also maybe a little bit scared, but she knew that it meant a lot to me. . . . [S]he was just really proud. I think that how proud she was of me, that's overshadowed how scared she might've been maybe."[76] Jin and Ricardo's narratives make clear that while concern for family members' opinions and safety may influence the decision about whether to share one's story, this concern cannot predict whether individuals will choose to become public storytellers. Some young people who have no family in the United States still choose to stay quiet, and others whose families discourage activism decide to step up in spite of their warnings.

While there is no sure way to predict the conditions that will lead undocumented individuals into activism, there are some noticeable commonalities in the ways the narrators in this project talk about their motivations for cultivating a public voice. Specifically, several pointed to an internalization of Americanness and the importance of creating spaces of belonging as a strategy for grappling with a lack of legal citizenship. Some of the narrators explained to me their desire for US law to align with their own long-standing feelings of Americanness. Piash stated emphatically, "We're Americans. I think of myself as an American. [We want] to make sure people realize that we're Americans. We're not just illegal immigrants, we're Americans. You can call us whatever you want, but we feel American."[77] Ximena remembered a feeling of pride that swelled in them during an experience watching fireworks on July 4 with friends in Long Island. The feeling was tainted by the coexisting and pervasive reality of their undocumentedness. "I'm *so* proud to be an American," Ximena told me. "The level of exclusion that July 4th brings to a person who identifies as American but is pursued by the federal government—it's just ridiculous."[78] For these two, feeling American without having the legal status to corroborate it creates a kind of cognitive dissonance. Unable to legally claim a name with which they deeply identify, or to benefit from the rights it would afford, they are left with the burden of negotiating this dissonance themselves. Notably, what these narrators describe as lacking is not Americanness in the imagined sense,[79] but rather an inability to reconcile an external reality with an internal identity.

Storytelling is one means by which reclaimant narrators may negotiate the kind of cultural dissonance that Piash and Ximena describe. Berkeley law professor Kathryn Abrams asserts that participation in the immigrant rights movement allows immigrants to "enact, in daring and surprising ways, the public belonging to which they aspire," and that "a *feeling* of authorization" may accompany solidaristic actions in the service of reform.[80] In other words, immigrants who lack legal citizenship may attain, through their activism, a kind of cultural citizenship and sense of belonging. Of course, cultural citizenship is not a legal status and therefore not subject to governmental control and monitoring in the same way as legal citizenship. But by characterizing belonging according to and within the paradigm of citizenship, Abrams's notion of "public belonging" obscures the coalitional agency of activists to manufacture spaces that serve interests *outside* the unilateral goal of political acceptance and legal rights. In his senior thesis, Daniel—an undocumented community organizer who was born in the Philippines and arrived in the United States when he was five—writes about finding a space of belonging through sharing experiences with other immigrants in ways that complicate the kind of cultural citizenship Abrams describes:

> My immigration story is not uncommon, with many of my experiences shared by other undocumented immigrants I have met the last few years. . . . In the undocumented immigrant spaces I have visited and been a part of, I see many different people come together, united by the shared experiences of being undocumented in the U.S. and the different institutional barriers they face. These established safe spaces provide a place of comfort and belonging for undocumented immigrants in a nation that has continuously denied them of access to funding for higher education, public assistance, health care, and rights associated with citizenship.[81]

As Daniel elucidates, there are communal benefits to the role that storytelling plays in immigrant activism that do not result in general public belonging but rather aid immigrants in finding pockets of safe spaces even in the midst of a "nation that has continually denied them." In these spaces, immigrants claim the power to speak for themselves and share experiences of living in a political climate that is hostile toward them. Daniel's characterization of the "established safe spaces" created in and through sharing experiences and stories with other undocumented immigrants shows a paradox of immigrant storytelling. On the one hand, as Chapter 1 demonstrates, telling these stories to public audiences puts undocumented activists at risk; on the other, sharing them within the undocumented community may help mitigate the threat of loneliness and provide what Daniel calls "a place of comfort and belonging" that may be otherwise hard to come by.

It is important to remember that reclaimant narrators' goals differ from each other: while some are eager to perform Americanness as a demonstration that they deserve citizenship, others actively resist this performance. Adela Licona's notion of "third space" provides a clearer view of the more radical possibilities these latter activists may employ and offers another alternative to Abrams's notion of cultural citizenship.[82] As a starting point, Licona takes Gloria Anzaldúa's poetry about "borderlands," or spaces around the boundaries that constitute belonging and exclusion from which marginalized groups might speak. Licona reveres Anzaldúa's work but fears that because "borderlands" connote the existence of a single, linear boundary, the concept obscures everything but the desire to fit neatly on one preferred side. She explores the "unrealized potential" of Anzaldúa's concept by proposing the existence of "third space"—a coalitional site for activism inhabited by individuals "whose geographic location is not the border" but who exist on the sociopolitical fringe even as their lives are firmly situated within the communities that consider them illegitimate outsiders.[83]

Licona suggests that "in third space, borderlands rhetorics and their representational potentials emerge to reclaim and resignify language practices beyond dichotomous borders."[84] In other words, reading "borderlands" through "third space" allows a reclamation of language practices that are freed of the inside/outside binary that a border suggests. Applying Licona's logic to reclaimant narration by reading legal status as a border makes clear how activism may involve creating and maintaining coalitional sites that disrupt simplified dichotomies between il/legal, un/documented, non/citizen bodies and provide speaking spaces for the proclamation of value and selfhood outside these binary titles. It is certainly the case that activist storytelling is designed to advance goals that often involve a pathway to citizenship. But reclaimant narratives also function as refusals to accept secondhand characterizations quietly and as assertions of a right to personhood irrespective of the nation's laws and policy.

The decision to tell one's story for oneself presents an opportunity to redefine what it means to be an immigrant, or, as undocumented writer Gina Diaz explains, "to deconstruct the word 'immigrant' and construct its real meaning every time you create a sentence describing yourself."[85] In this sense, to participate in reclaimant storytelling is to exclaim, with a slogan of the immigrant rights movement popularized by activist Julio Salgado (Figure 2.1), "I exist!"[86]

Alcoff posits, "In speaking for myself, I am also representing myself in a certain way, as occupying a specific subject-position, having certain characteristics and not others, and so on. In speaking for myself, I (momentarily) create myself—just as much as when I speak for others I create their selves."[87] Alcoff's view of the self-making potential of first-person narrative is directly applicable to the immigrant rights movement; her assertion illustrates that the outcome of reclaimant narratives is not merely public

FIGURE 2.1. © Julio Salgado 2013 (juliosalgadoart.com)

and single faceted. Instead, the decision to participate in narrative activism produces both an immediate effect and an after-effect. In the immediate, activism allows undocumented individuals to constitute their selves and assert their rights within a constructed "third space" of belonging. This act stands in direct resistance to the reality that undocumented immigrants in the United States are frequently spoken *for*—in education, governmental discourse, and news media—rather than recognized as having a right to speak. The after-effect involves the publicity of the message as it finds its way into public discourse and the influence it has on activists' future social and legal positions.

When undocumented young people come to see themselves as part of the story of immigrant activism and begin to share their experiences publicly, stories become a form of capital. David told me, "We might not have a lot of money, we might not have all of these other resources, but we do have people." The goal in David's work is to get people who may be "wary about sharing" to the point of readiness to speak about what he calls their "story of self." The decision is a weighty one; when immigrants use their selves—that is, their experiences, emotions, and fears—as the material for story crafting, they put their very lives on the line. This is not a legally protected form of activism such as the constitutional right of citizens to exercise free speech, but instead a vulnerable one. The "story of self" requires a kind of baring of one's person without being assured of any positive outcome.

As the narrators in this chapter suggest, few undocumented immigrants who arrive in the United States as children understand the full implications of their lack of legal status until later in their lives; before they can share their stories with others, they must learn it for themselves. They come, in the words of Gonzales and Chavez, "face-to-face with illegality," sometimes over several years of discovery.[88] As the narrators explained, communication—with parents, peers, and in mediated accounts—is central to their evolving understanding of undocumentedness. Sometimes, these encounters are empowering; too often, they are traumatic. For the narrators I interviewed, coming to terms with one's undocumented status is almost always accompanied by questions of belonging and feelings of isolation. Recognizing the diverse ways immigrants navigate and negotiate their experiences can shed light on the reasons they may decide to confront the risk of exposure and share their stories.

Undocumented storytellers are stuck between two worlds and fear they may never fully belong in either. Even as they persist in the campaign for a right to citizenship, the possibility that they will see this goal realized for themselves and their parents is raised by the failures of the movement to realize promise of advancements such as the DREAM Act and by setbacks such as Donald Trump's dissolution of the DACA program. Faced with the idea of living entire lives without citizenship rights in the city they consider home, these undocumented storytellers have worked assiduously to strategize about what kinds of stories to tell. In Chapter 3, several narrators recount their first steps into activist storytelling and the narrative strategies they employ along the way.

CHAPTER 3 | Reclaiming the Story and Finding the Frame

AS A COMMUNITY organizer for Revolutionizing Asian American Immigrant Stories on the East Coast (RAISE), an immigrant rights group in New York City, Daniel spends a great deal of time evaluating the most successful ways to frame the story of undocumented immigration for public audiences. This undertaking is not only professional; it is deeply personal. When he was five years old, Daniel's family immigrated to New York from the Philippines, and when he was in high school, he learned he was undocumented. Daniel began paying attention to portrayals of undocumented immigrants in mainstream media, and they frustrated him. "I always saw on TV these organizations and rallies and protests, but the faces you see don't look like you," he explained.[1] He saw mostly Latino activists. As a young adult, Daniel started thinking strategically about how to get more diverse groups of immigrants involved in the movement toward the goal of immigration reform. He began working with other activists to plan events in New York City where immigrants could perform vignettes for audiences to defy stereotype and provide a view into the complexity of being undocumented.

One of these performances included comedic skits where undocumented actors recreated instances in their lives when people said discriminatory or patronizing things to them. "It was just awesome, just retelling that story in a really funny way. It was like a big 'fuck you' to those people who really made bitter impacts in our lives," Daniel remembers. The humor was cathartic. He told me it served as a "creative way for us to really reclaim our stories and tell it how it is."[2]

At other events, the messages were less comedic but similarly impacting. One evening, the team of activists gave a sobering performance, sharing experiences about their mixed-status families being separated or surviving domestic violence. Daniel remembered, "That was a really real night [about] us really just owning our story."[3] These performances gave the group of activists a chance to take back their stories from those they believe had misrepresented them. By reclaiming these narratives and performing them publicly, they sought to put their stories to work, using their experiences as capital to invest in their own goals.

The insights that Daniel and the other narrators share in this chapter about their struggle to reclaim their narratives and brand the immigrant rights movement reveal the power of storytelling and the centrality of strategic communication to social movements. In this chapter, I offer both theoretical and pragmatic contextualization as the narrators describe the ways they present and negotiate narrative frames and strategies toward the goal of immigration reform and a path to citizenship. I chronicle the public work of a diverse group of reclaimant narrators who use their own stories as activism in creative contexts. Instead of beginning with a historical account of immigrant-produced media,[4] I begin with the narrators I interviewed and foreground their voices as they weigh the pros and cons of different messaging strategies. I illuminate the strategies the narrators describe by way of textual analysis of some exemplars of each, demonstrate the ways members of the movement have advocated for shifts in strategies, and explore how these shifts are promoted and implemented.

A good deal of immigrant rights activism takes place at rallies and protests. Here, I focus on mediated activism, much of which takes place in digital contexts because it (1) is recorded, preserved, and thereby available to both primary and secondary audiences; and (2) holds greater potential for inclusivity of individuals who wish to remain anonymous and/or are reticent about appearing physically in public spaces and revealing their status in order to advocate for immigrant rights.

Speaking for Others

It would be a mistake to describe the strategy of the immigrant rights movement as if it were a unified and unanimously agreed-upon plan of action. In fact, reclaimant narrators and immigrant rights organizations employ types of activism that vary greatly and sometimes even oppose each other. In the following pages, I demonstrate some of the major and recurring storytelling strategies employed by undocumented activists who share their status publicly. Because no one immigrant or immigrant rights organization can effectively represent the whole group, I use philosophy scholar Linda Alcoff's "The Problem of Speaking for Others" throughout this chapter to make sense of the power and limitations of embodied activism in instances of contested representation and social location.[5]

When undocumented immigrants perform their own reclaimant narratives, these tend to bear little resemblance to the oversimplified representations that appear in US political and news discourse. More raw and less deferential, these stories are often born out of frustration with the incessant casting of immigrants as stereotypes. Firsthand undocumented narratives like the ones described in this chapter are powerful and creative, but also risky; because they position themselves in direct opposition to oversimplified narratives of pitiful victims or fully assimilated and docile aspiring citizens, the authors of these new frames may rattle some comfortable presumptions and disrupt what US audiences think they know about undocumented immigrants.

Many of the individuals I interviewed described this reclaiming of the narrative as empowering. As Magdalena Bobowik, Nekane Basabe, and Dario Paez remind us, "Stigmatized individuals are not passive victims of prejudice and discrimination, but rather act to deal with their negative identity in order to preserve their well-being."[6] Harnessing the power to speak for themselves after being spoken for in so many contexts has proven empowering for many of these activists. But the benefits and consequences of these performances are perilous, and activists' firsthand accounts of their frustration do not always resonate with audiences as well as the picture of compliant and hopeful youth that the DREAMer movement has popularized. Many reclaimant narrators instead express their disappointment with Washington's failure to pass comprehensive immigration reform, their frustration with US citizens' ignorance about immigration policy, and their resentment toward a community that rejects their presence without understanding their predicaments. The resulting messages may appear as threatening to those concerned with maintaining privileged societal positions.

Throughout this chapter, I emphasize the frames that appear in reclaimant narratives. I use "frames" (framing, framework, framing theory) in the tradition of the field of media studies. Framing theory allows for analysis of the *way* a story is told to an audience and reveals that choices about inclusions and omissions always influence the way the audience interprets any given message.[7] It follows Fisher's narrative paradigm in viewing "people as storytellers, as authors and co-authors who creatively read and evaluate the texts of life."[8] Using the metaphor of a framed photograph, which always both contains and excludes some visual information, one might analyze how a photographer employs certain devices and not others in an effort to evoke a particular response. In this way, framing in immigrant rights storytelling involves strategizing about the angle, breadth, and duration of whatever messages appear in the chosen frame.

In a 2013 interview in the online magazine *Cultural Organizing*, CultureStrike director Favianna Rodriguez described the importance of strategy in activism. "Now I see the value of cultural strategy, which means to me that we are thinking about culture as a tool that can move our ideas forward," Favianna explained.[9] "When artists are organized, it means we have an awareness of the political strategy, and the general direction the movement is trying to go in, so that we can position ourselves. This is why I think it's important to use the word strategy." Strategizing about the way to frame a message does not ensure that undocumented activists will achieve their desired effect, but when undertaken collectively and with consistency, it does increase the ability of organizers to influence the ways the narrative of the immigrant rights movement appears in public.

Sometimes, individuals make grassroots decisions about undocumented activism strategy; in other instances, immigrant rights organizations (made up of both immigrants and immigrant allies) determine a strategy that they deem most likely to succeed and then provide talking points that they encourage their members to stick to. After President Obama passed his executive action to expand DACA and quell the separation of families in 2014, the immigrant rights association United We Dream posted on its website a document entitled "How Do I Talk to the Community about What the President Announced?"[10] The document provides interpretations of the executive action ("This is a major victory, but we did not get everything we wanted") and instructions about how to respond to assertions that the president's executive action was not legal ("The president has the authority to decide how to enforce our country's laws"). These talking points serve the dual purpose of increasing shared understanding among immigrant rights' activists and influencing how they talk to others about the executive action.

Both organizational and grassroots framing and strategy are dynamic, meaning successful frames must respond to evolving current events and changes in policy because they exist within a milieu of other messages and movements. For this reason, any analysis of storytelling strategy should recognize frames as partial accounts of larger contexts. Given the obstacles to professional work, education, and travel that undocumented immigrants face, my analysis considers what means of strategic activism are available to undocumented immigrants, and who has the power to speak for the movement and enact these strategies.

This is a chapter about what happens when undocumented immigrants reject stereotypical portrayals and decide to tell their own stories. To comprehend what is at stake when immigrants organize together to lobby for their rights, one must remember that the social location of undocumented immigrants is not fixed; individuals may access more power in certain situations than others. Moreover, not all undocumented immigrants hold the same potential for advocacy. Certain bodies, professions, ages, levels of language comprehension, access to resources, amount of education, and other kinds of experience may grant access to or prohibit certain groups from effective activism.

To sort out both how and why this happens, we might resurrect questions originally posed by Michel Foucault: "What difference does it make who is speaking?"[11] and, "From where does [a message] come, who wrote it, when, under what circumstances, or beginning with what design?"[12] These may appear at first as simple questions—matters of fact—but the answers demand closer inspection because they hold the power to sway both the content and the effect of any message in any context. Alcoff asserts, "We must finally acknowledge that systematic divergences in social location between speakers and those spoken for will have a significant effect on the content of what is said."[13] She argues that there does not exist a "neutral" position from which to speak, though sometimes speakers attempt to conceal or supersede their positions to accomplish their purpose.

Much of the variance in strategy within the immigrant rights movement can be read as a response to differing opinions about who can or should speak for whom. As explained in the preceding chapters, undocumented immigrants often lack the ability to represent themselves in mainstream media; when they do appear, it is often as tokens. Tokenism occurs when some perfunctory gesture is made to include a member of a minority group in some action or message and often involves a request or expectation that this one individual represent an entire group. One immigrant activist told Walter Nicholls about witnessing tokenizing while attempting to work alongside some pro-immigrant rights politicians: "Whenever a politician needed one of us, they would say, 'Hey, bring a student, we need him at this press conference.' There were many among us who felt like puppets."[14] Instances of tokenism of the undocumented community lead many immigrants to the weighty realization that when they speak, they cannot simply "speak for themselves"; they implicate other undocumented folks through their words and actions.

In the following pages, undocumented activists express understanding that their words influence each other. Because the act of storytelling is social rather than isolated, immigrants work together to find collective frames and strategies that offer them a shared platform on which to base their arguments. Daniel believes immigrants must pursue a "decentralizing from individualized narrative[s]" and collectively recognize that "it's not about 'you.' It's really about the people you're fighting [for], whose lives you're trying to fight to make better."[15] The extent to which undocumented immigrants see themselves as responsible to each other varies from person to person. But because they are portrayed in public discourse as belonging to the same group—despite originating from all over the world and holding diverse viewpoints, beliefs, and values—even if an undocumented immigrant wishes to distance himself or herself from the group and speak publicly only as an individual, such isolation may not be possible. As Alcoff contends, "The declaration that I 'speak only for myself' has the sole effect of allowing me to avoid responsibility and accountability for my effects on others; it cannot literally erase those effects."[16] As immigrants grapple with the effects their own words have on each other, they must make difficult choices about which parts of their lives to make public and which goals their activism should try to achieve. This requires both perseverance and some collective agreement about which frames to employ when sharing stories.

The impossibility of speaking only for oneself is further complicated by the presence of stereotype threat. In a 2013 study of undocumented college students, Lauren Ellis and Eric Chen found that several of the individuals who participated in their research interviews felt "a responsibility to counteract negative stereotypes of their ethnic communities as well as stereotypes of undocumented immigrants."[17] One participant admitted, "I feel like I represent Latinos everywhere. . . . I can't just say BS in class because then the stereotypes are perpetuated, and I feel like it's my job to, to break that."[18] As a result of stereotype threat and tokenism, undocumented immigrants' words are always implicating and constituting each other. This realization has led to a commitment on the part of immigrant rights activists to find a frame that works not just for individuals but that will benefit the group as a whole.

The search for an inclusive strategic frame that works for diverse groups of immigrants has not been a simple undertaking. Members of the undocumented community cannot or do not always want to coordinate their efforts, but there are many grassroots groups and immigrant-led organizations working tirelessly to establish and maintain a workable set of storytelling frames. Sometimes well-intended frames have unexpected consequences that demand revisions and reworking. In the next sections, the narrators describe three of these significant revisions in strategy that have occurred in contemporary undocumented immigrant activism, and their reactions to each.

From "No Fault of Our Own" to Celebrating Courageous Parents

When the DREAMer movement began to gain steam in the early 2000s, it garnered a great deal of support through messaging that emphasized that children who were brought to the United States before they were old enough to make their own decisions arrived through "no fault of their own." This rhetoric was successful enough to permeate both conservative and liberal discourse. In the attempt to garner support for the DREAM Act, and again after it failed to pass in 2010, former president Barack Obama lamented the lack of options for undocumented youth brought to the United States as children. In a Rose Garden speech in 2012, he remarked, "That can't be who we are, to have kids—our kids, classmates of our children—who are suddenly under this shadow of fear through *no fault of their own*. They didn't break a law. They were kids."[19] In a letter of support for allowing undocumented immigrants to qualify for in-state tuition, a group of New Jersey mayors charged that requiring undocumented students to pay out-of-state tuition is an "unfair punishment on children who find themselves in an immigration status limbo through *no fault of their own*."[20] As recently as September 2017, Donald Trump used this language on Twitter to describe the young people who had received temporary protection under DACA. "They have been in our country for many years through *no fault of their own*—brought in by parents at [a] young age," he tweeted.[21]

The "no fault of their own" frame also found its way into immigrant rights associations' discourse. In 2011, a staff writer for the *Define American* campaign explained, "Undocumented students graduate from our high schools every year. They came to this country illegally through *no fault of their own*."[22] In a webpage devoted to quick facts in support of the DREAM Act, the American Immigration Council explained the impact of illegality on DREAMers: "Through *no fault of their own*, their lack of status may prevent them from attending college or working legally."[23] Though useful for framing young undocumented immigrants as innocent victims of unfortunate circumstances, this kind of rhetoric has had the unintended but precarious effect of criminalizing undocumented parents. That is, the exact frame that exonerates immigrant children implicates their parents by transferring the full weight of fault onto them.

In June 2016, I interviewed Jung Rae Jang. Jung Rae was born in South Korea in 1990, arrived in the United States on a tourist visa with his mother when he was fifteen, and now has temporary protected status under DACA. Jung Rae works as a community organizer for the immigrant rights focused MinKwon Center for Community Action in New York City, and he has noticed a difference in the ways the American public sees his generation and his parents' generation. "I think they're more sympathetic toward us, knowing that we came here against our choice and we're just going to school and we're just working," he told me. He remembers that in the early 2000s, immigrant advocates believed there was a very slim chance that comprehensive immigration reform was a realizable goal, so activists decided to "just push for the DREAM Act," which would grant a path to citizenship for children who arrived in the United States but exclude their parents. Since that time, undocumented activists have had to choose whether to support comprehensive immigration reform (CIR)—a significant change in legislation that would include paths to citizenship for parents—or the DREAM Act, which has been touted as much more feasible and likely. This choice to focus on securing their own futures or committing to the potentially unattainable possibility of CIR puts many activists between a rock and a hard place. Jung Rae told me,

A lot of the advocacy work [included] that rhetoric like, "Oh, those kids," like, "It's not their fault that they came here and they're just good students. Let's provide them a path to citizenship." . . . But when it comes to our parents, they are really, I feel like they are vilified and very marginalized in a way. Some of the remarks [were that] they're rapists and killers and whatever—how ridiculous it sounds. Those are not really comments that are directed towards undocumented youth, they're comments directed toward our parents or older generations of undocumented people.[24]

Jung Rae is not sure how to feel about these perceptions. "I have a very mixed feeling about that," he explained. "I mean, sure, like in a very, very technical sense, yes, my mom came here with a tourist visa and she overstayed her visa, but we've really got to see the side that says . . . *why* would the parents come here, risk everything they have in their country and be undocumented? There is a human reason for that and that's something that people do not see often."

As undocumented youth began to recognize that the success of the "no fault of our own" frame led to and allowed the criminalization of their parents, many began to question and disavow this language and to change the way they told their stories in public. Jung Rae told me that this frame is "a rhetoric that we don't use anymore" and that his own message has shifted to emphasize that "it's not just the kids that are not criminal, but everybody [is] not criminal. Our parents, they are hardworking, they pay taxes, they just want a better future for their kids, [they are] law-abiding. I think those are the rhetorics that we're trying to use around now and push for."[25] The shift in strategy away from the "no fault of our own" frame opened up a space for undocumented activists to honor their parents and consider how much courage it took them to leave their lives behind and travel to the United States in hopes of something better.

Daniel also explained to me his frustration with the "no fault of our own" frame and how it "definitely victimizes parents and shifts the blame onto them also." Daniel believes the idea that "DREAMers are deserving immigrants because they came here as children without making conscious decisions" is faulty logic because no matter what your age, "You *can't* really make a conscious decision when your options are so limited and maybe you're facing violence back home."[26] The move toward a frame that celebrates parents instead of criminalizing them reveals undocumented immigration as a multinational, rather than single-nation, problem. It allows audiences to consider the political, social, and cultural climates that may prohibit some individuals from accessing well-being, safety, and security for themselves and their children in their home communities. One activist explained in an interview with Walter Nicholls, "We no longer say 'through no fault of our own.' We now say we were brought here by our parents who are courageous and responsible and who would not let their children die and starve in another country."[27] This shift creates a more inclusive rhetoric for all immigrants rather than exonerating only some.

Jenny, who was born in Hungary and arrived in New York with her parents and brother when she was twelve, believes this shift is necessary because, she explained with some exasperation, "It's not fun to pick up your whole family—they're not doing it just to joke—and people that actually do come across the borders, they risk their lives coming here for an opportunity. Like other people like us, my parents sold everything they had, so if this didn't work out, we were going to go back to nothing. I think that's what [people] don't understand."[28] Debates about immigration to the United States can gain a fuller view of the "big picture" by pulling back to a wider framing of the issue that allows for a consideration of the motivating factors that would lead adult immigrants to leave their homes.

The "no fault of their own" frame lost its status because it inadvertently excluded parents, not because it was false. It certainly is the case that some young immigrants were not old enough to decide for themselves whether to come to the United States. I interviewed one young man who was born in Jamaica and arrived in the United States when he was only one month old and thus has lived as an "alien" without legal status for essentially his entire life. Such narratives challenge the oversimplified categorization of migrants as either "voluntary" or "forced."[29] Undocumented immigrants brought to the United States as very young children may not have experienced coercion, but neither did they "volunteer" to be resettled as aliens in a nation that would prohibit them from basic rights and freedoms.

While some young immigrants do express frustration with their parents' decision to bring them without papers to the United States, the shift in framing toward esteeming parents is also more inclusive of young immigrants who are grateful that their mothers and fathers risked their own safety and security to search out a different life for their children. In May 2016 I interviewed Felix, who was born in El Salvador and brought to the United States when he was five. "I think about it all the time and, honestly, it was probably the best decision my parents made for me in my life," Felix told me. "I have a couple cousins over there [in El Salvador] that have college degrees and they can't even get a job and they're older than me. I sit back and think about it. What if that was me at twenty-five, twenty-six years old, no career, living at home, basically no future because there's really no opportunity to prosper? What would I do at that point? I'm very thankful that my parents made the decision for me."[30] As undocumented youth age and face the reality of their own uncertain futures in the United States, many are also coming to terms with the hardships their parents faced when they left everything behind and are beginning to understand the larger forces that influence such a decision.

Daniel recalls, "For a long time, I had resented my family and blamed them for our situation, rather than understanding the larger processes that had brought my family to where we were—the larger structural forces that had moved us away from our home in the Philippines."[31] This same realization led Josue, who arrived in the United States with his parents from Mexico when he was seven, to believe that the immigrant rights movement needs to "pay more attention to the parents of undocumented immigrants because they're struggling to help us make it here." Josue sees now that his parents' lives revolve around his own success. "My mom and my stepdad,

I don't think they have any plans after I graduate and after I find a career. The only reason they're here is for me," Josue explained. "I think we definitely should pay more attention to the parents and try to find ways for them to also remain in the country. Ways for them not to feel unsafe and like they have to leave because they should be able to stay here with the kids if they want to, they shouldn't be separated."[32] This understanding has led Josue and others to purposefully include messaging about their parents' bravery and selflessness in their activism.

A 2013 article called "Celebrating Parents, The Original DREAMers" on DefineAmerican.com reads, "Now, in that space 'DREAMers' created, there is great opportunity to push back on a narrative that has at times painted the noble sacrifice of parents as irresponsible. Parents are speaking out, allies are speaking out and the narrative is changing." In a *Huffington Post* article, undocumented student Lisette Candia wrote,

> I am not brave. No, the brave ones are my parents. My parents who left their native country, who left everything they know, in order to give me a better future. My parents who drive my siblings to school, despite not having valid licenses. My parents, who despite the many injustices they face, still choose to pay taxes to the country that still does not recognize them as contributing members of society, but instead portrays them as criminals in the media.[33]

In a YouTube video called "What my undocumented parents sacrificed for me," and produced by MiTú, a media brand that features Latino content creators, a montage of immigrants thank their parents and honor their struggles. "Our parents have sacrificed the unimaginable to give us better opportunities. Their struggles give us the strength to pursue a higher education and work harder to thank them for what they've done," the video's description reads.[34] Through tears, one young woman faces into the camera to say about her mother's decision to come to the United States, "It's impacted me so much, and I really do appreciate her for her sacrifice."

The unintended consequences of the "no fault of our own" frame and the subsequent response of activists to reverse this effect reveal the power of a compelling story on a public. A US-centric view makes it easier to blame parents for jeopardizing their children's futures, but a transnational view reveals that this choice often results from the fierce desire to protect children's lives in the midst of insurmountable hardship or danger. The newer frame of positive parent-centric messages resonates within the undocumented community and contributed to the momentum behind Deferred Action for Parents of Americans and Lawful Permanent Residents

(DAPA),[35] which would have granted some undocumented parents protections similar to those DACA recipients received, including a work permit and a temporary exemption from deportation. Proposed by former president Barack Obama, DAPA faced an injunction after several states filed lawsuits in 2015 against the federal government. The Supreme Court agreed to hear the case, but on June 23, 2016, a four-four tie prevented any lifting of the injunction, prohibiting DAPA from passing. Today millions of undocumented parents continue to live without protection.

From the Cookie Cutter Frame to Inclusivity of Difference

The early stages of the DREAMer movement attempted to counteract stereotypical portrayals of criminal immigrant job stealers by highlighting the successes of undocumented young people who were among the best and brightest youth in the nation. To accomplish this, the movement publicized success stories of college bound, community-involved youth in graduation regalia speaking American English without an accent. As the former director of the California Dream Network described, "We have focused on the crème de la crème, the top students, the 4.3, the valedictorian. We have always been intentional in choosing the best story, the most easily understood story, the most emotionally convincing story."[36] The exceptional youth featured in these stories have managed to overcome significant legal, financial, and social obstacles to achieve an impressive amount of success.

Several of the narrators I interviewed described these kinds of emphasized stories as "cookie cutter" portrayals because of the ways they repeat each other with little variation. The cookie cutter frame provides a classic underdog narrative that still dominates some pro-immigrant political discourse. But this narrative does not sit right with many immigrant activists because it does not accurately represent the realities of many of the 11.3 undocumented immigrants living in the United States today.

The "cookie cutter" narrative holds a good deal of potential because of the ways it aligns itself with dominant US values of education, ambition, and self-reliance. But ultimately it is both reductive and exclusionary because not all undocumented immigrants have the same access to or desire to achieve these values. The cookie cutter frame presents a role that only certain kinds of immigrants can play. The role reifies what Karma Chávez calls "dominant imaginaries of belonging within the U.S. nation-state" through sustained attention to the ways the brightest undocumented immigrants resemble the brightest Americans.[37] This performance begs a question, asked previously by James Scott in *Domination and the Arts of Resistance*: "How do we study power relations when the powerless are often obliged to adopt a strategic pose in the presence of the powerful and when the powerful may have an interest in overdramatizing their reputation and mastery?"[38]

Nicholls explains, "Producing a good front stage persona of the DREAMer" meant that "backstage complications and identities of real immigrant youths, their complicated national loyalties, sexualities, conduct, and so on, could not be allowed to seep onto the public stage because they would complicate the core message and imperil the cause."[39] Lisa Marie Cacho points out that undocumented immigrants have attracted a public gaze "only by conforming to those U.S. heteronormative 'morals' and 'standards of living' that, ironically, have been defined over and against their very communities and their communities' survival strategies."[40] Conformity to US ideals allows only a contingent potential for acceptance; because the cookie cutter frame operates as a success-driven narrative, those who are included and praised within this frame are granted consideration because of their accomplishments, not their personhood.

The proposed DREAM Act entailed specified eligibility requirements each time it was proposed to Congress—including limits on the age at which immigrants were brought to the United States, enrollment in school, and continual residence—but the cookie cutter narrative reveals requirements for eligibility that supersede mere demographics and appear as more implicit boundaries. To fit the cookie cutter, immigrants must demonstrate eagerness for citizenship, publicly espouse normative American values, and silence the parts of themselves that diverge from the dominant narrative.

Upon critically evaluating the role of this frame, Daniel recalled thinking, "It doesn't make sense for us [because] a lot of our members didn't immediately go to higher education. Some are in community college and that's fine with them. Some never graduated from high school. Some never finished college or high school or had to put things on hold. The majority of us were like working class people really [just trying] to survive." Unquestionably, this frame has little room for immigrants without "enough" education, for undocumented victims of sex trafficking or asylum seekers, or even just older adults, immigrants still learning English, and those unwilling to play the role of model potential citizens. There are many immigrant stories that simply do not appear in newsworthy or emotionally compelling ways. While some undocumented youth certainly do fit the cookie cutter frame via their wish to go to college, volunteer in their communities, and live lives within the boundaries of normative American citizenry, others do not or cannot.

The interviewees in this project seemed particularly troubled by the proliferation of accounts of this cookie cutter frame. "You'll see a lot of that during election season," Angy explained during an interview. "A lot of the perfect DREAMers and the good stories that we want to highlight. The DREAMers that support Obama and the DREAMers that love the Democratic Party. But you won't see the DREAMers who actually are really disappointed with Obama because he has deported the most immigrants in our history. Those aren't the ones that you want to hear on the news." Angy works with the New York State Youth Leadership Council and supports more undocumented representation in media, but she believes these idealized narratives are not the solution.

When overly positive stories are highlighted, Angy explained, "that drowns out a lot of other stories that have had different experiences." Daniel agreed and explained, "DREAMers have been used as the face of the movement, sending out a very specific message about the value of higher education and racializing immigration as Latino centric. It erases the narratives of other immigrants of color and those who do not fit the mold as higher education aspiring."[41]

Beyond only emphasizing the most admirable traits of a select group of young undocumented people, the cookie cutter narrative often frames immigrants as a promising but ultimately helpless group of victims, powerless to overcome the obstacles facing them, and willing to do whatever it takes to become model citizens. Daniel explained, "It's such a familiar story. It's meant to draw pitiful kind of feelings from people [who will] sympathize with them. I was like, I don't like that. That's not empowering for me. That puts me in a place where it's like I'm begging for some sort of reprieve from the state, which has *caused* my existence to be like that, rather than questioning or being more direct and understanding why we are here or why we are undocumented."[42] Because Daniel sees his undocumented status as directly related to deep flaws in US immigration policy, he is uncomfortable subordinating himself to this policy in order to plead for some reprieve.

Sonia also expressed her frustration with monolithic portrayals of undocumented immigrants as suppliant victims. She told me, "I like to stay away from immigrant media because it just shows people as victims instead of showing people that we're a force to reckon with."[43] Stories of distress and hardship may pull on US-born citizens' heartstrings and engender sympathy for immigrants, but, as these narrators explain, the collateral damage of such portrayals includes their inability to account for the reality that undocumented immigrants are a heterogeneous group with agency who may desire to be seen as activists rather than victims.

Counteracting the cookie cutter frame requires the inclusion of narratives in the immigrant rights movement that do not simply reiterate the hopes and dreams of the best and brightest. Evolving this frame into one that better serves more undocumented people requires highlighting the great deal of difference and heterogeneity that exists in this group, but this task is formidable, and the means are not always clear.

Pang's idea is to attempt, in the future of her filmmaking career, to commit to working with undocumented individuals whose stories are not likely to appear in mainstream media. She told me, "I would probably want to work with—not to be selective—but maybe now that I'm seeing these generational gaps I would want to tell more stories about older generations, or first generation undocumented immigrants . . . because they're a different face in the undocumented world, they're a different scenario."[44] Providing audiences opportunities for encounters with this difference, Pang believes, may shift individuals' understanding about all the varieties of experiences that exist under the title "undocumented immigrant."

Activists who wish to contest the cookie cutter frame must confront the reality that inclusivity of more diverse stories is likely to prolong, rather than expedite, the possibility of immigration reform. But for some, such a deceleration is warranted if it means ensuring greater inclusivity and guarding against idealizing some immigrants at the expense of others. David explained,

> The struggle that we always have is that the media is always looking for people that fit their bubble. . . . [W]e realize that if we do that, we're throwing people that may not fit that perfect bubble under the bus for the benefit of a few, and if we're going to get change we need to include all the people. We need to make sure that our movement is inclusive, so more and more our stories are highlighting the people that have been pulled over, that may have committed a crime, that may have, I don't know, have a drug conviction. All of those different things. And even if progress might be a little slower, that's okay, because we're including more people in our movement and we're including all of the different stories that are darker, that are not the perfect ones, but it's beautiful in its own right. Those are the stories that we want to have.[45]

Whereas at first glance David's determination for inclusivity may appear at risk of minimizing the reality that many undocumented immigrants have *not* been pulled over or convicted of drug charges or other crimes, in fact, his logic serves a protective function that safeguards such individuals. If immigrant rights rhetoric rests on the premise that undocumented people deserve reform because they are a faultless group, then just a single instance to the contrary can dismantle this argument. But if, as David suggests, the movement can make room for stories that depict a broader array of experiences, single pieces of anecdotal evidence may be prevented from achieving such dominating power.

David's reflections complicate some of the existing scholarship on the immigrant rights movement, like Nicholls's, that suggests in order to be successful, immigrant activists "must craft representations that . . . build a sympathetic public portrait of their group . . . [by] silencing those other aspects that may distort their central message" so that they are perceived as "a coherent and deserving 'group.'"[46] David's strategy of amplifying difference—rather than silencing it—suggests a coalitional possibility that does not sacrifice imperfect and dissimilar immigrants for the benefit of a few.

One of the most popular immigrant-produced media strategies designed to invite variations on the cookie cutter frame is found in the work of Jose Antonio Vargas, a journalist who came out as undocumented in a groundbreaking essay published by the *New York Times* magazine in 2011. Vargas's aforementioned *Define American* project includes a digital archive of stories designed "to elevate the conversation around immigration and citizenship in America."[47] *Define American* offers one digital space where divergent and varied undocumented voices are gathered, welcomed, and placed side by side to emphasize the reality that being undocumented is not a single story; it is many.

Vargas has received more journalistic and popular attention than most undocumented immigrant-produced media makers. He has been interviewed multiple times on Fox News, and quoted or mentioned in such mainstream media as *Time*, the *Washington Post*, the *Atlantic*, and *USA Today*. Vargas testified in a Senate Judiciary Committee in February 2013,[48] regularly appears at both Democratic and Republican political campaign events, and tweets to his more than 74,000 followers on Twitter several times a day.

The front page of DefineAmerican.com offers several invitations and calls to action. "SHOW YOUR PUBLIC SUPPORT" and "SHARE YOUR STORY," two large links beckon. Below that, a box appears where readers can "Stay connected to Define American" by entering their names, email addresses, and phone numbers. A link for readers who want to "Share this story" succeeds each of the headlines that cycle through on a timed rotation. Of course, the name of the initiative is a call to action in itself. *Define American* contests mainstream US media portrayals of immigrants through emphases on heterogeneity and humanization. These two traits are often lacking in mainstream representations of immigrants, which lean instead toward homogeneity, dehumanization, and criminalization.[49]

The "Stories" page of the *Define American* site invites visitors to watch a multitude of short films of reclaimant narrators talking through their pasts. Some of the stories look professionally produced, others appear to be filmed using the front-facing camera on a cell phone held by the storyteller. Many of the immigrants featured in these stories hold little in common with each other beyond having lived for a time as undocumented. Some still lack documentation, others have temporary protection under DACA, and others have gone on to receive permanent residency or even citizenship through successful claims of asylum or through the petitioning of a citizen spouse or family member. *Define American*'s ability to crowd-source an ever-growing corpus of stories and share them instantaneously is a hallmark of the power of digital media for reclaiming immigrant rights rhetoric and resisting the cookie cutter frame.[50] When these reclaimant narrators are able to speak for themselves despite a lack of congruence with a preferred mold, they defy presuppositions and assert their own humanity.

Recovering the validity of stories that do not fit an idealized form has both symbolic and pragmatic implications. Daniel explained to me that when diverse perspectives "are invisible, it kind of alienates people from being involved in any actions or seeing themselves as part of that movement." Following this logic, individuals who *do* encounter stories that detail a wider range of relatable struggles may be more likely to envision themselves as part of the movement. Daniel's proposal is consistent with research suggesting that people identify more with leaders who look like them or share their race or gender.[51]

The presence of difference among stories placed side-by-side reveals the unreliability of generalizing from a single undocumented narrative or conflating multiple ways of being into an oversimplified account. Indeed, resisting the cookie cutter frame challenges both dominant media and also immigration studies scholarship that casts undocumented immigrants in the same light regardless of diversity. When scholarship generalizes undocumented immigrants as holding, for instance "common hopes, obstacles, fears, and dreams," it falls prey to the danger of speaking for others in ways that are academically tidy but realistically ineffectual.[52]

From One Note to More than Immigrants and Solidarity with Other Groups

Much of the narrative activism undocumented immigrants produce foregrounds the effect of immigration status on one's life. A lack of documentation is, after all, the crux of the issue these activists seek to rectify for themselves and their families. But by continually pointing to immigrants' lack of legal status, this frame fails to emphasize that the storytellers are *more* than immigrants, and that they lead lives full of ambitions, fears, relationships, insecurities, and challenges—some of which are related to their immigration status, and many that are not. When immigrants fashion reclaimant narratives that highlight multiple dimensions of their identity, this dynamism resists essentialism that fosters dehumanization, and reveals them as individuals whose lives very much resemble those of other members of their communities in most ways except one. If audience members cannot relate to being undocumented, they may be able to relate, for instance, to the pressures of dating, or the stress of college, or the excitement of a new baby in the family.

"One-note" narratives—a metaphor I borrow from theater, in which a performance fails to engage an audience because of monotony or stagnation—show immigrants as undocumented but nothing more. This frame is hazardous because it neglects revealing the relatable humanity of immigrants' day-to-day lives, instead emphasizing their foreignness. Joshua Meyrowitz asserts that contemporary media engage with a public "fascinated with exposure";[53] but he demonstrates that "ironically, what is pulled out of the closets that contain seemingly extraordinary secrets is, ultimately, the 'ordinariness' of everyone. The unusual becomes usual."[54] Revealing immigrants as *usual* rather than *other* has the power to counteract American resistance to immigrants that stems from fear of the unknown or an inability to relate.[55] Reclaimant narratives that show immigrants as more than undocumented hold a good deal of potential to remind audiences of the similarities rather than differences between people with documentation and people without.

Esther, who was born in Spain and arrived in the United States when she was three, explained to me why more narratives need to exist that include "storytelling that doesn't limit our identities to just being immigrants."

When Esther begin to seek out other firsthand undocumented stories on-line after receiving DACA protection in 2012, she explained,

> It just seemed like everyone was following this outline for their story, and it often felt preachy. I don't know. I thought that there should be more creative ways that weren't just about us as immigrants, but also showed us as people and people with hobbies—I like my bike, and I like movies, and I don't just like social justice movies, I also like watching *That '70s Show* right now and also having a sense of humor. That's something that I think is still missing from our movement.[56]

Sonia reinforced this view. She explained, "I'm at a point where I don't want to create work about my undocumented status. Now I just want to create it about me. It's like . . . I'm more than undocumented—*I get it*, I'm undocumented. Now I want to know who I am outside of being un-documented."[57] These insights underscore that immigration status is just one facet of individuals' identities—a reality that demands two necessary recognitions.

First, any account of undocumented activism must be contextualized—indeed, even radically contextualized so as to avoid the propensity to con-sider immigration status as isolated from other facets of identity.[58] Second, many undocumented immigrants in the United States face double binds due to the interaction of their undocumented status with other facets of their lives. Being undocumented puts individuals at greater risk for un-fair treatment, issues related to a lack of available health care, and sexual assault, but immigrants may not know where to seek help, and even if they do, they may demonstrate reticence to seek it out because of real or imagined threats to their safety or well-being.[59] Describing an abusive re-lationship she experienced wherein her boyfriend threatened to have her family deported if she broke up with him, Sonia recalled, "I had no idea that you could get a restraining order and be okay and be protected. I just didn't know. I had no idea where to seek help."[60] Considering the challenges un-documented immigrants face requires an approach that avoids one-note essentializing and instead considers different facets of identity in tandem.

Kimberle Crenshaw, in her groundbreaking essay "Demarginalizing the Intersection of Race and Sex," writes, "Because the intersectional ex-perience is greater than the sum of racism and sexism, any analysis that does not take intersectionality into account cannot sufficiently address the particular manner in which Black women are subordinated."[61] While Crenshaw wrote primarily of the necessity of analyzing discrimination on the basis of gender and race in tandem, we might easily apply her argument about intersectionality to the necessity of considering immigration status alongside identities such as ethnicity, age, sexuality, gender, ability, religion, and/or class. Such a view allows for a consideration of the ways intersecting facets of identity may compound the likelihood of acceptance or discrimination, and it reveals the great differences that exist between undocumented individuals' lived experiences.

Pairing Crenshaw's intersectional approach with Karma Chávez's notion of *interactionality* may work to further redress the problems affiliated with one-note narratives of immigrants. As I discuss in the introduction, interactionality resists the notion that oppression, identity, and social location are fixed realities in order to show the dynamic nature of these entities. Chávez demonstrates how attending to identity's dynamism promotes a focus on "possibilities for creative and complicated responses to oppression" through emphasis on the evolutionary, rather than stagnant, facets of one's self.[62] Reclaimant narratives that acknowledge the dynamism of heterogeneous identities through intersectional and interactional perspectives work to counter oversimplified rhetoric about immigrants and to point to creative alternate possibilities for representation and activism.

To push back against one-note narratives, some undocumented activists have employed creative means for highlighting the ways that their undocumented status intersects with other parts of their identities. The organization that Daniel organizes with, RAISE, coined the hashtag #UndocuAsians to show that "people are really three-dimensional people and have to go through a lot of different things. . . . [W]e're not just undocumented." But Daniel wants to go even further than acknowledging simple intersections. "Beyond just being undocumented and Asian, what does it mean to be undocumented and Asian *and* a woman *and* queer *and* not East Asian *and* darker skinned?" he asks. He believes facing into these questions is "an impactful way to kind of really reclaim spaces where we have been kind of pushed out even within our own movement . . . and really connect with an audience that has a potential to help us steer not just the narrative but where legislation can really help create beneficial impacts for us."[63] Recovering the possibility of speaking about intersections may counter the belief that being undocumented supersedes other facets of identity or disallows one from the right to request or receive help.

One young woman I interviewed, who was born in Mexico, courageously shared her story on a Facebook group for undocumented immigrants at the City University of New York. She wrote,

After the prom, back in High School, I was sexually assaulted in a party that I went to with my friends. A lot of issues came after that. I got posttraumatic stress disorder (PTSD) and depression; but these are things that many people like us don't really talk about when we are undocumented because we are already dealing with the situation and feeling that we don't belong here. . . . I started thinking, "I want to take my life. I don't even want to live anymore. I don't see the point for it." Somehow I gained courage, and spoke with my parents about my disorder instead.[64]

The effect of such messages on both author and audience should not be underestimated. In the responses below this post, one commenter wrote,

You are not alone. I agree with you, less people talk about their traumatic experiences because, of course, it's like opening old wounds, but even less people talk about it when they're undocumented, with thoughts like "I don't belong here." I agree, I feel for you, I'm here for you, and I thank you from the bottom of my heart for sharing this piece of you because it gives other survivors the courage to move on, and maybe share their own.[65]

In such moments, addressing the interaction of immigration status with other experiences and identities allows for greater understanding of the ways these realities co-constitute each other.

In 2011, Angy released a five-minute YouTube video called "Dating While Undocumented."[66] In the film, Angy faces the camera and talks informally about some of the awkward scenarios that are likely on dates when one person is undocumented. "There's the one where you don't want to tell them you're undocumented," Angy describes. "Because you feel like that doesn't define you—that's not who you are, they shouldn't focus on that." She talks about another possibility where immigrants do tell their dates about being undocumented. Angy describes wryly, "They're obviously going to use this line on you: 'So why don't you just get your papers?' Then you have to try to school that person on immigration laws. . . . [S]ometimes you want to go on a date and you don't want to talk about immigration, you don't want to talk about politics." The video currently has 109 comments; six express anti-immigrant sentiment,[67] and the remainder show support for Angy.

One commenter posted, "As a white girl, I can preach all I want about how immigrants should have the same rights I have, but what really makes a difference, is when those people learn that someone they care about [is] undocumented. . . . Keep up the good fight! In solidarity." Another lamented incurring additional difficulty when trying to date while "not only [undocumented] but being queer on top [of] that," and offered relational support for Angy. "Even though you are on the other side of the country you have my friendship and my love if you will take it," this commenter assured. Others mentioned the desire to use the video as a device for opening a conversation. Someone wrote, "I had to revisit this . . . imma use it as a conversation starter with the guy I'm dating and we'll go from there." Throughout the thread, Angy responds to encourage those who write in with concerns. "Hang in there we'll get thru this. just understand that you're valuable too regardless of status," she assures one of them. When I interviewed her, Angy explained,

> That video in specific is interesting because we get so caught up in the legislation, and laws, and bills that would impact immigrants that we forget that this immigrant person still dates, and goes shopping, and needs to pick up a package but doesn't have an ID, and what that is like. We forget that immigrant people also love, and deserve love, and how hard that is when you don't have papers, and all the stuff that comes up when you're trying to date and you want to have a normal life, but you're still undocumented and what that's like. Those are things that we kind of don't really think about. We just focus on laws, laws, laws.[68]

Angy's work serves as an exemplar of the "more than immigrants" frame because of its ability to take up intersectional and interactional identities in tandem.

As Alcoff reminds us, "We might say that I should only speak for groups of which I am a member. But this does not tell us how groups themselves should be delimited . . . how narrowly should we draw the categories?"[69] She contends, "No easy solution to this problem can be found by simply restricting the practice of speaking for others to speaking for groups of which one is a member."[70] Instead of claiming to speak for the entire population of undocumented immigrants in the United States because of a shared lack of status, the "more than immigrants" frame allows reclaimant narrators to address the reality that they all belong in multiple and sometimes overlapping identity groups.

These efforts open up intersectional spaces like the #EndTransDetention campaign, which addresses the reality that lesbian, gay, bisexual, transgender, and queer (LGBTQ) immigrants in detention face more risk than others for sexual harassment and assault, and also allow for solidarity with other movements. This message appears clearly in artwork by Yocelyn

Riojas that states *TU LUCHA ES MI LUCHA*—"Your fight is my fight" in English (Figure 3.1).

In a recent Tumblr post called "8 Black Immigrant Organizers You Should Follow on Twitter," Angy wrote, "The Black Lives Matter movement and the immigrant rights movement are not mutually exclusive. Many folks exist and organize at these intersections."[71] By refusing an oversimplified frame that highlights only one's undocumentedness, these narrative activists tell about their intersectional lives and reveal the complexity of humans previously cast as a single-issue crowd.

In Chapter 1 I suggested that one of the primary challenges facing undocumented immigrants who use their stories for activism is that their reclaimant narratives are complicated and diverse. A second challenge arises from the reality that due to this diversity, the undocumented community does not always agree upon or wish to use the same strategy to pursue reform. For this reason, it remains impossible to talk about immigrant rights strategies as though they are consistent or stagnant. Instead,

FIGURE 3.1. © Yocelyn Riojas 2017 (yocelynriojas.com)

frames and strategies are dynamic and porous. Because activists may employ more than one at a time, or shift their approach according to the sociopolitical moment in which their activism appears, this chapter should not be read as an exhaustive or prescriptive description of all immigrant rights strategy. Instead, it offers illumination of some of the major recurring and contested themes in contemporary narrative activism, as described by reclaimant narrators themselves. This analysis allows a view into the power of storytelling strategy to define a movement and the potential effect of framing in instances of desired social and political change.

One should keep in mind that shifts in framing like the ones described above do not necessarily represent or require shifts in the storytellers' selves or ways of being. A frame can morph, disappear, reappear, and be manipulated irrespective of any change in the reality to which the frame attends. As Olga Kuchinskaya found in her analysis of the ways the Chernobyl nuclear accident was framed for public audiences, "Older themes can be overshadowed or (temporarily) disappear, while other perspectives can reemerge. Yet new interpretations do not fully replace the existing ones; they supplement them. Even with the most radical historical transformations, the whole discourse cannot be assumed to change and be transformed into a new discourse."[72] Here, Kuchinskaya demonstrates that what changes during these thematic evolutions is not the accident itself but rather the way public discourse reinvents and reinterprets the accident in the minds of its audiences.

Likewise, Walter Nicholls describes in his work how "immigrant youths [c]ould be transformed from threats to the national community into sources of economic, civic, and moral rejuvenation" simply "by representing them as virtuous Americans."[73] But notice that, similar to Kuchinskaya's work, what shifts in Nicholls's example is not who these immigrants *are*; the individuals in question may retain the same beliefs, values, actions, and personalities as they always have, yet be perceived differently by audiences because of a shift in a representational frame.

Considering the negotiation of narrative frames demonstrates the import of dynamism and flexibility within a social movement. It is not always possible to know for sure what effect a reclaimant narrative might have on audiences before it is implemented. In cases where unanticipated results incur negative consequences for immigrant activists, adaptability is imperative for progress. As new media become ever more accessible and immediate, activists have greater ability to react and respond quickly, so that shifts in storytelling strategy that used to take much longer and were difficult to coordinate over any distance can now be implemented almost instantaneously. Because the effect of digital media in this respect has been so profound, it demands a closer look. To investigate the potential and limitations of digital narrative activism, I analyze this phenomenon in detail in the following chapter.

CHAPTER 4 | The Search for Connection Online

IN 1987, ESTHER MEROÑO Baro was born in Cartagena, Spain. Her parents were members of the Church of Latter Day Saints, and when Esther was still a child, the family moved to Utah to join the largest concentration of Mormons in the United States. At fifteen, Esther wanted to apply for a job at a local movie theater in Salt Lake City. That's when her parents told her that she was undocumented. Esther was livid, and recalls telling them, "Well, you really messed up. You messed this up for me. How are you going to fix it? I want this job. I need to be able to work." Ultimately, Esther did not have as much trouble finding work as she expected: "I look and I sound like a white American woman," she explained. "So that let me have a lot more job experience than other undocumented youth."

Today, Esther has the protection of Deferred Action for Childhood Arrivals (DACA) and works as a digital organizing strategist and communications manager at Auburn Seminary, a leadership institute in New York City that partners with other faith-rooted social justice organizations to advance progressive change. I met her in her office at Auburn for an interview just as the sun was setting outside her window over the nearby Hudson River.

Esther kept her immigration status a secret until she successfully applied for DACA in 2012. Afterward, she found the courage to go public about her status in a post on her personal blog, which bears the headline "Bringing my whole self, one piece at a time." The post begins with a photo of her, smiling into the camera, holding a sign that reads "#undocumentedandunafraid" and ends with a call to action:

> Now that you know who I really am, I hope that those of you with questions won't hesitate to ask, and that rather than dismiss me and the cause, you'll consider how you can become more informed on this very critical topic, and

join the campaign for change. There are millions of people like me—your neighbors, your classmates, your coworkers—who, in their hearts, are just as American as you are. Please, help us gain "human being" status in the only place we call home.

When I asked Esther about her decision to tell her story publicly after she had kept her status a secret for over a decade, she told me, "I think it's really important for people to see their experiences in art and in media. It kind of validates your identity in a way." She is optimistic about the power of digital media in particular to effect change: "Media basically drives the fabric of society. It gives a glimpse into other people's lives and tells us what to think and builds our view of each other and even ourselves. It's really powerful." She believes that a profound exchange takes place when undocumented people encounter each other's stories—their identities are validated as they view others' experiences and offer their own.

Esther's optimism about the power of digital media is contagious, and I left our interview feeling hopeful about the potential of this medium for undocumented immigrants who may be geographically isolated or reticent to connect offline with others without legal status. I also left with questions: How and why are undocumented immigrant media makers choosing to tell their immigration stories online, and to what degree can immigrant-produced digital narratives work to abate the effects of isolation for undocumented immigrants and serve as a means of communal coping among individuals without legal status? What drawbacks and dangers are specific to digital contexts, and how do these risks figure in immigrants' decisions to share their reclaimant narratives digitally?

Because many undocumented immigrants face barriers that make higher education and/or professional employment infeasible, many reclaimant narratives find their homes on the internet, where production costs are low, amateur professionalism is the norm, and the option for anonymity is still vaguely present. Some undocumented storytellers produce digital content using pseudonyms for fear of detention or deportation; others are forthright about their identities despite the risks. The resulting stories work to counter more mainstream discourse, trading faceless narratives for individuality, and revealing relatable individuals who elsewhere have been vilified by stereotype and presupposition. These activists' reflections on their digital presence as well as the responses from their audiences reveal a good deal about the current public perception of immigrants in the United States and the power of narrative media to affect that perception.

The undocumented content creators in this chapter explicate how and why they choose to refute mainstream discourse with digital reclaimant narratives and assert an alternative view of immigrants. This chapter chronicles the self-reported positive effects that these narratives have on their creators in digital contexts, including the ability to negotiate the effects of social stigma, abate isolation, and advocate for social change. Some of the narrators confirm, as Radha Hegde and Katheryn Abrams have asserted in their work, that cultural citizenship is enacted through communicative processes that may provide a sense of belonging even when legal citizenship is unattainable.[1] But others reveal that this enactment comes at a cost, and the optimism I felt as I left my meeting with Esther was soon tempered by interviews with immigrants who are frustrated with digital activism.

Three themes emerged from this variety of perspectives. First, digital media provide a respite from the isolation that is all but unavoidable in undocumented immigrants' lives by offering an opportunity for connection that may seem impossible or too dangerous in the offline world. Second, as is evident from my analysis of the plentitude of comments that respond to digital reclaimant narratives, this context provides an unprecedented forum wherein US-born citizens and immigrants can interact, share opinions about immigration, and learn from one another. Finally, for some, participating in digital activism incurs unintended negative consequences that outweigh the positive potential of this medium. It is clear that creating reclaimant narratives in digital contexts incites particular hazards including the difficulty of gaining an audience for heterogeneous perspectives, the normalization of free labor, the facilitation of hateful and xenophobic responses, and the perpetuation of the confirmation bias.

"Internet Is Everything": Digital Media's Promise

I interviewed Freddy in March 2016. He arrived in the United States from Ecuador when he was two years old and was recently featured in a digital article from a major news source about undocumented students receiving tuition refunds.[2] I asked Freddy if he was nervous about going public about his immigration status in the article, and—unlike many other narrators—he told me he was not at all. His focus instead was on his story's potential. "My situation has helped others come up and show that they're having the same problem, something that they probably have not done before," Freddy explained. "The point of me doing this and being open about it is so others can follow—a domino effect. Make a difference. A big difference."

I asked Freddy if he had been featured in any other types of media after the *Huffington Post* article came out online. He confirmed: "There were TV stations calling for me but I really wasn't too crazy about those. They don't really show what is really going on a lot of the times." To make sure I understood, I asked, "Did you feel more comfortable on the internet than you did [about] television?" "Definitely," he replied. "The internet is very open. It's open to everyone. Everyone can see it. The TV is focused on popularity . . . and it's focused on [whether] this situation is going to make [it] more popular [with viewers]." He explained, "The internet is open for everyone. There might be a lot of wrong information there, but there's also a lot of good information, accurate information, information that is not altered by these big companies on TV. I think that's the difference. The internet is great." Freddy believes digital media has the ability to foster small-scale activism in a way older media—such as television and newspapers—could not.

While the fear of detention, deportation, or family separation drives many undocumented immigrants to silence and fear, the narrators in this chapter chose another path. Each of them has shared a reclaimant narrative—an experiential, partial, public, oppositional, and incondensable story about life without legal status—in a creative digital project. For these narrators, digital platforms facilitate prosumerism, amateur professionalism, self-disclosure, and perceived privacy. In this chapter, several narrators share their belief in the unique power of digital media to evoke empathy from audiences.

Most of the immigrants I interviewed are millennials—they grew up in the age of what Alvin Toffler calls "prosumerism," wherein previously existing boundaries between producers and consumers of media are blurred.[3] Because of the rapid rate of production made possible in digital contexts, prosumers may watch, read, or listen to media while they simultaneously create and respond. In addition, digital media has normalized a kind of amateur professionalism wherein traditional forms of expertise are dismantled through peer-to-peer training and the sheer abundance of available information about any subject of interest.[4] Esther describes her own experiences with amateur professionalism this way:

Technology has opened up popular education for anybody. Like you can go on YouTube and learn almost anything. You can go on Tumblr and start and make a beautiful website for fifteen dollars. Yeah, I mean, I definitely wouldn't have been able to do all these things twenty years ago. Internet is everything. . . . [When I wanted to] make a video, a documentary about my experience and story, I was like—I don't know how. I have no clue how I'm going to do this, but if you'll give me some time, I'll teach myself. I spent the next three months on YouTube learning how to edit in Final Cut. I borrowed some equipment from some neighbors. I made my own mic . . . out of an old set of headphones. All of that is available for anybody.

Amateur professionalism is not specific to undocumented immigrants. But it is especially salient to these individuals because of the barriers facing them in work, civic life, and education as they cannot accept federal financial aid or present documentation that would authorize them to vote or pursue professional careers in many fields.

Ricardo Aca, a twenty-five-year-old photographer who crossed the Mexican border into the United States when he was fourteen, described his digital photography this way in a recent film his friend posted to YouTube: "It also gives me a voice. I can't vote, but I can take photos and share the stories of people like me. You know, Trump keeps pointing out all these immigrants who have done all these terrible things, but those aren't the immigrants that I know. That's not what we're like, and photography is a way for me to show that." Ironically, until recently Ricardo worked in a restaurant in one of Donald Trump's towers in New York. The YouTube film, posted under the title "Meet the Undocumented Immigrant Who Works at a Trump Hotel," got 20,000 hits the first day it was posted; as of March 2018, it has almost 450,000 views.

Existing research has noted the ways digital culture has fostered a greater penchant for self-disclosure within the millennial population than was found in preceding generations.[5] When I asked Ximena (whose preferred third-person pronouns are "they" and "them") why they decided to share their immigration status publicly in a video on the *Define American* website, they told me emphatically, "Because I'm the social media generation—I have to talk about life! I have to tell people what things are like. I have to let people know I have to say something. I had to because it's so infuriating to know that nobody knows what it's like." Ximena thinks people too often highlight the ill effects of social media and forget that it also offers several benefits. They explained,

I feel you keep some things inside but given the correct environment, a correct website, you can tell people anything—and then you'll hear encouraging words and you'll hear support and it's like, yeah, people want to demonize social media but I feel like there's support to sharing your life on social media that a lot of people would not have gotten if it didn't exist.

A lot of people would have had this bigger sense of isolation and this bigger sense of lack of normality if it wasn't for the fact that we can share our struggles. I'm very pro-internet. I'm very pro-social media.

Other narrators echoed Ximena's enthusiasm, but described the strain that telling their stories online may create in conversations with members of older generations who are less accustomed to such unbridled self-disclosure.

Sonia remembers that before she posted both digital music and short films about her immigration status online, "any time that I would do something that would be heading towards becoming public, my dad would be like—he would make me question myself, like, 'What are you doing? What do you think can happen if you do this? You could have us all deported.' " Though her father's actions gave her pause, Sonia ultimately decided to move forward. Today her music and films are publicly available online.

Pang credits her generation's penchant for self-disclosure for helping to reduce the anxiety that might otherwise be affiliated with sharing a reclaimant narrative online. She explained, "People who are much younger, they grew up in this culture where it's like everything is shared and media is so readily available that they're not afraid to talk about it. . . . [People] who are more outspoken because they grew up in this outspoken generation, you know, we need more people I guess like them to really come out." Pang's encounters with other people's "coming out" narratives online gave her the courage to share her own story through film. She told me, "I would've sat on that piece forever if I could, and only shared it with family and friends. It's through the courage of these young undocumented, seemingly American youth that are really paving the way for people like myself to be more open." It is clear from Pang's reflections how digital undocumented storytelling self-perpetuates through the courage gained from encounters with others' stories.

One factor that influences millennials' penchant for self-disclosure in this context is the reality that digital platforms engender a perception of privacy that may reassure anyone fearful about the implications of revealing their immigration status in a public context. Angy developed and manages a Twitter-housed immigrant advice column; as she explained it to me, it gives undocumented immigrants in the United States "a place to ask questions anonymously, or without being judged, or forced to make a decision about something, having to show up in person, and having to fill out applications and forms." Angy clarified, "Mostly, I think, at least immigrants that I've met, are more comfortable searching online and trying to do things on their own than they are showing up to a place or coming in person to things." The motivation for this preference is simple; as Angy pointed out, "The news is not going to know that you don't have papers." A 2013 report by Kimberly Kahn, Katherine Spencer, and Jack Glaser suggests that in fact anonymity online is declining in recent years due to a combination of institutional factors (such as Facebook's policy that users display their real names) and social trends (e.g., the movement away from avatars and fictional identities online).[6] Regardless of this decline, the authors suggest, *perceived* privacy subsists in online contexts, so that undocumented prosumers may feel anonymous or invisible online even when this is not the case. As Freddy explained,

> A lot of us are very shy—they're very scared to even talk about it. To ask someone or try to find [something out] through the means of another person who knows, it would be very difficult for us to actually go and see what's going on. The internet lets you do it all on your own, which is good. Also, if you get over this shyness and you look for people who are actually trying to help, it would also be great, once you get over that shyness. For those who aren't, who are still afraid, then definitely the internet is the first step, I would say.

Freddy's view of the internet as a private and safe space to make a "first step" toward sharing one's experience and connecting with others reveals the medium's unique function in the lives of immigrants without legal status. To participate in the exchange that the internet offers this group, individuals do not always need to leave their homes, reveal their real identities, or have the training or education necessary for participating in more traditional forms of media.

Piash was born in Bangladesh in 1990 and arrived in the United States with his parents on a tourist visa when he was ten. After they overstayed their visa, Piash and his family became undocumented, and his father was deported back to Bangladesh in 2006. The event frightened Piash and reinforced for him the importance of hiding his status. "It felt like America was just a giant prison," he told me. But there was one place where Piash felt safe seeking out information that could help him:

> I started doing research online trying to see what is available. . . . I found a forum for undocumented students, DreamAct.info, I think. It was actually a relief when I found that site because I finally realized I am not alone. There are thousands of students just like me trapped in this horrible situation.

That actually really calmed me down almost because it is like I'm not alone in this.

Piash felt safe in the forum because none of the participants used their real names; instead, they had user names they created for themselves. The group felt that this choice protected them both from government monitoring and from "trolls" who would visit the forum just to post hateful messages.

But the feelings of relief Piash experienced in this space did not last for long. He began to feel "really helpless, because all of us are just unable to do anything, [we were] just talking about our situation online in a forum, and that's as open as we could be without risking getting into trouble or getting INS [Immigration and Naturalization Services] involved." Soon, he began to identify people in the forum who he "could tell were interested in doing something"; they started to message each other privately on AOL Instant Messenger, where they finally exchanged their real names. When the DREAM Act went before Congress in 2010, Piash went to Washington, DC, to meet some of these friends from the forum to rally. His mother was furious. "She was like, 'They could just be crazy people or it could be the government people, they're trying to get you,'" Piash remembers. But he felt so desperate for change that he thought, "If they want to come find me, come find me." Piash and his new friends rallied bravely, but to their disappointment, the DREAM Act failed in the Senate after passing in the House of Representatives.

Today, Piash is outspoken about his status and participates in a good deal of immigrant rights activism, both online and offline. In this sense, his experience confirms Freddy's view that the internet may act as a "first step" toward participating in other kinds of activism. But Piash still uses digital media to navigate the limitations of his status. Last year, he was diagnosed with colon cancer; since he has no health insurance, the medical bills for the removal of his tumor totaled around $225,000. His friends created a GoFundMe crowd funding website to help him with the expenses; it has raised just under $13,000.[7]

Piash is so optimistic about digital media's potential to aid the immigrant rights movement that he even attributes Obama's DACA program to digital activism:

Basically, digital media helped us so much because finally we could get organized together, through Facebook, through these events, through Change.org. I feel like if there was no digital media, this would not have happened. . . . If we didn't have that option of finding each other through online, I don't think the Deferred Action that President Obama passed—that wouldn't have even happened. . . . Without the digital media, I don't think we would have made that much progress at all.

Katherine, whose story appeared at the beginning of Chapter 1, agrees. She told me, "I don't think that DACA and DAPA[8] would have been possible without media—without digital media. I just think that it would have been impossible. It's what connected all of our stories." The belief that digital media provides connections that were impossible in older forms of media testifies to Manuel Castells's notion of digital media's creation of a "network society."[9] Castells posits that the internet has driven a decentralization of information hubs away from geographic centers and toward a more unrestricted system of nodes and flows of communication within a network that allows multiple points of juncture and connection. Though a networked society cannot claim to have thoroughly democratized information sharing online, it makes many-to-many connections more available than any medium before it.

Beyond the perceived anonymizing and democratizing features of digital media, the narrators revealed the ways that digital media may simply be more convenient than other mediums for undocumented audiences. Angy explained, "I think TV is still valuable, and news channels are still valuable. It's just a little bit difficult to navigate because a lot of our immigrant families maybe work really long shifts and aren't home when the news shows. They don't have nine to five jobs where they're able to be home in time for it." Undocumented immigrants are often paid less than US-born workers for the same work so that they may need to work longer hours to earn the same salary.[10] Moreover, these jobs are likely to have unstable or difficult schedules and offer few, if any, benefits.[11] Under these conditions, the internet's convenience, mobility, and availability at free cultural institutions such as libraries provides more access than older media.

Of course, not all undocumented immigrants have access to the internet—language barriers, the cost of devices, or a lack of understanding about libraries and other available resources prohibit some from access—but for the young immigrants who participated in this research and who grew up in New York City, digital culture is a ubiquitous and integral part of day-to-day life. When I asked her why she chose this medium for her story, Esther explained, "It was just what I had immediately. It's what was there. I didn't want to endanger the [publication company employing me] so, yeah, my blog was what was there available immediately." Digital media's pervasive presence and its ability to facilitate instantaneous publishing make it appealing for millennials in general. But undocumented populations have more to gain from its unique features because of the barriers to interaction and information they encounter on a daily basis in the offline world.

Several of the narrators I interviewed are working, either independently or with immigrant rights organizations, to try to get more undocumented stories online, believing that if audiences encounter the narratives of individuals who speak firsthand about the experience of being undocumented, it will engender empathy and an openness to immigration reform. Working for Change.org—a website that has hosted petitions for immigration reform as well as a range of other issues including environmental protection, education, and police brutality—Piash was tasked with posting a story of a different DREAMer each week. It was not always easy to find people willing to tell their stories, but Piash would encourage people by talking with them about the change their narratives would have the potential to make. He explained,

> My job was actually to find undocumented students and have them talk about their stories every week. Every week I'd find someone—online basically. I would email in this forum or I'd post in this forum, or on Facebook or somewhere else. I would be like, "Okay please send me a story. If you don't want your name, you don't have to put your name on it—just your first name. We just want exposure, and we want more and more people to come out and say, 'Yes, I'm undocumented, I'm in this position.'"

This tactic is effective, Piash believes, because the posts gives activists a chance to change the stereotype that Americans are used to hearing about "illegal" immigrants. "You have to give them a different version of the story than they are hearing," he explained. "All the people hear from politicians or people in power is like 'Oh undocumented immigrants, they are killing this country, taking our jobs, terrorists are pouring through the border, yada yada.' [But] if you look at the story, you're like, 'Wait—this story is talking about a boy or girl and his *struggle to live* in this country.'" The possibility of evoking empathy and getting as many names as possible onto a digital petition becomes a way for Piash to participate in civic engagement for the benefit of the undocumented community.

By providing inroads for amateur professionals without advanced educational or professional training, encouraging a culture of self-disclosure through prosumerism, and offering access even to those who may have limited ability to engage with other mediums due to fear, work schedules, or lack of resources, digital platforms provide a means through which undocumented immigrants may be able to counter isolation and become civically engaged. It is clear that telling digital narratives has led to unique outcomes for the undocumented storytellers I interviewed. In the following pages, they reflect on the nature of these outcomes, and I elucidate the implications for others who may wish to follow in their footsteps.

"We All Can Stand Together": Reflections on Sharing Reclaimant Narratives Online

The top level of Abraham Maslow's famous hierarchy of needs is "self-actualization." Self-actualization is a quest for fulfillment and contentment that "involves the individual doing what [s]he is fitted for. A musician must make music, an artist must paint, a poet must write, if [s]he is to be ultimately happy. What a [wo]man *can* be, [s]he *must* be."[12] According to Maslow, an individual will not likely engage with this need until lower-level needs, such as a sense of belonging, are met. The narrators in this study complicate Maslow's hierarchy, however, by demonstrating that the pursuit for self-actualization, as enacted through creative output about one's immigration status in online contexts, may be conceived as a path *toward* belonging rather than the other way around. As the narrators demonstrate, sharing reclaimant narratives online may lead to a greater sense of self-awareness and empowerment that results in fulfillment of the need to belong.

The narrators stated consistently and repeatedly the ways sharing their stories online enabled them to self-actualize—that is, to discover or uncover parts of their identities they had previously been unaware of or worked to hide. Esther told me,

> While I was making [my] documentary, I had to write out what I wanted to say and put it on a teleprompter app on an iPad. I couldn't have anyone else in the room. I would just sit in front of the camera by myself and read what I had written and speak to the camera because I couldn't even remember what the story was that I wanted to tell and say it the way that I wanted to, because I just didn't know who I was anymore. . . . [I]t mostly gave me confidence.

"Creating things has allowed me to accept myself," Sonia shared. I asked her how she felt after putting her first autobiographical storytelling project online, and she replied, "I felt great. It was like finally just letting it out." Angy emphasized the importance of storytelling for her: "It has pushed me to see myself in a different way. To be able to tap into things that I kept ignoring for a long time, or I thought they didn't bother me, but they did."

When Pang reflected on sharing her story online, it was clear that the process not only worked toward her own self-actualization but also toward the goal of relating to others in similar situations. No one outside Pang's family knew she was undocumented until she decided to tell about her life in a documentary film she produced for an art school project in 2014. In the film, she described what it felt like to carry the burden of her immigration status as a secret throughout her youth. The experience of screening it for her classmates was both nerve-wracking and liberating. "It's completely changed who I am," Pang told me. "After I made the piece, I felt better. I felt more like an actual person, whereas before, really half of a person because I felt like people didn't really know who I really was." Pang's film is now available online to watch free of charge and was recently picked up by a national newspaper. She told me, "After the piece came out, I've been slowly getting responses from people who are undocumented—'If you can do it, I can.'"

These reflections of self-discovery that occur as a result of the production of creative public content testify to Linda Alcoff's assertion that when one speaks for oneself, she or he is "participating in the creation and reproduction of discourses through which [his or her] own and other selves are constituted."[13] Other scholars have likewise demonstrated how such self-making is cyclical and reifying. In her book about *Queer Latinidad,* Juana María Rodríguez shows how "subjects mobilize identities and are in turn mobilized by those identity constructions."[14] Likewise, Judith Butler demonstrates how a "'doer' is variably constructed in and through [a] deed."[15] But the narrators in this project reveal that such reification is not boundless by pointing to the inherent limitations of what possibilities for identity are available to and restricted from immigrants who wish to go public about their status.

It became clear over the course of this project that many of the narrators do not view their digital story sharing as a purely personal process but rather as a way to reckon with the limitations of their status alongside others facing similar circumstances. Psychologists Renee Lyons, Kristin Michelson, Michael Sullivan, and James Coyne argue for a reconceptualization of coping that recognizes the action as one that may take place socially rather than individually. The authors describe communal coping as an "appraisal of a stressor as 'our' issue" and the initiation of a "cooperative action to address it."[16] Sonia illustrated this phenomenon clearly. "I feel like more and more, as I open myself up to seeing more things or being more educated about the undocumented, I am seeing other nationalities come out," she said. "It's been really empowering. . . . I felt like the more I shared [my film] the more empowered I felt. The more open I felt about being myself."

Pang too described her digital storytelling experience as a self-perpetuating and communal—rather than individual—way of coping with her status. "If it's out there, some undocumented person's going to see it, and that undocumented person might feel better about themselves," she told me. "If you can make it personal for someone else and they are affected by it, then maybe you can make it personal for two people. Then somebody else will come out and talk about it and they will make it more personal for four other people. I think that's where the media is really important." These reflections reveal the creation and dissemination of digital reclaimant narratives as a reciprocal and prosocial communicative process. In addition to the positive personal outcomes of sharing one's narrative, storytellers may also take comfort in and derive purpose from the idea that their experiences help others to cope.

Jin Park, an immigrant activist from South Korea who shared his story on DefineAmerican.com, explained to me,

> One of the biggest reasons why I decided to come out and be public about it was . . . Jose Antonio Vargas' piece in *TIME* and in the *New York Times Magazine*. I read that and I connected so much to it because he was like a dude from the Philippines. I felt that this is something that's much bigger than me, and I could possibly contribute to this movement or add my voice to this wide array of perspectives. That's when I realized that I could possibly have an impact. It empowered me.

The opportunity to become part of a digital community that is "bigger" than one's own story is enough to drive an increasing number of undocumented immigrants to share their narratives online despite the risks.

The decision these narrators made to share their reclaimant narratives demonstrates a belief that having their voices heard is more necessary and important than the risk of exposure. Over and over again during interviews with undocumented storytellers I listened as narrators described their concern for and responsibility to other immigrants without legal status. This concern in many cases was not limited to one's immediate community of family and friends; several mentioned the potential benefit that their story sharing online might have for undocumented strangers.

Piash explained, "Say you're a guy or a girl in somewhere middle of nowhere in America, [like] Wisconsin. You read the story [of another immigrant] and you're like, 'Huh. I'm *not* alone.'" He stressed, "This might be the first time they are reading this story and saying 'Wow—this person just shared this story and it sounds almost like mine. Maybe I want to do something.'" Though Piash is unlikely to ever personally encounter his hypothetical Wisconsinite audience member, his actions follow a sense of responsibility for such a person's well-being. As he explained, "It is our civic duty almost to talk about these issues, these sufferings." It is clear that this sense of responsibility, echoed by a number of the narrators, is due at least in part to the reality that before they went public themselves, most of the digital media makers in this project experienced firsthand the isolation and fear they now try to abate for others.

After making her documentary available online, Pang recalled, "I was really concerned about putting myself out there, and what it might mean for my family. . . . Is ICE going to come get me because it's out there? . . . I was really, really worried, and I guess I still am at times." But she felt she must persist despite the fear, because, she explained, "If I'm open about my status and I'm not scared about getting in trouble, maybe it'll help someone else come out. I'm fighting for us all to be equal. . . . My fears aside, I felt like this could be something good."

For Sonia, a sense of privilege she feels because of being a student at Harvard intensifies the burden of her sense of responsibility. Because she works full time while pursuing her degree, her time for unpaid creative production online is limited. Still, she explained,

> Harvard has given me a lot of leverage to be able to publish these things. I don't think I would've been able to—it wouldn't have been as appealing for Buzzfeed to publish [the article about my status] if I wouldn't have been a Harvard student. I do understand the privilege, and that's why I do feel like I have a responsibility to create and to publish and try to make the effort to publish as much as possible.

Similarly, Esther explained, "Before DACA, I'd been really scared to even go to protests and talk about immigration and speak out about it. I felt that I had a lot to catch up on and I owed a lot. Yeah, so what I wanted to do is be a voice for the movement in mainstream media and see if that was possible." I asked Esther whether it feels like the responsibility is an unfair burden to bear, and she confirmed: "Yeah, definitely. It isn't. It's not fair." But her confidence in the importance of undocumented representation in media and media's role in self-actualization compel her to continue writing about her status and collecting footage for a film she plans to release.

Digital reclaimant narratives serve more than a single purpose, and, as these narrators make clear, the act of story sharing online may serve as a path to self-actualization, help to mitigate one's fear and uncertainty, offer a means for communal coping, or satisfy a sense of responsibility that accompanies a feeling of privilege in some cases and a sense of debt to other activists in others. A close look at these varied and profound outcomes reveals digital reclaimant narratives as powerful tools in the hands of individuals who in other contexts face constant limitations.

Hazards of Digital Storytelling

For all the benefits that digital media offers reclaimant narrators, the hazards of storytelling in this medium may have negative implications, both direct and indirect, for undocumented immigrants. Digital work disrupts traditional pay structures and normalizes the prospect of creating and disseminating creative work without compensation for the labor involved. In addition, the perception of privacy—which earlier in this chapter I explored as a potential benefit of the medium—may also serve to attract hateful or xenophobic responses to immigrant media in ways that would be less likely in offline contexts. Finally, digital spaces regularly serve as echo chambers that create a feedback loop rather than reaching new audiences, so that undocumented reclaimant narrators often fail to reach the audiences they strive to engage.

The narrators I interviewed have struggled to reconcile the time and energy input required for digital production with the expectation of free labor in digital contexts. Nicolas Carr argues that the internet promotes "digital sharecropping" by "putting the means of production into the hands of the masses but withholding from those same masses any ownership over the product of their work [in order] to harvest the economic value of the free labor provided by the very many and concentrate it into the hands of the very few."[17] The digital media that undocumented storytellers produce is likely to cost money without resulting in any monetary return.

Sonia, whose music video work sometimes requires the construction of sets and costumes, spoke about this problem at length. She said,

> It's just hard, it's a lot of effort to create and to try to find places that will publish, at the same time, having a job and just paying for life—you are able

to humanize somebody by creating a narrative for them, but you can only do that with money, and I closed that page. I haven't really made as much of an effort as I once was in trying to publish things, because I just don't know how. . . . I would have to spend a lot of time on it, but at this time I just can't afford to spend time on it.

Because Sonia has the protection of DACA, she has legal work authorization that most undocumented immigrants do not. When faced with whether to spend time working a traditional job for money or dedicating her time to creating digital work that is unlikely to turn a profit, Sonia feels at this point she has little choice.

Esther pointed out that because immigrants without DACA often cannot legally receive payment for their creative work, she believes that "telling our stories can happen right now, but, I mean, getting compensated the way that we should be, the way that other artists are—and probably not as much as they should be—yeah, I mean that's going to require some legal help." Esther's reflection demonstrates that while digital sharecropping may affect anyone who performs digital labor, in the context of undocumented immigrants, this hazard is especially salient. In light of the fact that undocumented immigrants are underemployed and underpaid even when they are employed, digital sharecropping only compounds the problem of a lack of fair compensation for immigrant work.

Even when undocumented storytellers do have the resources they need to create digital reclaimant narratives, they may be discouraged by a phenomenon Chris Anderson calls "The Long Tail."[18] In this phenomenon, digital mediums trend away from a limited amount of mainstream creative products toward a broad repertoire of coexisting, distinct creative works. Adrian Athique argues that The Long Tail leads to an information overload and demonstrates that because "humanity possesses more talent than the market actually needs," it is becoming more and more difficult to stand out in digital contexts and garner an audience.[19]

The narrators in this project are familiar with the frustration of this feature of The Long Tail. Sonia explained with exasperation, "If you're putting something into an online platform, whether that be SoundCloud or YouTube, you still need viewers, so it's like, what's the point of me publishing it if it's not going to get views?" I reminded Sonia that one of her recent songs—a response to Donald Trump's disparaging comments about Mexican immigrants—got over 17,000 views. She shrugged. "That's not a lot. . . . There's so many kids creating so many things, that a video with 17,000 views—they're not that impressive." Sonia thinks the possibility of her overcoming this hurdle is unlikely. "It [would require] understanding the formula that's very rarely understood," she said. "It's like the chances of winning the lottery."

Jon told me, "There [are] just too many voices on the internet for the really important ones come up, in my opinion. There has to be some way to make a flag and say 'Read this—not that!' There's a lot more negative blogs out there spewing hate about undocumented immigrants than there are people saying, '[H]ere are the things about the real facts about undocumented immigrants.'" Without any such means for directing audiences as they wade through the abundance of information available to them, undocumented immigrant content creators risk spending a good deal of time and energy telling digital stories that only a few may encounter.

Another reality further complicates the sometimes-disheartening search for viewers: the notion that more views is evidence of more effectiveness may be a faulty premise, as demonstrated in the field of digital advertising, wherein metrics reveal that the number of viewers who "encounter"—that is, scroll quickly past an advertisement in their feed—has little correlation to the number of sales of a product. Because these encounters elicit superficial glances rather than meaningful engagement, they are not likely to spur potential consumers to action. While it is reductive to compare immigrants' personal stories to a product that can be either purchased or ignored, the parallel merits some consideration. Like a brand advertising a product for purchase, these narrators have some action-oriented goal for their audiences, and, like advertisements, their stories operate as a means of raising awareness about and motivating the public to achieve that goal. Without the meaningful engagement of audiences, undocumented narrators may be left to ask, like Sonia, "What's the point?"

Earlier in this chapter, I described the amateur professionalism that the internet allows as a potentially positive characteristic of this medium. But of course, not all amateur professionals have altruistic intentions, and sometimes this phenomenon leads to direct negative consequences for undocumented immigrants searching online for reliable information. Gabriela explained, "It can be confusing if you don't know how to search and what websites to use. It can be deceiving because there's so many articles and there's fraud." For this reason, Gabriela believes, "it's always good to double check with a lawyer or a good source that you trust to clarify." The potential of encountering fraudulent information—especially from individuals and organizations claiming to be immigration lawyers, is a major problem for undocumented immigrants in the United States.[20] Several of the narrators I spoke with reported histories in which members of their families or communities paid large sums of money to individuals who promised them sound advice that could lead to their legalization, only to find out later that the individuals who took their money have no authority to provide legal counsel. The internet allows for a level of removal between such individuals and their clients, and this type of fraud is becoming increasingly problematic. Because immigrants risk revealing their status if they have been victims of such a crime, they often have little recourse. These scams are now so common that United States Citizenship and Immigration Services (USCIS) devotes one page of its website to outlining the different ways immigrants may be taken advantage of online and how to avoid paying for services that will never be rendered.[21]

Beyond the reality that undocumented storytellers work long hours to produce media unlikely to generate revenue and the increasing prevalence of fraudulent transactions online, several of the narrators in this project pointed out another drawback of digital platforms for reclaimant narrators. Earlier, I elucidated the potential benefit of perceived privacy online; this perception may allow immigrants who are too fearful to connect with others offline to have the courage to interact with each other online. But perceived privacy online also has a detrimental effect; it may provide anti-immigrant audiences more "keyboard courage" or confidence to display prejudicial attitudes and discriminatory behavior than they would in off-line contexts.[22]

Several narrators told me about firsthand encounters with this problem. Angy explained, "I've seen people who will sit there and watch an entire YouTube video that I made and still comment on it and say 'Oh, you're il-legal. Go back to Mexico. You're dirty.' I think the internet has been great at being able to hide, and being able to write an email, anonymously, hor-rible things. But would they say that same thing to my face? I don't know. Probably not." Besides the fact that Angy is from Colombia, not Mexico, posts like these demonstrate the type of rhetoric often used in media to de-humanize immigrants.[23] In comments and emails responding to her advice column, YouTube videos, and a film that recently featured her, Angy has been called a leech and a cockroach, encouraged to commit suicide, and physically threatened.

In their 2015 narrative analysis of hate group websites, Marco Gemignani and Yolanda Hernandez-Albujar remind their readers that individuals such as those Angy mentions above, who hatefully oppose un-documented immigrants, often act out of a perceived ethical obligation. The authors share findings that suggest that "group members feel the moral responsibility to respond and act upon the threat that illegal immigration poses to supposed US values."[24] Likewise, sociologist Bernadette Nadya Jaworsky finds that in the digital rhetoric of organizations that advocate for a decline in immigration, "legality was constantly refracted through moral lenses—it simply wasn't fair to break the law."[25] These findings complicate and caution against reductionist characterizations that render digital hate speech as just impulsive or mindless trolling, and demonstrate how hateful messages may, though virulent, be motivated by perceived moral justifications.

The likelihood of encountering hate speech leaves undocumented media makers who hope to connect to their US-born audiences in a difficult position; digital contexts provide all kinds of built-in means for discussion and exchange, but the decision to engage in this discussion is too often met with a barrage of hateful replies. It is difficult for Pang to resist reading the responding comments on her digital work, even though she knows she's likely to encounter discrimination. "People are empowered to sit behind a computer and say whatever they want," Pang told me. "When my piece was picked up by [a major online news site], I couldn't help but read all the negative comments, and I take what they say to heart. . . . My boyfriend used to tell me, 'They are going to say what they want to say, we can't change them, can't change their minds.' I completely have stopped reading the comments because it was really hurtful. I felt really hurt."

Angy's decision to make use of opportunities for response and interaction online depends on her mood and sense of stamina. She told me, "On some days I want to read and I want to see what's out there, and then on other days I'm just tired and overwhelmed by all of it that I don't want to see it because it gets tiring of all that abuse and violence, and seeing it all the time. Sometimes I just try my best not to read it, or if somebody shares something I try to ignore it. Then other days I want to read and see what's going on." Pang's and Angy's reflections offer an important reminder about digital interaction: just because a digital context offers opportunities for feedback from audiences does not mean that creators will wish to take advantage of this opportunity. They may instead purposefully avoid interaction in order to mitigate the risks of engaging with hateful and xenophobic responses.

In the instances above, narrators describe situations where non-undocumented audience members encounter and respond to undocumented narratives. But reaching these audiences in the first place is not an easy task. Despite the fact that the narrators continue to produce digital media about undocumented immigration, several of them are pessimistic about the ability of media to ever reach the intended audience. Instead, digital media too often supports the confirmation bias, wherein individuals seek out information that confirms what they already believe.[26] Chris told me, "What social media has done is it's made it easier for people to get more information, but that means to get more information that appeals to what already align[s] to what they believe. So you've made it so much easier for people to stick to their own ideas, and a lot of those ideas are wrong." The confirmation bias is a symptom of a larger problem in digital media; because of both human actions (the choice of search terms, one's community membership) and machine actions (algorithms, cookies), many groups end up reaching only audiences who already support them. In this sense, digital storytelling risks serving as a feedback loop, confirming for users what they already expected to hear, and connecting them with people who are similar in circumstance and goal.

The likelihood of a feedback loop is supported in recent research. Pablo Barberá and his coauthors found that in the case of political issues, Twitter users are, on average, more likely to share information with other users who share similar ideological preferences.[27] Flaxman, Goel, and Rao examined the web-browsing histories of 50,000 online newsreaders in the United States and found that social media usage increases the likelihood of ideological segregation; their report shows that online newsreaders are more likely to choose news outlets that align with their own political ideology.[28] While users have the potential to be exposed to opposing viewpoints online, these authors argue, many users choose instead to "exist in so-called echo chambers."[29] These findings draw into question the ability of online activism to reach audiences prone to disagree with its message, and offer a reminder of the gap that exists between the *ability* to reach an intended audience and the *probability* that this may occur. I discuss this problem in more detail in Chapter 5.

When I asked Piash whether the stories he gathered for Dream.org were intended for US citizen or immigrant audiences, he responded, "They're for U.S. citizens, definitely." I reminded him that in the examples he had given me—including the one above where an undocumented person reads an immigrant's story and then is inspired to share her own—the audiences appeared to be undocumented. But Piash stressed:

We wanted as much exposure as possible because we were trying to change people's minds. An undocumented immigrant—we know he's going to agree with us, with our position. . . . Our goal was for U.S. citizens—for them to change their minds. For them to think, "Wait a minute. This story may not be as simple as: Oh, you can come here illegally? Go back home. We don't want you here."

I asked Piash, "Did you see any evidence that the stories that you were sharing on Change.org were having the intended effect on Americans?" He replied, "I mean at the time I would say yes." After a pause, he continued,

> Looking back on it I feel like we were preaching to the choir. It's like people who go to Change.org usually are very liberal as it is. . . . You want to convince the people that don't feel the same way about you. Talking about it with people who already agree with you doesn't really help them. You might feel better. I could see, oh wow all of these people care about me. They feel my struggle, they see how bad it is. At the end of the day I feel like our job was to find people who were either neutral or against it. People who are very against it, it's very hard for you to change their mind. At that point they were done. Our goal was definitely to get the people that are neutral that didn't know too much about it either way and we wanted to present them a heartfelt story about real people and not just some person in the shadows stealing your jobs.

If a mediated message intended for audience persuasion never reaches its intended audience, it cannot have its desired effect. Indeed, for undocumented storytellers, the likelihood of butting up against the problems of confirmation bias and feedback loops is potentially devastating to their goals. Unless the narrators' stories extend beyond the undocumented community and reach audiences who hold voting power and citizenship privilege, their power to advance reform is severely limited.

James, who works for the Minkown Center, an Asian-American immigrant rights association in New York City, believes that the ability to reach more people is directly correlated to resources: "Money do[es]n't just grow on trees. We have to get people to support us financially to reach a broader audience too." He is optimistic about digital media's ability to move beyond what he, like Piash, calls "preaching to the choir." I asked James what he believes is the key to moving beyond undocumented audiences. He answered, "Now that we live in [the] twenty-first century and we have access to a lot of networks outside of the physical networks that we have, definitely exposure to other networks does help."

But when pressed further, it seemed he was not quite sure how this would work. "I'm not entirely sure about the logistics behind it, so I can't really say—like Facebook, YouTube—it just takes one person who becomes famous on YouTube or Facebook to show, to share. I'm not entirely sure, to be honest." Part of the lack of surety stems from a unique facet of digital media—at a physical rally or protest, one might count members of an audience or record their observable demographics. But when immigrants share their stories online, it may be difficult or impossible to tell how many people encounter the post, how long they linger over its contents, and whether that encounter has any effect at all on their opinions or actions.

David, who worked for a time with James at the Minkwon Center, created a series of digital zines to share immigrant narratives to a broad online audience. He told me, "Through the zines, we're targeting people who identify with us, [but] you never know who the audience is. You can't tell who's undocumented. . . . You never know who you might actually touch or impact. Who knows?" Though he cannot be sure who is reading the work, David hopes it finds its way to audiences with formidable resources—"just people who can really help kind of expand our work and support our work, financially maybe, that would be very nice."

James reminded me that even when undocumented media makers *do* reach their intended audiences, those audiences may not respond in the way immigrants hope they will; persuasive media is not guaranteed to incite some preferred action. In James's experience, "people do get affected to some extent, but not to the extent where they actually do something about it." From this view, it is clear that non-undocumented audiences must pass through several degrees of action for these undocumented storytellers' goals to be achieved, and each degree is less likely than the one before it. First, audiences must find the narratives among a barrage of other work vying for their attention. Then, they have to linger long enough to digest the complexity many of these narratives contain, and to connect in their minds the hardships the narrators discuss to some change that could relieve the hardship. The work must then persuade audiences to take action in favor of that change or to publicly express their solidarity with the movement.

The ever-increasing volume of available stories of undocumented immigrants is often framed as a mark of the movement's progress. As more and more individuals share their stories online, the act itself can become normalized, undocumented individuals can access and take comfort in narratives that hold some similarity to their own, and some of the social stigma affiliated with living without legal status may be lessened. This result should not be minimized, as its potential to affect the day-to-day lives of immigrants for the better is profound. But the increasing volume of publicly available stories may also serve to disengage an empathetic audience of viewers who come to equate listening to stories with being a part of the advancement to reform. In other words, the proliferation of stories may have the unintended effect of mollifying the very audience they hope to activate.

The argument that some media may placate instead of energizing their audiences is not new; in 1948, Lazarsfeld and Merton suggested that media may incite a "narcotizing dysfunction" wherein audiences come to "mistake *knowing* about the problems of the day for *doing* something about them."[30] Concerned with a society that seemed to be taking in an awful lot of radio programs and sometimes reading as many as two newspapers a day, Lazarsfeld and Merton feared this intake served both to assuage the audience of any kind of motivation to act and to engender a sense of mastery over the media's content: "His[/Her] social conscience remains spotlessly clean. [S]he *is* concerned. [S]he *is* informed. And [s]he has all sorts of ideas as to what should be done. But, after [s]he has gotten through his[/her] dinner and after [s]he has listened to his[/her] favorite radio programs and after [s]he has read his[/her] second newspaper of the day, it is really time for bed."[31] More and more time spent consuming, these authors argued, leaves little energy or drive for organized action.

But Lazarsfeld and Merton could not possibly have anticipated the evolution their narcotizing dysfunction would confront as a result of the internet. Viewers of activist stories today are served both by the number of stories available and the medium that layers them one on top of another, side-by-side with a viewing potential that could outlast the energy of even the most persevering viewer. Those empathetic to the cause encounter no lack when seeking to have their fill of affective personal accounts of undocumented life. The need to feel involved and familiar with the problem is assuaged; and once they are sufficiently fatigued, audiences can move on to more pressing concerns. If narrative fatigue is a true adversary of the immigrant rights movement, then the call for more and more undocumented immigrants to share their stories requires a close critique.

To advance immigration reform, reclaimant narratives must simultaneously equip their audiences with knowledge and spur them to action. If not, the very stories designed to aid the movement may instead foster its stagnation. The possibility of passive story-binging necessitates an updating of Fisher's narrative paradigm to the digital age in which the narrators in this book are living and creating stories. Two facets of Fisher's paradigm are challenged in this new context. First, whereas Fisher seems to presuppose that audiences will approach narratives with logic, applying "good reasons" and thoughtfulness, and assessing stories "by the principles of coherence and fidelity," the narrators' experiences with their digital audiences often reveal their audience members to be unpredictable passersby who may fail to offer any sustained attention at all, and who, when they do, often respond in haste rather than with measured deliberation.[32]

Second, for Fisher, audiences are always active; he characterizes them as "co-authors who creatively read and evaluate the texts of life."[33] The possibility that audiences may instead encounter narratives while passive and narcotized is left out of Fisher's paradigm. To recognize that audiences may be, in Chris's words, much more likely to "stick to their own ideas" rather than to engage in any active response, requires a less celebratory view of audiences than Fisher maintained. Access to a glut of stories may fail to inspire action—indeed, may even have the opposite effect, so that storytellers end up expending great amounts of time and energy on content that mollifies rather than activating audiences.

Though the narrators in this chapter tell their stories online to spur interaction, invite advocacy, and advance reform, the stories' volume and availability in digital spaces put them at risk of inviting sedentary bingeing and even voyeurism. [34] Social activist bell hooks calls such voyeurism "eating the other"—a satisfaction of a kind of sensual longing for difference. She argues that "cultural appropriation of the Other assuages feelings of deprivation and lack."[35] The prevalence of digital narrative activism allows users of digital technology to acquire intimate knowledge of the lives of others without ever having to engage in conversation or make contact.

The parallel to bell hooks's notion of "eating the other" is evidenced in the reality that often the most dramatic, heartbreaking, unbelievable epics receive the most attention from mainstream outlets, leaving little room and interest for more mundane or typical narratives that struggle to compete. The culture of binge watching, self-disclosure, and fascination with the most dramatic of personal narratives may result in an eager audience, but one eager for consumption rather than action.

Certainly, digital media is a promising outlet for undocumented immigrants in the United States who are seeking to abate isolation, engage in communal coping, and advocate for reform. But until that reform comes to fruition, immigrants without legal status must continue to navigate the tension between the detriments of isolation and the risks of exposure.

CHAPTER 5 | In Pursuit of an Audience

When La Migra truck arrived, an officer
who probably called himself Arizonan,
Hispanic at best, not Mejicano
like we called him, said *buenas noches*
and gave us pan dulce y chocolate.
Procedure says he should've taken us
back to the station, checked our fingerprints,
etcetera. He knew we weren't Mexican.
He must've remembered his family
coming over the border, or the border
coming over them, because he drove us
to the border and told us *next time, rest*
at least five days, don't trust anyone calling
themselves coyotes, bring more tortillas, sardines,
Alhambra. He knew we would try again.
And again—like everyone does.

—from "Let Me Try Again" by Javier Zamora[1]

JAVIER ZAMORA WAS born in El Salvador. His parents left for San Francisco when he was only a few years old, and his grandparents cared for Javier until they sent him with a *coyote*—a person who is paid a fee for helping immigrants across the Mexico/US border—to reunite with his mother and father when he was nine years old.

When he was in high school, Javier started writing poetry as a way of working through his feelings about his lack of legal status. "I just started writing for myself," he remembers. "It was just a means to deal with happiness. I've always struggled with me being in this country and writing has really helped me." In his early work, Javier was not comfortable talking about being undocumented explicitly, but poetry gave him a way to express himself under the safety of creativity and fiction. "I started reading my poems at protests just to [say], 'Hey, I'm undocumented, and this is what happened.' Through a subtle way—I wasn't still saying that sentence like, 'I've been undocumented.' It was like, 'Here's a poem.'—It was my entryway." The practice of publicly reading poetry about immigration has slowly given Javier more courage over the years, but he still wrestles with his reality. " 'Yes, I crossed the desert when I was nine years old,' is still a sentence that is hard for me to say even, but the more I say it, the more comfortable I get with it to this day," he told me.

I was surprised to learn that Javier feels more comfortable sharing his poetry with strangers than friends:

> There's still the stigma within myself. I don't want to be viewed by those around me that know me that can see me a certain way through this lens of, "Wow," and like, "Shit. You came here when you were nine and you crossed the border." I don't want that to be the first thing that my friends see me as. For some reason, I don't care if strangers see me that way. I'm more comfortable with strangers viewing me that way because I'm never going to be in their life per se. I don't have the hopes of becoming somebody's friend. Strangers always come up to me like, "Thank you for writing." . . . Other people, like immigrant moms, would cry when they heard me read. I was like, wow, maybe it matters what I'm doing. Those are the reactions that I get, but with my friends I don't really share that.[2]

The ability to connect with strangers offers Javier a sense of fulfillment—his poetry describes emotions that other immigrants can empathize with and relate to, even without any personal relationship to Javier himself. His work demonstrates the power that reclaimant narratives have to bind members of the undocumented community despite their differences; though their origins and lives might look quite different from one another's, each has reckoned with and can relate to the penalties of life without legal status.

When I met Javier in March 2016, he was having a great year. A prestigious press had accepted his book, he had received a large writing grant, and he had found out just the week before our interview that he would be awarded a fellowship at Stanford. But he was concerned that these successes were creating a rift between himself and the only group who could truly understand his struggle. "The more of these [opportunities] I get, the further I am from my community. I'm not there out in streets," he explained. Javier has begun to notice that his audience is changing—it is no longer made up only of individuals like those who stood in front of him at protests and share a similar history. With his new notoriety come audiences who have never felt the sting of undocumented life. He explained,

> I started there with reading my poems at protests and doing all this work like marching, but I think it would be a lie to myself if I told you that I am there. I don't think that I am. It distances me from it. In that way, I have lost some of that audience, but in another way, I have gained a new audience for the future because a historian or somebody would see, "Who is this person? He is an immigrant who has got his shit at Stanford?" I think that it's huge, and just me being there physically, I have gained an audience for the future and an audience now. I think having those titles next to my name has already gained me more of an audience. That doesn't always happen and this is a very rare thing that it's happening to me.[3]

As his audience transforms and grows, Javier has had to decide whether to write his poetry in English or in Spanish, and to think about how that decision influences who can access his work and who feels a connection to it. "[When] I am writing in English . . . that also distances a population," he explained. Recently, he's decided to write more poetry in Spanish and to publish new work in both languages, in hopes of reconnecting with immigrant readers while maintaining his enlarged readership.

As I read Javier's poetry, I looked for clues about how he constitutes his implied audience. Some of his work, like the poem "Let Me Try Again" that opens this chapter, contains only implicit allusions to a reader. In others he directly addresses a particular audience, like in this selection from his "Looking at a Coyote":

> gringos why do you see us illegal don't you think
> we are the workers around you
> we speak different accents yours included and we know
> también the coyote is suspect of what we say[4]

Here, Javier not only implicates "gringos" as his implied readers, but he also speaks in solidarity with other immigrants. The "we" and "you" dichotomy he maintains throughout the poem fosters a linguistic alignment with one group while addressing the other. Javier rhetorically constructs two audiences, here—the one he speaks to and the one he speaks with and for.

Talking with Javier and reading his work helped me to understand why it is not enough just to collect and analyze immigrant-produced stories themselves. "How do I explain it? You need people in order for change. You need policy. You need people in the streets who are actually protesting [and] you need someone to be recording it. You need the policy maker and you need the people in the streets. In *all of those*, there is an audience," Javier stressed. In the preceding chapters, this book explored the kinds of messages that undocumented activists create and disseminate. But, as Javier makes clear, to understand how reclaimant narratives function within the immigrant rights movement more broadly, one must also consider whom these stories address and when and how the audience responds.

As they have related in the previous chapters, undocumented immigrant activists and immigrant rights associations spend a great deal of time, energy, and money learning how to tell their stories in strategic ways for the benefit of the movement and teaching others the techniques of effective storytelling. Within the undocumented community, these narratives have the potential to relieve some of the feeling of isolation that is common in undocumented immigrant experiences and to facilitate a kind of communal coping with the realities of life without legal status. But unless these stories extend beyond the undocumented community and have an effect on the audiences who hold the power to vote and to advance immigrant rights using the full resources offered by citizenship, they have limited potential to advance reform. Stated plainly, immigrants have a narrative to share, but they need an audience to listen.

A story may contain all the necessary elements of a masterpiece—thoughtful design, relatable characters, a grand arc of intrigue—but if it lacks an audience, the narrative's influence is suppressed. The act of telling a story can have an impact on the narrator, surely, but it cannot change the perceptions of those who never encounter it. In Javier's words, "If you don't record it, it's like nothing ever happened."[5] A story becomes part of the mythos of a community when it is recorded in some way and thereby preserved for an audience who encounters it, spends time with it, interprets it, and then tucks it away in its collective memory to be called forth when needed.

In this chapter, I turn from undocumented creators to their audiences to illuminate how immigrant storytellers conceive of and characterize US citizens who encounter reclaimant narratives. The narrators describe their frustration with citizens' apparent lack of knowledge about immigrant rights and policy. I illustrate the link between US audiences' perceptions of immigrants and the tropes present in mediated portrayals of immigrants in public discourse, and the narrators describe their own reactions to these portrayals. Finally, in response to the question "What do you wish US citizens knew about undocumented immigrants?" the narrators explain why it is so important that citizens (1) recognize immigrants as human, (2) take a bigger picture view of the historical reality of undocumented immigration, (3) acknowledge the factors that lead immigrants to give up their homes and communities and flee to the United States, and (4) understand the privilege of citizenship.

Analyzing the Audience

Research from the field of audience studies reveals that members of potential audiences avoid even messages crafted especially for them for all kinds of reasons.[6] If individuals experience fatigue from too many messages, if they consider a narrative irrelevant to their needs, or if they are preoccupied with other concerns, they may never encounter a message at all. But even when non-undocumented audiences do find their way to undocumented narratives, there is a substantial likelihood that they will turn back instead of pursuing the actions and adopting the attitudes many of these stories encourage. If audiences hear something that offends them, lose interest after an election cycle, or simply fail to relate to the performers of the narrative, they may see little reason to settle in and pay attention. Audiences are fickle, and immigration is complex.

When I asked the narrators how much they thought US-born Americans know about undocumented immigration, the responses were grim. Ximena told me: "Absolutely nothing. Nobody has any idea what immigration laws are. It's so frustrating. Everybody has this concept—'You just got to do it legally. Make a line like everyone else—like *our* ancestors did—and then just, you know. Pay your dues.' "[7]

Answers like Ximena's were common. Some narrators thought a lack of education or information may be to blame for the deficiency in US citizens' knowledge about immigration. Javier told me, "I think the education in this country is terrible and I think that's why people don't really understand the facts."[8] Josue said, "I think schools should definitely be teaching something like that. I don't remember any of my classes speaking about documented and undocumented people. They should tell their students;

there should be articles in textbooks." Jon explained, "There's a lot of ignorance and it has to do with the fact that a lot of people's notions aren't founded upon any evidence. [That] is probably the reason why there's so much fear and so much anger. If there was more information out there, if people knew more why there's people coming to this country and their methods and what's their background, there would be a lot more understanding."[9] Daniel pointed out, "A lot of people are not taught to critically think, which is so unfortunate. [For] a lot of people it's so much easier to blame those in proximity to you that are going through the same shit as you, rather than understanding why are we both suffering and why are we fighting each other?"[10] He went on, "I think I'm still shocked when people don't understand what being undocumented means. They're like, 'Oh, so why don't you go back to your country?' I'm like, 'If I go back, I can't come back. The Philippines has like a ten-year ban on anyone who overstays their visa.'" Daniel thinks "it's those kind of basic facts" that first have to be cleared up for Americans before they can even begin to understand why immigration reform is necessary. Katherine told me,

> I know people from the university I attended, I know academic professors, I know economists, folks who [have] the word "Emeritus" at the end of their signature on their email, who were not aware of the plight of undocumented youth until they met me. Which terrified me. I remember thinking, if *you* don't know that, then there is a lot of people in middle America who are not aware of it and whatever they learn of it is going to be—may not necessarily be nice. I think it's something that very few people know about.[11]

Many of the narrators find it difficult to understand how Americans could not have more understanding about immigration, considering how much publicity it has received and what a contentious issue it has been in recent presidential elections.

Sometimes, even the narrators' American friends and family members demonstrate a lack of understanding about immigration, suggesting that firsthand experience or a close relationship with an undocumented person may not be sufficient for abating ignorance. Omrie gets frustrated when his friends act "nonchalant" when he worries about his status. "They're always, 'Oh, it'll be fine, man, you're a good-looking guy'—I don't want to hear that! I really don't want to hear that," he told me.[12] Esther remembers that her friends once asked "why I was undocumented, why I didn't have papers. A lot of them didn't understand the system at all or its complications and kind of related being undocumented . . . to coming from

South America or Mexico, and so some of them asked like, 'What? But I thought you were from Spain.'"[13] A few days later, in an email Esther wrote me, she went on,

> I know that most native-born citizens who don't have undocumented parents . . . know very little about immigration. From the reasons that drive people here, especially North America's role in perpetuating violence and poverty in South America, to the complicated, expensive and time-consuming application system, and especially the limits and restrictions undocumented folks have without legal documents. And I know this from the ignorant comments I've seen and that have been directed at me when I've posted my story online, all of the questions I got from friends and acquaintances when I came out, and I know that even my best friends are still confused. They often forget that I can't leave the country when they make travel recommendations.[14]

Here Esther charges that US-born Americans' lack of knowledge about immigrants spans the length of the immigrant experience rather than merely a part. The Americans she has encountered fail to understand the reasons immigrants leave their homes in the first place, the prohibitive nature of the immigrant permissions application system, and the day-to-day social and legal restrictions immigrants without documents must navigate.

Jenny, who was born in Hungary and arrived with her family in the United States when she was twelve, recounted a similar frustration and revealed that even her husband—an American citizen whose parents are immigrants—lacks a basic understanding of the implications of undocumented status. She explained, "His parents, they came from Poland, but I think even he doesn't understand to a point because growing up, he had everything. It's like they don't understand coming here—I tell him, but he doesn't understand the actual getting up and leaving."[15] The inability to relate that many immigrants' friends and family members demonstrate can leave them with a feeling of dismay and a lack of confidence that US immigration reform will ever come to fruition. If Americans do not even *understand* the problem, why would they make the effort to work toward a solution?

Some of the narrators think US ignorance about immigration is a symptom of some larger deficiency. Ben, who was born in Uzbekistan, told me, "Some of the real Americans don't know even geography. You tell them where you came from; they'll be like, 'What? Is that [a] country?'" He estimated that when he attempts to talk with Americans about Uzbekistan, "ninety percent of [the time], they don't know where exactly the country is."[16] While Ben seemed somewhat incredulous about these experiences, others were more forgiving about US ignorance. When I asked Jin how much he thought US-born citizens knew about undocumented immigration, he shrugged and told me, "It's not something you have to deal with if you're not undocumented. That's why I really understand to a certain extent about a lot of people's misunderstandings, because there's no reason to have to think about those issues."[17]

After I interviewed her, Ahram wrote to me in an email: "I do think that about ten percent of U.S. citizens might know about how broken (as well as racist and classist) our immigration system is, perhaps know undocumented immigrants themselves, [and] understand what their limitations and struggles are."[18] Likewise, Mitasha observed, "They're not purposely—it's not their fault that they don't know that they're oblivious of the fact. I'm sure that they know there's undocumented immigrants in America but they don't understand it because they are citizens."[19] While these reflections on Americans' lack of understanding about immigration are forgiving, there may be a less innocent explanation for these narrators' experiences: ignorance diffuses responsibility.

If US citizens do not understand the ways that contemporary immigration policy allows for the separation of family, the exploitation of immigrant workers, the mistreatment of LGBTQ detainees in detention centers, the disproportionate amount of domestic violence in mixed-status relationships, or the normalization of xenophobia toward the foreign-born population in the United States, those Americans can claim plausible deniability; their lack of knowledge pardons both disinterest and inaction.

Undocumented immigrants who seek US audiences for their narratives do not merely pursue these audiences for the sake of entertainment or empathy. Within all of the possible audiences for undocumented narratives in the United States, of particular concern to the narrators I interviewed are the perceptions of audiences who vote—that is, citizens, over the age of eighteen, living in the United States, and not convicted of any crimes that would prohibit them from voting. Voting Americans have the potential to be advocates for or against immigrants at the polls. Without any political representation of their own, undocumented immigrants' fate exists at the mercy of those who hold the legal power to influence legislation.

The audiences of undocumented storytellers do not consider reclaimant narratives in isolation but rather in tandem with all kinds of other messages they receive about undocumented immigrants, and reclaimant narrators are keenly aware that their stories make up only a fraction of the messages about immigrants that are available to US citizens. Like citizens, immigrants too are audiences of the political speeches, fictional representations, and US news discourse that regularly portray undocumented people from secondhand perspectives and often lack nuance and perpetuate stereotypes. Many narrators expressed their frustration with mainstream portrayals of immigrants as criminal or economic threats to America and the disservice these representations do to reclaimant narrators working to show their audiences the opposite.

Encounters with and Responses to Mainstream Portrayals of Immigrants

Scholars across sociology, communication, American studies, and journalism have analyzed portrayals of immigrants in mainstream US media and found they are often racialized, rife with negative metaphor and stereotype, and pay homage to an ideological cultural narrative of a more "pure" America that existed before an influx of immigrants.[20] By speaking for immigrants while simultaneously highlighting their otherness, US discourse paradoxically presents immigrants as both known and strangers—all similar to each other and yet different from "us," wholly familiar and yet fearfully strange.

One cannot speak of US media as a generalized whole; narratives vary by political leaning, medium, and geographic location. Coverage about immigration in US news tends to focus more on illegality the closer the media organization is located to the US-Mexico border.[21] While mainstream portrayals of undocumented immigration in the United States are not unanimously alarmist and sometimes include neutral or positive portrayals of immigrants,[22] analyses dating back to the early 1900s reveal the widespread prevalence of mediated narratives that present immigrants as "indigestible food, conquering hordes, and waste materials."[23]

The subjects of mediated immigration metaphors are rarely human; objects and animals are more common. J. David Cisneros reports that through the use of "similar techniques as the news media coverage of pollution," news media portray undocumented immigrants as "stationary pollutants contaminating communities and the environment."[24] Jonathan Xavier Inda reveals how "nativist rhetoric implicitly figures the immigrant . . . as a parasite intruding on the body of the host nation, drawing nutrients from it."[25] Sheila Steinberg has compared newspapers from the southwestern United States and found that "the most common term is 'illegal aliens,' which attributes a certain 'non-human' quality."[26] Likewise, Sylvia Mendoza argues, "word choice used by the media to cover immigration issues is already biased and dehumanizing. Words like illegals, terrorism, racist, discrimination, DREAMers and illegal aliens strip away positive emotion and relatability."[27] This is not merely a matter of words. As Jean Kilbourne contends, dehumanization through objectification is "almost always the first step towards justifying violence" against a group.[28] To know the implications of the prevalence of dehumanizing portrayals of immigrants in media, one must carefully consider the nature and scope of media's power to shape public sentiment.

Mass media act as an increasingly central avenue for audience discovery of information about undocumented migration, especially when direct contact with the subjects of mediated texts are unavailable, as is often the case with undocumented immigrants. Because of the concentrated geographic dispersion of the majority of undocumented immigrants in just a few states, many US born citizens may experience few or no face-to-face interactions with this group, giving mediated representations of immigrants an outsized ability to control public perceptions about this group.

Of course, the ways US media portray immigrants holds little significance without an understanding of immigrants' encounters with and responses to these portrayals and recognition of the ways this discourse may affect the lived experiences of both immigrants and US-born audiences. While much scholarship exists that chronicles the ways immigrants are portrayed in media, more work is necessary that gathers and explores immigrants' reactions to these portrayals so that the scope of their tangible and intangible effects is observed rather than hypothesized.

Angy told me the mainstream media she's encountered about undocumented immigrants is

> always racialized. It's always stereotypes. It's always men. It's always poor brown men, men of color, men who are Mexican. Diseases, illnesses immigrants bring over. All kinds of infections. . . . It makes it seem like, like immigrants are only of one nationality, they only come from the same country. It's always negative portrayals of immigrants. . . . If an immigrant kills somebody, that's the first thing that will be on the news. But it won't ever be about all the other stuff that happens. We start associating stereotypes with immigrants, and then by default a specific nationality, and race, and group. I think a lot of people tend to forget that immigrants come from all over the place because of that. [29]

Angy's observations are consistent with King and Punti's findings that "nearly all media images and public discussions of undocumented individuals focus on border-crossing Latinos,"[30] and they emphasize the prominence in immigrant-related discourse of metaphors like disease and infection.

Moreover, her reflections indicate the necessity of questioning both broad and more nuanced ways of describing immigrants. The political leaning or aim of any piece of media may be found embedded in its rhetorical choices. Faist and Ulbricht note that journalists often refer to highly skilled immigrants with terms like "mobility" and "cosmopolitan," but low-skilled individuals as simply "migrants."[31] These semantic differences function as cues for the audience, suggesting how they should interpret the subjects in question.[32] Media representations contain countless numbers of these cues, which may exist in the words used to describe immigrants or in production and layout choices, such as the story's placement or context and its visual elements.

J. David Cisneros analyzed a televised CNN report from 2009 depicting two Hispanic men scaling a sizable border wall under the cover of night. Cisneros explains that, as in many similar representations, in the CNN report "the camera is positioned on the American side of the border, while immigrants scale or duck fences to sneak toward the viewer."[33] This use of perspective may discourage viewers from considering the points of view of the immigrants themselves and instead encourage alignment with the nation into which they are arriving.

Just as perspective in the CNN report emphasized a relationship between viewer and nation in opposition to immigrants, media about migration to the United States may make rhetorical choices that trigger correlations in viewers' minds, so that "subtle changes in the descriptors used to characterize objects can shape a range of social judgments made by the audience."[34] Such leading language remains difficult to study in most cases because its effects occur discreetly; audience members may pick up on a particular trope pertaining to immigrants in news media, incorporate its meaning into their beliefs about immigrants, act according to this gained "knowledge," and yet never explicitly state—or even recognize—what influenced their perceptions.

Although a news writer or director cannot control the interpretation of a report fully, she or he can attempt to influence "how the minds of recipients are 'managed' by such discourse structures" by using dominant codes with largely naturalized meanings.[35] These codes prove indicative of cultural, personal, or corporate attitudes toward any given subject because they point to a widely familiar concept in order to achieve coherence with the audience. Stuart Hall describes the effect of such a tactic when he writes that "certain codes may, of course, be so widely distributed in a specific language community or culture, and be learned at so early an age, that they appear not to be constructed—the effect of an articulation between sign and referent—but to be 'naturally' given."[36] These implicit links between sign and referent are "strengthened each time they are activated in tandem" so that news stories—which tend to use recurring language and format in order to reinforce audience perceptions of consistency and professionalism—may create, sustain, and reinforce particular conceptions of immigrants in the minds of their audience members.[37] Although implicit mediated cues and tropes remain difficult to quantitatively measure, their presence in media about undocumented immigrants is ubiquitous.

Media representation has the power to work in favor of or against immigrants in ways that often have direct and immediate implications, both positive and negative.[38] When I interviewed Pang in May 2015, she had temporary protection from deportation through DACA. She told me, "The only reason I was aware about DACA was, I was listening to NPR, and they mentioned it." After the radio broadcast, Pang told me she immediately called a lawyer and figured out how to apply.[39] In this case, media representation of immigration policy had a direct and positive effect.

But the narrators in this project more often expressed discomfort and frustration with the negative effects of stark omissions in the portrayals of immigrants in US media. Chris, who is sometimes mistaken for being Latino despite his Filipino roots, believes that US media's overemphasis on Mexican immigrants—who make up about 52 percent of the estimated undocumented population[40]—has the effect of excluding other populations from the cultural narrative. "Immigration is often seen as a Latino issue," Chris told me. "And that does a lot of, like, hundreds of thousands of African undocumented immigrants or European undocumented immigrants, Asian undocumented immigrants, that does us a disservice, [because] you end up identifying illegal immigration with Mexicans or Hispanics in general."[41]

Whereas one might believe that a lack of media attention could in fact benefit the groups Chris mentions by avoiding potentially negative portrayals, existing research shows the opposite may be more likely. Bloemraad, de Grauuw, and Hamlin demonstrate in their discussion of newspaper coverage of immigration that, in fact, "a lack of media coverage could keep issues of concern off the agenda, render immigrant hardships and accomplishments invisible, and make it difficult for immigrants to be seen as legitimate stakeholders in their communities."[42] When non-Latino undocumented immigrants' narratives are left out of media representation, they are excluded from the few conversations about immigration that do receive some neutral or positive public attention, and underrepresented in public imaginations of the characteristics of undocumented immigrants more generally.

Pang noticed a paradox in how undocumented immigrants are portrayed in mainstream US media. She explained, "From where I grew up, it was in the country, and I know that the way people took undocumented people and portrayed them in the media was that we were sort of, for the lack of better words, like a plague on jobs, and—I guess what I just remember is negative stereotypes. Lazy, but at the same time—it was a paradox. It was, lazy, but we're taking all the jobs from United States citizens."[43] Sonia, a musician and visual artist who was born in Mexico, believes that beyond being stereotypical, these portrayals measure immigrants according to their economic value and nothing more. She told me, "We're always placed against the economy. We're never really humanized as people—we're more like a product . . . in the media you mostly just hear people like Donald Trump and his comments. That's the main narrative that I see."[44] Sonia's analysis testifies to Leo Chavez's review of the ways mediated representation encourages " 'illegal aliens' and 'immigrants' [to] become abstractions and representations that stand in the place of real lives. . . . [T]hey are aggregate figures melded into cost-benefit analyses."[45] In such representations, the experiences of immigrants' real, multidimensional lives are obscured in favor of oversimplified myths about the threats they pose.

Other narrators mentioned the feeling that immigrants are found media-worthy only when they do something wrong. Javier told me, "Two days ago, there's this news trending about four Guatemalan men, [and I thought] why is this trending? Because they got drunk, they assaulted a couple and they stabbed the boyfriend and they wanted to, or did, rape the girlfriend. Why is *that* trending and not everything else?"[46] Ricardo reiterated Javier's frustration. "Let's say an undocumented immigrant attacked somebody—that's what people like to highlight more," he charged.[47] Freddy echoed, "We don't see in media 'This undocumented student did something fantastic.' They just show these people being deported or people getting arrested or riots or these gang related people."[48] Such problem-oriented coverage, typically related to criminal acts, highlights an individual's immigration status while downplaying other personal attributes, and hyperbolize immigrants' likelihood to commit criminal acts.[49]

These narrators' reflections on the impact and implications of mediated representations of undocumented immigrants underscore that it no longer makes sense to discuss media and migration as separate entities; they are increasingly intertwining, always constituting and informing each other. Media has an outsized effect on public perceptions of undocumented immigrants because of the power of fear-inducing representations of "others" rife with harrowing metaphors and dehumanizing rhetoric. These media demonstrate to reclaimant narrators what they are up against; not only do undocumented storytellers encounter audiences who know very little about the needs of undocumented people but also audiences who have been predisposed through mediated encounters to associate immigrants with criminality and economic threat.

It is for this reason that I characterize reclaimant narratives as counternarratives. As I indicated first in Chapter 1, some reclaimant narratives directly address and respond to the prevailing stereotypes and presuppositions that result from mainstream media portrayals, while others may contest existing narratives only implicitly, choosing an offensive, rather than defensive, posture. Both of these strategies contest and complicate oversimplified and generic accounts of living undocumented and thus appear in opposition to mainstream mediated representation. This is not to say that reclaimant narratives always contradict all manifestations of dominant portrayals of immigrants; rather, in order to recognize the potential and limitations of undocumented stortelling, one must consider reclaimant narratives in light of the other messages about immigration that storytellers' audiences receive.

What We Wish They Knew

The activists I interviewed are rightfully concerned that the outcome of their futures rests in the hands of citizens who hold the right to participate in American democracy but are likely to encounter persistent negative portrayals of immigrants as criminal and economic threats. Many expressed the importance of strategically reshaping audiences' perceptions of immigrants so that they become more likely to vote in favor of representatives who will work toward immigrant rights and a path to citizenship. But it became clear throughout this project that reclaimant narrators wanted to communicate to American audiences something *more* than the importance of voting in favor of immigrants. To gain clarity about what this desire entailed, I asked almost all of the interviewees, "What do you wish US-born Americans knew about undocumented immigrants?" As one would expect, the responses varied a good deal. Still, the more interviews I conducted, the clearer a few key messages became.

Specifically, the narrators wished that US-born citizens would (1) recognize immigrants as human, (2) take a bigger picture view of the historical reality of undocumented immigration, (3) acknowledge the factors that lead immigrants to give up their homes and communities and flee to the United States, and (4) understand the privilege of citizenship.

David talked about these goals at length and was careful not to essentialize. "I don't think there is a one single thing that people should know," he explained. David went on,

> I think what we need to emphasize is that we need to view immigrants— whether documented or undocumented—as people, not just as a policy or as this thing. Once you start viewing people as people, as humans, you start wanting to get to know what may have motivated them to come to the [United States], all of that stuff. There is that lack of wanting to understand people that is really harming that discourse. . . . If you actually take the time to get to know people—like my parents, who work their butt off to support me and my brother to go through college to actually make a living here—if you got to know all of these other people that come to this country, you'll realize that it's not easy to move across state let alone a whole country. These parents and these folks are making that sacrifice for not just themselves but for their future generations to say, "Hey, I might not be able to make a living here but let me try to support [my family]." Also, a lot of people that are motivated [to immigrate] here, especially like the Central American migrants, they come here because at any day they could lose their life. If you put yourself in their shoes, wouldn't you make that same decision? I would really stress [that] people [need to] look at the humanity of people and get to understand them before making a decision.[50]

Like many of the narrators, the knowledge that David seemed to wish most insistently to communicate to citizens was not an explanation of which laws and policies would need to change in order for immigration reform to be realized but rather a much simpler message: his desire for undocumented people to be seen as human.

Jin described, "We have dreams and aspirations. It's hard to communicate to someone how important my goals and dreams are, but I have them, you know? We're human beings."[51] Likewise, Jung Rae emphasized, "One thing that I want to—if I could tell U.S.-born citizens, is that we are not some people that you just see working in restaurants or mowing your lawn. We are your classmates. We are neighbors. We are the people that you talk to on the street. We're the people that ride the subway with you."[52] James stressed that he wants citizens to know that "We are people that want to better ourselves, better our communities and contribute. Grow a family, grow ourselves, be a part of the American culture. That we aren't criminals, that—just the word 'human.' "[53]

The narrators' desires to be seen in US culture as more than dehumanized economic or political problems echo concerns that appear the work of writer Gloria Anzaldúa, who grew up along the Texas/Mexico border. In her book, *Borderlands/La Frontera*, Anzaldúa wrote, "We need you to own the fact that you looked upon us as less than human, that you stole our lands."[54] Whether Anzaldúa was writing here about the Treaty of Guadalupe Hidalgo, which made much of Mexico into what is now the southwestern United States, or in reference to her Native American origins, Anzaldúa's aim is one that reverberated in many of the interviews for this project. She calls for citizens to both own up to the ways they have dehumanized those they render as outsiders and accept responsibility for their historical role in creating and benefiting from a place that prohibits some bodies from belonging.

Several artists and activists I interviewed expressed their desire for US-born citizens to understand from a more transcultural perspective the complex processes that inform and provoke migration, and the ways the United States may profit from these phenomena. When I asked Sonia what she wishes Americans knew about immigration, she answered quickly, "How the economy actually works and the benefits that the U.S. receives from undocumented people and keeping people undocumented."[55] She believes this recognition is necessary "especially because of the history that exists, like the *Bracero* Program, which gave immigrants the ability to come to the U.S. and work, but after a while, it made them illegal." The Bracero Program was made up of several pieces of legislation from 1942 to 1964 to address the need for manual labor during World War II by providing the terms for the United States to accept "braceros"—literally, those who work with their arms—from Mexico. Throughout the 1950s, the United States brought in around 200,000 migrants for manual labor every year. [56] In the years leading up to the program's final termination in 1964, millions of workers—many of whom had come to see the United States as home or started families—were forced with the choice to return to Mexico or to stay and become "illegal aliens" in the country that had formerly welcomed them.

Looking back at the legislation around historical events like the Bracero Program has helped to clarify for several of the narrators why comprehensive immigration reform has not yet come to fruition. They point out that in contrast to reports that immigrants steal American jobs and drain the economy, in fact the US economy has been stimulated rather than depressed by housing a community of immigrants who fulfill a need for low wage and hard labor work, pay over $11 billion in state and local taxes each year, and are ineligible for many of the services that tax dollars provide.[57] Javier believes there is a direct correlation between these economic benefit and the reluctance of the US government to provide a long-term solution for undocumented immigrants.

Javier has to pay regularly to renew his Temporary Protected Status (TPS)—a status that was granted to around 200,000 Salvadorans after an earthquake forcibly displaced them from their homes in El Salvador in 2001. "That's every year," Javier emphasized. "It used to be every two years. Then they cut it to a year and a half. Now this last one that they gave me was only [for] a year. You imagine what money that is generating. If you give all [immigrants] a green card, that money is gone because they're not going to have to renew a green card." Several months after I interviewed Javier, Donald Trump announced his plan to terminate the TPS program. Salvadorans with temporary status now have until September 2019 to leave the country if they cannot obtain a green card.

While some of the narrators were forgiving of US citizens who know very little about immigration policy, others charged that citizens willfully turn a blind eye to the negative effects of historical US interventions in some of the nations that now produce the largest groups of undocumented immigrants. Angy remarked,

> I would want citizens to understand how much profit is made out of detention and deportation of immigrants, and how much the United States contributed to our migration. The way that, in Colombia, there's eight United States Army bases, and the United States gave a lot of funding to civil wars that left us in poverty and pushed a lot of immigrants north. . . . I think that that's a lot of the things we like to ignore, and we like to pretend that immigrants just woke up one day and decided to come to the United States. But it wasn't like that for us. I wish that we understood that more. I think that's not something we really like to talk about because then we'd have to start thinking about a lot of the stuff that the United States does, and does to other countries, and still does now.[58]

In Angy's view, not much is likely to change until US citizens stop willfully acquiescing to this lack of understanding.

The frustration Angy expresses above is congruent with research that reveals Americans are less likely than citizens of other developed nations to have a grasp of current events outside their national borders.[59] In this sense, American ignorance about undocumented immigration appears as a cultural and systemic problem rather than just an individualized lack of understanding. Immigration demands a transnational view that recognizes the benefits of an undocumented presence in the United States and also accounts for the push factors that motivate immigrants to leave their homes in search of relief.

It is clear from existing research from the field of migration studies that when people feel safe and secure, when their families are happy and healthy, and when they are able to make a living wage to meet their basic needs, they are unlikely to choose to leave their homes and enter another country without permission.[60] Much of the focus on the harm undocumented immigrants supposedly do to the United States fails to take into account the reasons immigrants leave their homes in the first place. Jenny told me, "I think people don't understand what immigration is and why people come here. They don't understand what kinds of lives other people have outside of the United States and why they're forced to [leave]." She stressed, "It's *hard* to come here, it's hard to make the decision to uproot your family and take them somewhere that you don't speak the language."[61] Likewise, Javier emphasized,

> We don't want to be here. . . . [I]t wasn't our choice to be here. I think that that is the most important aspect. Once a citizen knows that, they'll be like, "What? Why? You don't want to be here, but you're here." Then, that's a conversation. . . . I think for an immigrant, you ask any immigrant, there's always this nostalgia for the homeland because they didn't want to leave their homeland. Nobody. If I tell you now, "Hey, do you want to leave all your friends, all your people, the home where you grew up?" You're going to say no, but something—an outside factor has to push you out of that. I think that outside factor is what citizens need to understand.[62]

He went on, "You can say that [Salvadoran immigrants are] here because of the war that was predominantly funded by the United States during the eighties. Before 1980, there were only like 40,000 Salvadoran immigrants here. Now after the war, one million of the population—a fifth of the population came to the United States." Javier concluded, "I think there is a correlation there. I don't think we wanted to be here, but we were forced to flee."[63] The idea of undocumented immigrants who would have rather stayed in the homes of their youth and who arrive in the United States against their own desires is in direct conflict with portrayals in political and popular discourse of eager and greedy immigrants who pour into the United States for personal gain.

During our interview, Francisco emphasized the normalcy of undocumented immigrants' decision to move by explaining how immigrants' reasons for relocating have been consistent throughout human civilization. For Francisco and his family, coming to the United States from Ecuador seemed like their only viable option. "Back at home, we were having economic problems," he began. "We just want to make our lives better in the same way that people throughout history go to different places, looking for a better future—that's what we want. We came here to the U.S. to get a job, and study, and get a career, and then make money and contribute to society, not just take."[64] Behind Francisco's profound and succinct explanation is the simple truth that people have been moving for the same reasons for as long as humans have had means to travel. Some have been criminalized for these decisions, and others have not.

No immigration to the United States was illegal until the government began to require documents for entry in the late 1800s. Thus, the difference between the immigrants celebrated today on Ellis Island and those hiding in the shadows for fear of deportation is not in the individuals themselves or even the decisions they make, but rather the ways these decisions have been legally framed as guilty or innocent. In my experience, this reality appears more perceptible to anyone who has ever moved from one country to another—with legal documentation or without—than it is to those who have never had to consider leaving their homes.

People who are born in the United States, whether to immigrant or US-born parents, receive *jus soli* citizenship.[65] They do not have to earn or demonstrate their entitlement to citizenship in order to reap its benefits, which include being able to vote and run for public office, having legal authorization to work, eligibility for services provided by tax dollars, receiving preference when petitioning for other family members to come to the United States, and traveling internationally with a US passport.[66] As is clear in the work of scholars of privilege such as Peggy McIntosh and Allan Johnson, it is often the case that because privilege feels normal to those who benefit from it, its power remains invisible and thereby unexamined.[67]

When I asked Javier what he believes contributes to US citizens' ignorance about immigration, he quickly answered, "Privilege—that they don't understand that being a citizen is a privilege."[68] For immigrants who risk their livelihoods to advocate for their own right to a path to citizenship, the fact that anyone would take citizenship for granted seems absurd.

Freddy explained the frustration of encountering normalized citizenship privilege. He has noticed that a lot of US citizens choose not to go to college even when they have the means to do so. Freddy wishes he could tell these folks, "Don't take it for granted. We have a whole group here who wants to *be* you, who wants to have what you have, the freedom that you have, the part of this country that you have. You're given this chance— this amazing chance—don't take it for granted. That's all I have to say."[69] Kattia explained that having to manage paying for school without being eligible to receive any federal financial aid felt "very unfair, because I felt like I did deserve to get a scholarship, or I did deserve to get financial aid because I worked so hard or I kind of went through a lot more than citizens go through here to be able to go to school." Omrie told me with some exasperation,

> I live with Americans—I live with them. I have friends who are married, all of them are citizens, all of them have IDs and most of them are procrastinators, lazy. I tell them that, I preach that to them. "Do that change man, you're doing this, you're doing that, you have so much opportunity. Go to school—you can apply for financial aid. Well, take it out, and don't worry about it." They don't want to hear that from me, and I don't get that. I don't get it! It bothers me so much. It's like, let's just trade for a day and you will see the difference.[70]

Adam agreed, "Nobody really teaches them what it means to be an immigrant because they're just born with everything, basically, almost privileged."[71]

Readers who are US citizens may experience frustration upon hearing these criticisms, especially if they have encountered some hardship in their own lives. But, as Allan Johnson reminds us, "Privilege does not necessarily lead to a 'good life,' which can prompt people in privileged groups to deny resentfully that they even have it."[72] The privilege of citizenship does not remove all obstacles from citizens' lives but rather ensures that they do not have to face the additional hurdle of a lack of legal status.

The insights the narrators share above reveal the importance they attribute to audience knowledge about immigration and their belief that the policies surrounding immigration would likely look vastly different if US citizens and legislators would take a humanistic approach to immigration, allow for a bigger picture view of the global historical reality of immigration, acknowledge the push factors that lead immigrants to give up their homes and try to get by without legal status in the United States, and recognize the privileges of citizenship.

Increasing attention to and information about undocumented immigration should logically result in greater public understanding of the economic and legal realities of undocumented immigration. However, the narrators in this chapter describe repeatedly confronting a lack of understanding in American audiences about even the most basic tenets of immigration policy and immigrant life. Accounting for this discrepancy requires a close look at the nature of the public discourse that Americans encounter about undocumented immigrants as well as the ways immigrants interpret and respond to these portrayals. Because analysis of immigrant-related media itself offers only part of the story, this chapter has chronicled the experiences of individuals who are directly affected by these representations and who amplify the weighty implications of audience perceptions and understanding

Though pervasive negative media attention drives many undocumented immigrants to silence and fear, the storytellers in this project have chosen to counter dominant mediated tropes with their own narratives. These storytellers have had varying degrees of success with the US audiences they strive to engage; while some have been encouraged through encounters with audiences who respond positively, others remain disheartened by the lack of understanding their audiences demonstrate. Until comprehensive immigration reform comes to fruition, competing discourses of undocumented immigrants will continue to work for and against those who strive to convince their US audiences that immigrant rights deserve their attention.

| Conclusion

THIS BOOK FOLLOWS the reclaimant narratives that appear within and weave throughout the immigrant rights movement. I have demonstrated both the power and limitations of these first-person narratives by tracing the circumstances under which undocumented immigrants decide whether or not to develop a public voice, and the narrators have elucidated how they negotiate this voice when stories fail to achieve their desired results or have unintended consequences. These stories have direct and meaningful implications for the more than 11.3 million undocumented immigrations living in the United States today, as well as those yet to arrive.

The future of immigration reform hinges on the power of storytelling. Both immigrant activists and those working toward stricter regulations against undocumented immigrants recognize and act according to the belief that the US-born public is not likely to pursue any exhaustive understanding of immigration policy—indeed, it is complex and of interest mostly to those who are directly implicated by its sanctions. Instead, American audiences remember the emotions that linger after hearing a story of immigration—the disquiet one feels after watching a horror film alone in the dark; the warmth that lingers in a crowd after seeing a dramatic love story performed in a theater. These sensory experiences may provoke or discourage action, depending on the degree to which they resonate with audience beliefs and values. As Fisher writes, some stories "are better stories than others, more coherent, more 'true' to the way people and the world are—in perceived fact and value."[1] Reclaimant narratives that manage to ring true with their audiences have the potential to advance cultural support for reform. But as the narrators described in the preceding pages know, finding the most persuasive frame for these stories requires creativity, strategy, and persistence.

Knowledge, Ignorance, and the Future of the Immigrant Rights Movement

In an interview for the *Nation,* Jose Antonio Vargas admitted, "I underestimated the gap between what Americans know about immigration and what the reality is about immigration." Vargas explained, "The fact that people ask me, 'Why don't you just make yourself legal?' or 'Why don't you wait in the back of the line?'—that proves to me that fundamentally the American people do not have an understanding of how immigration works in this country."[2] Vargas and other activists and scholars have attempted to redress ignorance and misinformation about immigration by reporting the dropping numbers of incoming Latino immigrants without documentation, highlighting the amount of income, property, and sales tax undocumented immigrants contribute, offering evidence that immigration strengthens the US economy, detailing the reality that there is currently no path to earned citizenship for undocumented immigrants, and demonstrating that many undocumented immigrants have no memory of or familial connection to the "home" country from which they came.

In search of meaningful conversations about immigration reform, Vargas traveled throughout the United States to capture the public's knowledge and ignorance of immigration on camera. During a key scene in his 2013 documentary film *Documented,* Vargas holds a sign at a Republican campaign event that reads, *I am an American w/o papers.* As the event concludes, an unidentified man approaches Vargas and inquires about his status. "Are you in line?" the man asks. Vargas responds, "No. But sir, there is no line. I was brought here when I was twelve. I didn't know I didn't have papers until I was sixteen. My grandparents who are American citizens didn't tell me. I just want to be able—as you said—to get legal, to get in the back of a line somewhere." Curtly, the man suggests, "Go back to Mexico." Vargas replies, "Well, I'm Filipino." "Well then," the man persists, "Why don't you become legal?" Vargas repeats slowly, "Because *there is no way*, sir."[3]

Understanding the relationship between recent attention to undocumented immigration in public media and US citizens' continued misunderstanding about the options available to undocumented immigrants requires that we look beyond simple explanations such as pure xenophobia or a lack of available information. In the example above, the man who approached Vargas was both willing to speak with an undocumented immigrant and was presented with some basic facts of immigration policy. But these two factors appear to have made little difference to the man's opinion.

A March 2016 Gallup poll reported that 60 percent of Americans said they worry about illegal immigration "a great deal" or a "fair amount."[4] But to understand the perceived threat undocumented immigration poses, one must first consider the nature of what citizens know about undocumented immigration, and then ask, what might citizens have to lose by gaining knowledge about immigration?

If one is not careful, it can feel quite natural to take what one knows and does not know as a kind of natural and inevitable reality. Getting beyond this reality requires critical and difficult self-interrogation. In the case of undocumented immigrants, one might ask: *What do I know and not know about undocumented immigration? How did I come to know or not know these realities? Whom did I entrust with informing me about what I need to know about undocumented immigration? What gives this person/organization/government the power to speak as an expert on the topic? What questions have been left unanswered by those I consider experts on the topic?* Only by wrestling with such questions might one begin to defamiliarize "knowledge" and dismantle its power. Mills argues that "if there is a sociology of knowledge, there must also be a sociology of ignorance"; the two are indissociable because ignorance is not a lack of knowledge, but rather, as Shannon Sullivan argues, "an active production of particular kinds of knowledges for various social or cultural purposes."[5] So understood, knowledge and ignorance are reciprocal and self-perpetuating.

The ways knowledge and ignorance operate in tandem is not specific to narratives of immigration; knowledge and ignorance are always informing one another, though often in ways difficult to perceive. The establishment of experts and institutional support of their expertise has an effect on what one might believe one knows. Experts hold authority over one or more areas of knowledge and serve as gatekeepers for truth claims. As philosopher Linda Alcoff charges, "Some of us have been taught that by right of having the dominant gender, class, race, letters after our name, or some other criterion, we are more likely to have the truth."[6] But, as Charles Goodwin contends, "victims do not constitute a profession," and therefore no "expert" can rise up from this group to represent or speak with the same degree of power that another is granted via accepted societal institutions of education, citizenship, and profession.[7] The barriers that, in many cases, exclude undocumented immigrants from higher education and professional careers also serve to prevent them from being able to make a claim to expertise from which to combat the kinds of ignorance that, in turn, ensure their subjugation.

Ignorance is ideological, not neutral. It might spur or hinder some social movement, sustain a problematic belief, or serve the interests of those for whom an increase in public knowledge would be detrimental. Interrogating ignorance thus promises to reveal not only areas where more information or education is necessary but also instances in which knowledge and information are not capable combatants of naivety because of more powerful oppositional forces.

As I discussed in Chapter 2, ignorance about immigration can be attributed in part to the legal, institutional, and social barriers preventing undocumented immigrants from self-representing in mainstream media, participating in immigration debates, and belonging to certain workforces and communities. Considering not only who is able to self-represent in media but also who is not able to and what occurs as a result of this lack provides a telling glimpse into the power and limitations of media in our everyday lives. But the ways ignorance is sustained even as more and more undocumented storytellers make their narratives available to public audiences requires a greater recognition of the purpose and power of ignorance.

During our interview, Javier suggested, "I think all citizens need to check themselves and look in the mirror. Most people don't do that. Most people don't want to do that, because it's hard."[8] For citizens who do not want to face the reality of the systems of inequality created and sustained by contemporary immigration policy, ignorance about immigration may seem the only viable option. Angy shared, "I don't even know what there is to know anymore because I feel like so much information is accessible now that I think sometimes we just choose to ignore it on purpose so that we could just remain ignorant about things." It is important to take notice here that what Angy describes is not a lack of knowledge that results from a dearth of information but rather a kind of willful ignorance—a decision to ignore information that may cause discomfort or require one to take action rather than to maintain the status quo.

I do not include these reflections to suggest that all US-born Americans do not care about or will refuse to listen to messages about undocumented migration—indeed, there are many Americans who eagerly serve as allies to the immigrant community. Moreover, one should be careful not to equate a lack of knowledge about some subject to an equal measure of ill will toward the subject. In fact, a recent Gallup poll showed that 66 percent of adult Americans oppose or strongly oppose deporting all immigrants without documentation back to their home countries, and a full 84 percent favor or strongly favor "allowing immigrants living in the U.S. illegally the chance to become U.S. citizens if they meet certain requirements over a period of time."[9] These polls have confirmed that the majority of both Democrats and Republicans favor a path toward citizenship for some undocumented individuals.[10] But these findings become more complicated when measured against other evidence that reveals how little US citizens know about immigration.

A 2015 Pew Research Report demonstrated that Americans have "relatively little knowledge about U.S. immigration facts": the majority of the more than two thousand interviewees significantly overestimated how many undocumented immigrants live in the United States and misidentified the leading nations of immigrant origin, and a full half of the respondents stated that they believe immigrants are worsening crime in the US.[11] A 2016 PRRI/Brookings survey reported that only 25 percent of Americans correctly believe that deportation rates have increased over the last several years.[12] Likewise, in her book *Everyday Illegal*, Joana Dreby interviewed two hundred parents and children in New Jersey and Ohio about immigration and found that American-born children often conflated documented/legal immigration with undocumented/illegal immigration, unsure of the difference, and often presupposed that any immigrant could be forcibly removed from the country. Notably, Dreby found that these children continued to "confuse being an immigrant with being illegal" even "after [she] gave them a definition of an immigrant as simply being someone who was born in one country and then moved to another country to live."[13]

These findings suggest that the voting power to advance immigration reform may rest in the hands of individuals who favor a path to citizenship but do not know what policy changes would be necessary for that to happen. This is what makes the incongruence between the type of narrative activism that many of the narrators advocate and the demonstrated areas of deficient audience knowledge a concern for undocumented storytelling. The findings above seem to suggest that while undocumented immigrants continually work to make more immigrants' stories available to US-born Americans, their audience's inaction might not stem from a lack of access to these narratives but rather from ignorance about what change is necessary.

The narrative evidence offered by storytellers without legal status holds a good deal of potential to confront a lack of understanding about law and policy, but this confrontation would require a narrative strategy that is not only inclusive of everyday lived experiences but also of the ways these experiences directly result from restrictive legal circumstances that deny undocumented immigrants the rights and resources that would allow them to thrive in the United States. While many activists include in their narratives the difficulties of living without legal status in the hope that audiences will see them as human and empathize with them, these narratives often do not include detailed information about immigration law and policy. Frequently, that detail is saved for activism created for undocumented audiences.[14]

One must keep in mind that ignorance about undocumented immigration does not lead merely to disinterest or a lack of adequate attention, as is the result of ignorance in many other cases related to contemporary politics. Rather, ignorance in this unique context feeds misinformation about undocumented immigration that drives and allows for active measures to be taken against this population, such as the dissolution of DACA, the deportation of law-abiding immigrants, and the well-documented mistreatment of immigrants in detention centers. Ignorance about undocumented immigrants results in an active and systemic exclusion rather than a passive disinterest.

By considering not only what US audiences know about immigrants but how they came to gain such knowledge and what is left out, one may begin to uncover the multifaceted ways communication sustains reality and to gain a clearer view of what reclaimant narratives are up against. That these narratives have empowered undocumented storytellers and have already succeeded in advancing a view of DREAMers as deserving of a path to citizenship is evident in the widespread bipartisan support for this path. But the narratives have not yet achieved the power to combat public ignorance about what steps immigration reform would require. This state of affairs points to an opportunity for a strategic intervention in narrative activism wherein reclaimant narrators more explicitly pair the stories of their lives with direct and clear indications of the steps voters must take for immigration reform to become a reality.

Nationalism and Citizenship: Looking Ahead

The narrative of undocumented immigrants in the United States begins and ends with nationalism. While there are some activists and allies who advocate for dismantling citizenship in a post-national society, most pro-immigrant reform rhetoric prefers a path to US citizenship for those who are undocumented. In this, the power and legitimacy of the nation is reified even by those who cannot currently access its benefits. Like an heir who cares little for a family heirloom until a visitor remarks on its value, Americans who previously took their citizenship privilege for granted or failed to understand its power may cling ever tighter to their position in the nation after encountering undocumented immigrants who desire a way in to citizenship.

Certainly, nationalism holds the immigration debate together. It is the spine of the story, the device without which the entire narrative would fall apart and become nonsensical. Without the boundaries of nationalism, undocumented immigration appears merely as people doing what people have always done: moving from place to place as a result of push and pull factors. Through this lens, migration becomes wholly unoriginal and quite commonplace—a stark contrast to contemporary narratives of criminal masterminds sneaking their way into a place where they have no legal right to stay.

Determinations of others always include some hint as to how people see themselves. While immigrants seek recognition and rights, US citizens simultaneously seek security and confidence in the United States' power and exclusivity. Joshua Meyrowitz suggests that "the widened public sphere gives nearly everyone a new (and relatively shared) perspective from which to view others and gain a reflected sense of self."[15] In Evelyn Glenn's words, "Rhetorically, 'the citizen' was defined and, therefore, gained meaning through its contrast with the oppositional concept of the 'non-citizen' as one who lacked the essential qualities needed to exercise citizenship."[16] This work makes clear that knowing and constituting an "other" is analogous to knowing and constituting one's self.

As Trebbe and Schoenhagen argue, "Perception of the other [always] includes the perception of one's own group and the feeling of being a part of this group."[17] Similarly, Edward Said posits that characterizations of an other follow a process of positive self-identification in which the familiar is set up as a standard with which to measure an outsider.[18] This reality helps to explain why so many responses to undocumented immigration include descriptions of Americanness and patriotism and serves as a reminder that the audiences of undocumented narratives are not merely neutral vacuums into which immigrants can insert their views; rather, audiences always arrive with needs, fears, and assumptions that inevitably affect how they interpret any story.

The narrative representation of undocumented immigrants as a threat to "America" subsists because of nationalistic fears of a waning homogeneity and a desire for those with sociopolitical power to retain their privilege.[19] As Jan Peiterse asserts, "Without reference to a prior pathos of purity and boundaries, of hierarchy and gradient of difference, the point of hybridity would be moot."[20] This notion of purity may initially seem a peculiar holding in a country that touts diversity with such pride and celebrates a history of immigrants who came to the United States in search of the American Dream. Unfortunately, the promise of the American Dream is accessible only when it serves the interests of the US economic and political climate. Otto Santa Ana explains:

> When the country is in the growth part of the economic cycle, cheap labor is at a premium. During these times U.S. commerce promotes the virtues of America, and its "American Dream" of the unbounded opportunity for the hardest worker, no matter who and from what circumstances. . . . The immigrants come, do the work, dream the Dream, and honor their commitment. . . . However, as the economic cycle wanes . . . then the immigrant is regaled as a burden and a menace.[21]

When economic times are tight, and US citizens struggle to find sufficient employment, popular and political discourse is more likely to characterize immigrants as not only unnecessary but also as an immediate and impending threat to hard-working Americans' jobs. In these moments of uncertainty, American citizens are called upon to "take care of our own" before considering the needs or humanity of any outsiders.

This trope found resonance in Donald Trump's 2016 campaign for president, in which he resurrected the phrase "America First"—a phrase originally used prior to World War II by isolationists who urged political leaders to refrain from involving the United States in the war against Hitler's Germany for fear that it would drain resources better spent elsewhere.[22] In a speech delivered in Washington on April 27, 2016, Trump promised: "My foreign policy will always put the interests of the American people, and American security, above all else. That will be the foundation of every decision that I will make. America First will be the major and overriding theme of my administration."[23] From the perspective of "America First," the American Dream is better interpreted in a more literal fashion than is typically employed. It is exactly as it sounds—a dream of and for Americans—it welcomes immigrants when welcome is in "America's" best interest and decries them when it is not.

The current political climate echoes a US history peppered with exclusionary immigration policies and necessitates a fresh look at the government's attempts to define, limit, and affirm the nation. Those who have critically interrogated nationalism in existing scholarship often point to contemporary parallels of historical exclusionary versions of the citizenship naturalization process that separated desirable from undesirable applicants through overtly racialized, gendered, or religion-specific eligibility requirements.[24] Looking critically into the ways the nation is preserved and sustained through immigrant-related processes and policies opens the door to more wide-ranging questions, such as the unstable fate of nationhood in a world in which ideas, people, and products move with increasing speed and agility across both political borders and cultural boundaries.

From the inception of academic discourse regarding globalization, considerations of the fate of nations have existed at the center. Early globalization research announced the looming demise of the nation-state.[25] While more recent accounts acknowledge that nations are likely to remain both ideologically and physically in place for the foreseeable future, many scholars analyze the shift that globalization has necessitated in previous conceptions of nationalism. This evolution threatens the taken-for-granted power of nations, drawing into question how much importance these imagined communities should continue to hold, and sometimes leading those whose identities or privileges are tied to nationalism to take a defensive stance that resists any indication of infringement.[26]

The current climate of fear and anxiety surrounding undocumented immigration is clearer when illuminated against this backdrop. In the face of such a threat, Madan Sarup suggests, a nation "draws in on itself, it tightens its cultural bonds to present a united front against its oppressor."[27] Anxieties about the state of the nation lead easily to nativism, or the implementation of and support for ideologies that privilege citizens at the expense of those who are rendered outsiders. Some scholarship suggests that a fear of immigrants is illogical or unfounded,[28] but when considering this matter of privilege, it becomes clear that immigrants—especially undocumented immigrants—do present a tenable threat. Because the immigrant rights movement requests a reconception of citizenship that transforms it into a right one might earn, those who benefit from traditional interpretations of *jus soli* citizenship stand to lose their monopoly on Americanness. Immigrants defamiliarize the norm of citizenship, thereby challenging the privilege others wish would remain unfettered and unacknowledged.

Jonathan Xavier Inda writes of nativism's "propensity to attribute social illness—the maladies of the nation—exclusively to external factors, to foreign bodies," and reveals how the logical end of such a construction is to reassure that public that by "expel[ing] the pathogen, the illness will go away, the nation will be cured."[29] Likewise, Aviva Chomsky confirms that "anti-undocumented sentiment plays into deeply held beliefs and fears about the state, the nation, and sovereignty. . . . It serves to preserve the privileged spaces for those deemed citizens and justify their privilege by creating a legal apparatus to sustain it."[30] Because the reasons for resisting or condemning immigration may have everything to do with maintaining the surety of the nation, one should not untangle the former from the latter.

The transnational flows of globalization call into question the authority and legitimacy of nationhood, so that the policies surrounding citizenship become sites for governmental reassertion and reification of the nation's strength, virtue, and necessity. Some of the narrators in this project who are determined in their focus on the goal of citizenship have conflicting feelings about how the pursuit of this goal reifies the exact sociopolitical structures that have worked in direct opposition to immigrants' well-being and ability to thrive. Esther envisions a world where citizenship is not a precursor to human rights. But she is realistic about what is possible. She wrote to me in an email following our interview:

> Our fight for now is limited to getting rights and resources provided through American citizenship, and the hurdle there is legislation, and the way we change that legislation is by engaging American citizens who are being fed fear, and the most powerful tool to overcome that fear are our personal stories of struggle, whitewashed and packaged into documentaries and campaigns with the goal to simply "start a conversation."[31]

Even when immigrants are wary about the paramount role of citizenship in the United States, they may feel they have little choice but to pursue it, as the alternative prospect of dismantling citizenship altogether remains incredibly unlikely. Indeed, even as they fight for the rights of citizenship, many immigrants view it with a critical eye informed by a life excluded from this unearned privilege.

By campaigning for the right to citizenship, undocumented immigrant rights advocates contribute reinforcing the importance of the nation. It is largely by aligning themselves with widely held national values, norms, and principles that undocumented immigrants have made any progress toward acceptance and inclusion at all. To achieve success, Walter Nicholls asserts, immigrants must "celebrate a nation's particular notions of justice and fairness and then assert that the exclusion of a certain group is morally wrong because it violates core national principles."[32] Instead of challenging the nation's power or the exclusionary construction of citizenship, the pro-citizenship immigrant rights movement reifies the nation, holding up its proverbial walls from the outside.

Citizenship is not a cure-all for the ills caused by undocumentedness, and the narrators in this project sometimes expressed their belief that the problems associated with being an immigrant would persist even if a path to citizenship was realized. Educational theorist Michalinos Zembylas argues that citizenship offers what he calls the "*re-humanization* of the Other";[33] once one has "put off" his or her former self, s/he is welcomed warmly into a new identity. But the narrators complicate Zembylas's argument by pointing out that even after historically marginalized groups *do* gain citizenship, they may not be perceived as "true" citizens. During our interview, Ximena reminded me, "To those in power, and to white people in general, Latinos are not Americans—whether they have an American citizenship or not—it is very difficult for American society to acknowledge that Latinos are Americans because the term 'American' is so synonymous with white."[34] Likewise, Jenny, who lived undocumented for over a decade before gaining US citizenship through her marriage to a citizen, told me, "Even though I'm a citizen now . . . I do have certain things, like an accent. So they still look at me like, 'Okay, where are you from?' Then they're like, 'Oh, okay, so you're not an American.' I'm like, 'Yeah, technically, yes I am. I can prove it to you.' Then they're like, 'No, but you're *not.*'"[35]

Ximena's and Jenny's reflections suggest that racialization and discrimination occur not only when determining whether particular groups are eligible for citizenship, but also after citizenship is conferred. Citizenship does not afford all of its constituents equal rights and privileges.[36] Even legal immigrants who become naturalized citizens may have their citizenship suspended or revoked if they are dishonorably discharged from the military or become affiliated with a communist or other totalitarian party within five years of their naturalization.[37] Likewise, as a result of a treaty at the end of the Spanish-American War, residents of Puerto Rico became US citizens, but today Puerto Rican residents cannot vote in national elections and have no representation beyond a non-voting symbolic seat in the House of Representatives. In addition, more than 5 million felons in several US states were banned from voting in the last national election. These instances of conditional citizenship reveal the necessity for a careful look at what a nation offers and withholds even from those who supposedly belong. There does not exist a simple or straight line between those who enjoy the full benefits and privileges of citizenship and those who do not.

Limitations of the Text and Cautions for the Reader

This book sought to resist the trend of academic work that speaks only for or about undocumented immigrants. By speaking *with* immigrants and foregrounding the work of undocumented activists, this work abides by a sentiment used widely during disability rights campaigns in the 1990s that has recently been taken up in the immigrant rights movement: "Nothing about Us without Us."[38] The brave and thoughtful insights that forty immigrant narrators generously provided in these pages have allowed this book to accomplish a number of objectives, but, like any finite project, it remains limited in some notable ways.

First, because this book highlights the work of so many immigrant activists, it risks overstating the likelihood that immigrants will reveal their status publicly. It is imperative to remember that while some undocumented and DACAmented activists are working tirelessly toward the goal of comprehensive immigration reform, many others who hold the same statuses and desire the same outcomes remain silent. This means that some directly relevant perspectives and stories are left out of the immigration debate—and out of this book—and that immigrants who are silent about their status publicly may be implicated by those who are more vocal, regardless of whether they agree with the positions of the activists. As is often the case with underrepresented minorities, the perspectives that are available risk becoming tokenized, as audiences may erroneously assume that these few represent the beliefs and values of the whole group. Readers should take care to avoid this fallacy.

Not all immigrants are interested or able to participate in activism, and so the work and perspectives of the narrators included here are not generalizable and should not be read as a deterministic or complete view of undocumented storytelling. Alcoff reminds us that "no embodied speaker can produce more than a partial account."[39] Since this is true, one must reckon with the power and limitations of these incomplete and sometimes conflicting accounts.

Readers should also guard against the presumption that failures in storytelling strategy are the only barriers to the immigrant rights movement's achieving its goals; even perfectly crafted or flawlessly delivered stories are not guaranteed to produce their intended effect. Audiences are active. They may encounter undocumented immigrants' stories and even be in favor of immigration reform and yet fail to take any meaningful action on the behalf of immigrants. As Columbia sociologists Paul Lazarsfeld and Robert Merton famously wrote, "To know the number of hours people keep the radio turned on gives no indication of the effect upon them of what they hear."[40] In other words, one must not take the connection of a message to its audience as proof of the inevitability of the message's effect. In light of this reality, one must consider not only the power of whatever stories exist at the site of analysis but also the power of audiences who encounter them to react in unexpected ways or not at all.

The notion that audiences retain such agency does not nullify the influence or potential of reclaimant narratives. As the narrators have attested, these stories have meaning and purpose beyond particular audiences' reactions. Measuring citizen or lawmaker audience reactions or responses alone would diminish the ways reclaimant narratives both affect those who tell them and function as important means of sharing and coping communally within the undocumented community.

Next, it is important for readers to avoid characterizing undocumented narrators as infallible actors in the pursuit of immigration reform.[41] It is problematic to assume that undocumented immigrants always know with perfect clarity how to employ the power of reclaimant storytelling most effectively. Holding this group to such a standard risks discrediting storytellers' expertise upon the first instance of a narrative inciting unintended consequences. There is more to gain by reckoning with the realization that both stories and storytellers are fallible. Sometimes, undocumented immigrants themselves do not fully understand immigration law or policy; one should not consider immigrants' knowledge as a standard by which to measure everyone else. As I noted in Chapter 2, undocumented immigrants may be afraid to seek out information about their status for fear of being apprehended, and so in some cases they are even less likely than others to understand the complexities of the law.

I was sometimes surprised by the ways the interviewees described other undocumented immigrants during the project. I noticed that Ben, who was born in Uzbekistan, was using the words "illegal" and "undocumented" to describe different kinds of immigrants during our interview. I asked him what he believed to be the difference between these two groups. He replied, "[An] undocumented immigrant could be someone who's not eligible to work without authorization, I believe. But illegal immigrants, that's the one who cross the border illegally [to arrive] here in America. That's the difference I think."[42] Here, Ben seems to be making a distinction between immigrants who enter the country without legal permission by crossing a border, and those who enter the country with temporary permission that runs out after a time, rendering them ineligible for work authorization. Ben himself belongs to the latter group, as he arrived in the United States with a student visa and became undocumented only after that visa expired. From the perspective of US law, there is no legal distinction between the immigration status of those who cross the border without permission and those whose legal residence has expired. But in Ben's mind the difference persists, and so he gives these two groups two different names.

During my interview with Esther, who was born in Spain and began her activism through a series of blog posts about being undocumented, we talked about the weight of the responsibility of immigration reform, and who is able to carry this weight. After remarking on American citizens' ignorance of the immigration system, Esther pointed out, "You know what, even undocumented people don't really understand the system either. I think that sometimes we also don't understand some of the things that oppress us and the ways that we oppress ourselves and each other. I don't think that it's just limited to native-born people. Yeah, I think that there needs to be . . . a better job of educating our own communities *and* of educating Americans."[43] Ignorance of immigration policy does not belong to any one party and will not be abated by addressing a single group's lack of understanding. But they also serve as reminder that no one group should be held to the impossible standard of a flawless understanding and knowledge of the problems of the current status of immigration law and policy.

Future Work

My interrogation of the frames employed by undocumented activists and storytellers is intended to recover from silence and omission those who have historically been left out of the grand narrative of the United States as a "nation of immigrants." Rather than discouraging others from pursuing related work, I hope the existence of this book will welcome to the table other scholars and activists to continue the conversation. Most of the existing academic work on migration comes from fields related to law and political science. But researchers in the humanities and especially scholars of communication are particularly well equipped to continue the project of critical/cultural studies of migration; indeed, narrative activism is a matter of communication. Researchers aiming to continue the field's long tradition of analyses of power, citizenship, and nationalism will find strong support from forerunners such as J. David Cisneros, Raka Shome and Radha Hegde, and Kent Ono and John Sloop.[44]

Those eager to pursue this work further will find that several proverbial stones remain unturned. Scholars compelled by the inextricable link between language and power will find the congressional hearings wherein the DREAM Act was proposed—and subsequently failed to pass—full of speeches and statements ripe for analysis. The language that appears in these hearings reveals much about the nature of potential threats posed and benefits offered by immigrants to the nation.

Though their presence in the United States is central to understanding contemporary notions of citizenship, undocumented and formerly undocumented voices are often left out in existing analyses of and public discourse about citizenship. In their review of Linda Bosniak's seminal *The Citizen and the Alien*,[45] Chhunny Chhean and Chia-Chi Li conclude that the book "provides very little testimony to the lives of actual alien citizens. Without knowing their trials, readers view the citizenship problem from a top-down approach."[46] Likewise, in the naturalization process itself, where eligible individuals born outside the United States become citizens, the possibility that a new citizen may formerly have been undocumented is rarely acknowledged. After attending thirty-six citizenship ceremonies and analyzing mediated records of forty-three more, Sofya Aptekar wrote, "None of the speakers at twenty-first-century citizenship ceremonies examined . . . referred to [citizenship's] unequal distribution among immigrants."[47] In contexts where undocumented immigrants *do* appear in public conversations about citizenship, it is often for the purpose of contrast. In public discourse, Aptekar points out, "Citizenship is held up as the opposite of undocumented status."[48] Future scholars concerned with this area of inquiry have much to gain by broadening the scholarly conversation around citizenship to include not only legal immigrants' perspectives but also the insights of immigrants who are excluded from the possibility of citizenship.

The majority of undocumented immigrants living in the United States today have no way to become citizens. But immigrants who are either petitioned through their marriage to or familial relationship with an adult US citizen, or who submit successful applications for asylum, may receive a green card that grants them legal residence and makes them eligible to apply for citizenship after a number of years. Six of the narrators I interviewed now have citizenship through one of these means; a few more are in the process. To determine how and why the United States excludes undocumented immigrants from a path to citizenship—despite the reality that the government was formed by individuals who arrived without the documentation required today—one could consider the ways the US government tells the story of citizenship and how undocumented activists respond by either trying to demonstrate how they fit this story or by resisting it.

More work is also needed that considers the means through which mythologies of citizenry and nationalism find their way into public discourse. This work could employ a social approach, similar to the one described by Alvin Goldman in his book *Knowledge in a Social World*. This approach allows one to interrogate the "spread of information or misinformation across [a] group's membership,"[49] rather than only investigating the ways that individuals seek out knowledge and information in personal and private encounters. Migration is a cultural phenomenon; while messages about "aliens" within US borders may indeed play to the fears and desires of individuals, they reach their full potential only when they become institutionalized through social and cultural constructs such as education, holidays, and political rhetoric.

Scholars of psychology would be able to lend insight into the positive and negative psychological effects of undocumented storytelling. Because the stories undocumented immigrants share are intrinsically personal, even intimate, several of the narrators explained that the act of telling them often has a powerful effect. "I was so used to just telling my story and people walking away with it," Daniel told me. Sometimes sharing his story at rallies and protests weighs on him. "I would just feel shitty. It's like, I'm left feeling horrible reliving my experiences," he described. As a result, Daniel wonders, "How do I tell the story where I'm not crying but they are, and I know they're going to help do something about it? I think that's where change really lies. It gives individuals a sense of power."[50] Kattia felt so relieved to have an opportunity to talk through her story that at the end of our interview, she offered a teary smile and said, "This feels like a therapy session!"[51] Whereas any scholar working with undocumented immigrants needs to ensure that the safety and well-being of the participants remain paramount throughout, more psychological research is needed to explain the benefits and risks of reliving the kinds of traumas that are common in undocumented narratives.

Finally, while this work included the perspectives of some survey respondents who oppose immigration, I chose to emphasize the perspectives of immigrants themselves rather than incorporating, for instance, oral history interviews with Americans who wish to see all undocumented immigrants deported. Fisher asserts, "To apply a narrative paradigm to communication is to hold, along with Aristotle, that people have a natural tendency to prefer what they perceive as the true and the just."[52] There are moral justifications for anti-immigrant sentiment that pro-immigrant forces too often ignore or essentialize. Future scholarship that did more to trace anti-immigrant sentiment back to its origins would likely yield helpful insights into the fears and desires that animate this stance.

Because of the social and economic barriers to higher education and work for undocumented immigrants, most undocumented writers are writing in informal spaces, like blogs, rather than in academic or mainstream news spaces. Since this will likely be the case until comprehensive immigration reform removes some of these barriers, there is a clear need for more work that addresses questions such as: Who counts as an expert on immigration? How can immigration scholarship be more inclusive of undocumented writing and creative work found outside the sources so familiar to academics? Writers who enjoy the privilege of documentation and citizenship must commit themselves to reaching beyond the academic canon to seek out the expertise of the undocumented community. It is only through these means that we can begin to reopen the door that has shut undocumented narratives out of the academy for so long.

Final Thoughts

This book represents a set of realities surrounding immigration bound by time. Immigration policy and protocol are revised recurrently due to ever-shifting political representation, the evolution of cultural understanding of equality and human rights, the long-lasting disagreement over whether immigrants are an asset or a liability to US economic well-being, and the unpredictable nature of migrant-producing conflicts and natural disasters around the world. Still, any given iteration of narrative in the immigrant rights debate promises a wealth of insight into the ways a national government sees its own influence over both citizens and those living without legal status. Through a close reading of these narratives wherever and whenever they are found, it is possible to interrogate the potential of stories to effect legal change, influence local sentiment, and promote self-actualization.

I encourage my readers to remember that the struggle for and against immigrant rights that is documented in these pages is not only a matter of federal law. Focusing only on a legal frame ignores the reality that the movement is also about a struggle for personhood within local communities. The solution to the immigration problem is not only a political change but also a cultural shift, and the narrators in this project stated clearly and consistently that the goal of their stories goes beyond a singular legal solution. The goals of reclaimant narratives range from increasing American understanding of historical international relations to simply overcoming individual isolation and loneliness. I have attempted a holistic view of immigrant rights narrative activism inclusive of these diverse goals.

Storytelling is self-making. It is a declaration of meaning. It is an act of defiance, bravery, and independence—a refusal to be spoken for, a simple yet powerful assertion of humanity. First-person reclaimant narratives told by undocumented immigrants reveal complex accounts of independence and activism—trailblazers pushing headlong into an uncertain future. But they also reveal human beings with fears, dreams, desires, and ambitions, pushing back against the ways that popular and policy discourse objectifies immigrants.

The hope of comprehensive reform is uncertain, so the final act of this story is unwritten. Until then, undocumented storytellers will continue to test the limits of narrative's reclaimant power to shape the world they know.

NOTES

Introduction

1. William Turner, *Libellus de re herbaria novus* (London: Priv. Print, 1877).

2. US Citizenship and Immigration Services, "Number of I-821D, Consideration of Deferred Action for Childhood Arrivals by Fiscal Year, Quarter, Intake, Biometrics and Case Status: 2012–2016 (March 31)," last modified March 31, 2016, https://www.uscis. gov/sites/default/files/USCIS/Resources/Reports%20and%20Studies/Immigration%20 Forms%20Data/All%20Form%20Types/DACA/I821d_performancedata_fy2016_ qtr2.pdf; Greg Sargent, "The First Big Political War of Trump's Presidency Will Be Explosive," *Washington Post*, November 10, 2016, https://www.washingtonpost.com/ blogs/plum-line/wp/2016/11/10/the-first-big-political-war-of-trumps-presidency-will-be-explosive/?utm_term=.6fac25981514.

3. See Roberto Gonzales, *Lives in Limbo: Undocumented and Coming of Age in America* (Oakland, CA: University of California Press, 2016).

4. See Carol Hanisch, "The Personal Is Political," CarolHanisch.org, 2009, http:// www.carolhanisch.org/CHwritings/PIP.html.

5. Walter Fisher, *Human Communication as Narration: Toward a Philosophy of Reason, Value, and Action* (Columbia: University of South Carolina Press, 1989), 18.

6. See Walter Fisher, "Narration as a Human Communication Paradigm: The Case of Public Moral Argument," in *Contemporary Rhetorical Theory: A Reader*, ed. Mark J. Porrovecchio and Celeste Michelle Condit (New York: Guilford Press, 1999), 266.

7. See Leo Chavez, *Covering Immigration: Popular Images and the Politics of the Nation* (Berkeley: University of California Press, 2001); "What's Next for Ethnic Media?," *Pew Research Center*, August 21, 2006, http://www.journalism.org/2006/08/ 21/whats-next-for-the-ethnic-media/; and Silvia Noguerón-Liu, "Usted Va al Capitolio También? Adult Immigrants' Positioning in Response to News and Digital Media about Immigration Policy," *Anthropology and Education Quarterly* 47 (2016): 113–29, doi: 10.1111/aeq.12144.

8. Jürgen Habermas, "Reflections on the Linguistic Foundations of Sociology: The Christian Gauss Lectures (Princeton University, February–March 1971)," in *On the*

Pragmatics of Social Interaction. Preliminary Studies in the Theory of Communicative Action, trans. B. Fultner (Cambridge, MA: MIT Press, 1971), 97.

9. Mike Corones, "Tracking Obama's Deportation Numbers," *Thomson Reuters* (blog), February 25, 2015, accessed September 16, 2016, http://blogs.reuters.com/data-dive/2015/02/25/tracking-obamas-deportation-numbers/; Tim Rogers, "Obama Has Deported More Immigrants Than Any Other President. Now He's Running Up the Score," *Fusion*, January 7, 2016.

10. "Independent economists say immigration reform will grow our economy and shrink our deficits by almost $1 trillion in the next two decades. And for good reason: when people come here to fulfill their dreams—to study, invent, and contribute to our culture—they make our country a more attractive place for businesses to locate and create jobs for everyone. So let's get immigration reform done this year" ("President Barack Obama's State of the Union Address," *White House, Office of the Press Secretary*, January 28, 2014, https://www.whitehouse.gov/the-press-office/2014/01/28/president-barack-obamas-state-union-address). See Dana Davidson, "Romney's Hispanic Chairman: Economic Growth Depends on Immigration, GOP Must Lead," *CNN*, last modified December 1, 2012, http://politicalticker.blogs.cnn.com/2012/12/01/romneys-hispanic-chairman-economic-growth-depends-on-immigration-gop-must-lead/; H. A. Goodman, "Illegal Immigrants Benefit the U.S. Economy," *The Hill*, last modified April 23, 2014, http://thehill.com/blogs/congress-blog/foreign-policy/203984-illegal-immigrants-benefit-the-us-economy; Diana Furchtgott-Roth, "The Economic Benefits of Immigration," *Manhattan Institute for Policy Research* (2013): 1–25, http://www.manhattan-institute.org/pdf/ib_18.pdf; Giovanni Peri, "The Economic Benefits of Immigration," *Berkley Review of Latin American Studies* (2013): 16–19, http://clas.berkeley.edu/sites/default/files/shared/docs/tertiary/BRLASFall2013-Peri.pdf.

11. Jens M. Krogstad and Jeffrey S. Passel, "5 Facts about Illegal Immigration in the U.S.," *Pew Research Center*, November 19, 2015, http://www.pewresearch.org/fact-tank/2015/11/19/5-facts-about-illegal-immigration-in-the-u-s/. In addition to advancing anti-immigrant sentiment, the majority of mainstream US media offers stereotypical, monolithic portrayals of undocumented immigrants that do not account for the great diversity in ethnicity, gender, age, and reason for migration that exists among this group.

12. See "Laura Wilkerson Confronts Jose Antonio Vargas on the Kelly File," filmed July 2016, YouTube video, 03:56. Posted July 2016, https://www.youtube.com/watch?v=LzR_A144gbw; Joshua Altman, "Romney Says Illegal Immigrants Should 'Get in Line,'" *The Hill,* http://thehill.com/video/campaign/196095-romney-says-illegal-immigrants-should-get-in-line; Sabine Durden, "Activist: Illegals Need to Get in Line," *Fox Business* video, 03:02, July 27, 2016, http://video.foxbusiness.com/v/5053905103001/activist-illegals-need-to-get-in-line-/?#sp=show-clips; Katie Pavlich, "Cruel Reality of Amnesty Continues: Illegal Aliens Given Priority over Legal Immigrants Already in Line," *Townhall*, May 19, 2015, http://townhall.com/tipsheet/katiepavlich/2015/05/19/cruel-reality-of-amnesty-continues-legal-immigrants-put-to-the-back-of-the-line-behind-illegal-aliens-n2000934.

13. See Chavez, *Covering Immigration: Popular Images and the Politics of the Nation* (Berkeley: University of California Press, 2001); Leo Chavez, *The Latino Threat: Constructing Citizens, Immigrants, and the Nation* (Stanford, CA: Stanford University Press, 2013); Regina Branton and Johanna Dunaway, "Spatial Proximity to the

U.S.—Mexico Border and Newspaper Coverage of Immigration Issues," *Political Research Quarterly* 62 (2009): 289–302, doi: 10.1177/1065912908319252l; Otto Santa Ana, *Brown Tide Rising: Metaphors of Latinos in Contemporary American Public Discourse* (Austin: University of Texas Press, 2002); and Rubén Rumbaut and Walter Ewing, "The Myth of Immigrant Criminality and the Paradox of Assimilation: Incarceration Rates among Native and Foreign-Born Men," *Immigration Policy Center* (2007): 1–20, https://www.americanimmigrationcouncil.org/sites/default/files/research/Imm%20Criminality%20%28IPC%29.pdf.

14. Rumbaut and Ewing, "The Myth of Immigrant Criminality," 1.

15. My use of the word "myth" here includes both common definitions of this term: (1) a story about the origins or early history of some community, and (2) a common but false belief.

16. Chavez, *The Latino Threat*, 16.

17. See Teun a Van Dijk, "Ideologies, Racism, Discourse: Debates on Immigration and Ethnic Issues," in *Comparative Perspectives on Racism (Research in Migration and Ethnic Relations)*, ed. Jessika Ter Wal and Maykel Verkuyten (Farnham: Ashgate, 2000), 91–115, https://faculty.georgetown.edu/irvinem/theory/SH-Encoding-Decoding.pdf.

18. Roland Barthes, *Mythologies*, trans. Annette Lavers (New York: Farrar, Straus and Giroux, 1972), 109.

19. Stuart Hall, "The Work of Representation," in *Representation: Cultural Representations and Signifying Practices*, ed. Stuart Hall (London: Sage, 1997), 1.

20. Karl Marx, *Capital: A Critique of Political Economy*, vol. 1, *Book One: The Process of Production of Capital*, trans. Samuel Moore and Edward Aveling, ed. Frederick Engels (Moscow: Progress, 1887), 27.

21. See especially Dan Berger, Peter Funke, and Todd Wolfson, "Communications Networks, Movements and the Neoliberal City: The Media Mobilizing Project in Philadelphia," *Transforming Anthropology* 19 (2011): 187–201, doi:10.1111/J.1548-7466.2011.01128.X; Magdalena Bobowik, Nekane Basabe, and Dario Paez, "'Heroes' of Adjustment: Immigrant's Stigma and Identity Management," *International Journal of Intercultural Relations* 41 (2014): 112–24, doi: 10.1016/j.ijintrel.2014.04.002; Samuel Byrd, "'The Collective Circle': Latino Immigrant Musicians and Politics in Charlotte, North Carolina," *American Ethnologist* 41 (2014): 246–60, doi: 10.1111/amet.12073; Christine Du Bois and Sidney Mintz, *Images of West Indian Immigrants in Mass Media: The Struggle for a Positive Ethnic Reputation* (New York: LFB Scholarly Publishing, 2004); Meenakshi Durham, "Constructing the 'New Ethnicities': Media, Sexuality, and Diaspora Identity in the Lives of South Asian Immigrant Girls," *Critical Studies in Media Communication* 21 (2004): 140–61, http://www.csun.edu/~vcspc00g/301/newethnicities-csmc.pdf; Edmund Hamann and Jenelle Reeves, "ICE Raids, Children, Media, and Making Sense of Latino Newcomers in Flyover Country," *Anthropology & Education Quarterly* 43 (2012): 24–40, doi: 10.1111/j.1548-1492.2011.01155.x; Ulf Hannerz, "Cosmopolitans and Locals in World Culture," in *Global Culture: Nationalism, Globalization and Modernity*, ed. Mike Featherstone (Thousand Oaks, CA: SAGE, 2004), 237–52; Jeffrey Jurgens, review of *Migrant Media: Turkish Broadcasting and Multicultural Politics in Berlin* by Kira Kosnick, *American Ethnologist* 37 (2010): 844–45, doi: 10.1111/j.1548-1425.2010.01287_14.x; Youna Kim, *Transnational Migration, Media and Identity of Asian Women: Diasporic Daughters* (New York: Routledge,

2011); Otto Santa Ana, "'Like an Animal I was Treated': Anti-Immigrant Metaphor in U.S. Public Discourse," *Discourse and Society* 10 (1999): 191–224, doi: 10.1177/0957926599010002004, and Rita Simon, *Public Opinion and the Immigrant: Print Media Coverage, 1880–1980* (Lexington, MA: Lexington Books, 1985).

22. See, for example, Leo Chavez, "The Power of the Imagined Community: The Settlement of Undocumented Mexicans and Central Americans in the United States," *American Anthropologist* 96 (1994): 52–73, doi: 10.1525/aa.1994.96.1.02a00030; Hillary Dick, "Making Immigrants Illegal in Small-Town USA," *Journal of Linguistic Anthropology* 21 (2011): E35–E55, doi:10.1111/J.1548-1395.2011.01096.X; Wayne Cornelius, "Interviewing Undocumented Immigrants: Methodological Reflections Based on Fieldwork in Mexico and the U.S," *International Migration Review* 16 (1982): 378–411, doi: 10.2307/2545104; Joan DeJaeghere and Kate McCleary, "The Making of Mexican Migrant Youth Civic Identities: Transnational Spaces and Imaginaries," *Anthropology & Education Quarterly* 41 (2010): 228–44, doi: 10.1111/J.1548-1492.2010.01085.X; Edmund Hamann and Jenelle Reeves, "ICE Raids, Children, Media, and Making Sense of Latino Newcomers in Flyover Country," *Anthropology & Education Quarterly* 43 (2012): 24–40, doi: 10.1111/j.1548-1492.2011.01155.x; Konane Martínez, "Thirty Cans of Beef Stew and a Thong: Anthropologist as Academic, Administrator, and Activist in the U.S.–Mexico Border Region," *Annals of Anthropological Practice* 31 (2009): 100–113, doi: 10.1111/j.1556-4797.2009.01021.x; Sylvia Mendoza, "Building False Crisis: The Role of the Media Covering Undocumented Immigrants," *Hispanic Outlook in Higher Education* 25 (2015): 10–12, http://www.hispanicoutlook.com/featured-articles/2015/7/14/building-false-crisis-the-role-of-the-media-covering-undocumented-immigrants; James Quesada et al., "'As Good as It Gets": Undocumented Latino Day Laborers Negotiating Discrimination in San Francisco and Berkeley, California, USA," *City and Society* 26 (2014): 29–50, doi: 10.1111/ciso.12033; and Marissa Raymond-Flesch et al., "'There Is No Help Out There and if There Is, It's Really Hard to Find': A Qualitative Study of the Health Concerns and Health Care Access of Latino 'Dreamers,'" *Journal of Adolescent Health* 55 (2014): S18–S19, doi: 10.1016/j.jadohealth.2013.10.051.

23. See Alyshia Galvez, *Guadalupe in New York: Devotion and the Struggle for Citizenship Rights among Mexican Immigrants* (New York: New York University Press, 2009); Sarah Mahler, *American Dreaming: Immigrant Life on the Margins* (Princeton, NJ: Princeton University Press, 1995); Jason Pribilsky, *La Chulla Vida: Gender, Migration, and the Family in Andean Ecuador and New York City* (Syracuse, NY: Syracuse University Press, 2007); and Robert Smith, *Mexican New York: Transnational Lives of New Immigrants* (Berkeley: University of California Press, 2006).

24. Jeffrey Passel and D'Vera Cohn, "As Mexican Share Declined, U.S. Unauthorized Immigrant Population Fell in 2015 Below Recession Level," *Pew Research Center*, April 25, 2017, http://www.pewresearch.org/fact-tank/2017/04/25/as-mexican-share-declined-u-s-unauthorized-immigrant-population-fell-in-2015-below-recession-level/.

25. See Hector Amaya, *Citizenship Excess: Latino/as, Media, and the Nation* (New York: New York University Press, 2013); Sarah Bishop, "Welcome Home: Examining Power and Representation in the United States Citizenship and Immigration Services' Guide for New Immigrants," *Journal of Intercultural Communication Research* 42 (2013): 155–71, http://dx.doi.org/10.1080/17475759.2012.756423; Çiğdem Bozdağ, "Policies of Media and Cultural Integration in Germany: From Guestworker Programmes

to a More Integrative Framework," *Global Media and Communication* 10 (2014): 289–301; Olga Bailey, Myria Georgiou, and Ramaswami Harindranath, *Transnational Lives and the Media: Re-Imagining Diaspora* (New York: Palgrave Macmillan, 2007); and Kent Ono and John Sloop, *Shifting Borders: Rhetoric, Immigration, and California's Proposition 187* (Philadelphia: Temple University Press, 2002).

26. Ono and Sloop, *Shifting Borders*, 5.

27. Lisa Flores, "Constructing Rhetorical Borders: Peons, Illegal Aliens, and Competing Narratives of Immigration," *Critical Studies in Media Communication* 20 (2003): 362–87, doi: 10.1080/0739318032000142025.

28. Radha S. Hegde, *Mediating Migration* (Boston: Polity Press, 2016), 21.

29. Josue D. Cisneros, *The Border Crossed Us: Rhetorics of Borders, Citizenship, and Latina/o Identity* (Tuscaloosa: University of Alabama Press, 2014).

30. Tatyana S. Thweatt, "Attitudes Towards New Americans in the Local Press: A Critical Discourse Analysis," *North Dakota Journal of Speech and Theatre* 18 (2005): 25.

31. Joachim Trebbe and Philomen Schoenhagen, "Ethnic Minorities in the Mass Media: Always the Same and Always Negative." Paper presented at the annual meeting of the International Communication Association, Montreal, Quebec, Canada, May 21, 2008.

32. Kristin M. Langellier, "Personal Narrative, Performance, Performativity: Two or Three Things I Know for Sure," *Text and Performance Quarterly* 19, no. 2 (1999): 125–44, 127, doi: 10.1080/10462939909366255.

33. Walter Nicholls, *The DREAMers: How the Undocumented Youth Movement Transformed the Immigrant Rights Debate* (Stanford, CA: Stanford University Press, 2013), 9.

34. Nicholls, *The DREAMers*, 9.

35. Lawrence Grossberg, *Cultural Studies in the Future Tense* (Durham, NC: Duke University Press, 2010), 116.

36. Grossberg, *Cultural Studies in the Future Tense*, 116.

37. Luke Walzter, "On Supporting Undocumented Students at CUNY," City University of New York, last modified January 25, 2017, https://tlc.commons.gc.cuny.edu/2017/01/25/on-supporting-undocumented-students-at-cuny/.

38. DACA recipients have no guarantee that this protection will be extended. At the time of this writing, the future of DACA remains highly uncertain.

39. Kate Willink, *Bringing Desegregation Home: Memories of the Struggle toward School Integration in Rural North Carolina* (New York: Palgrave-Macmillan, 2009).

40. See Donna Haraway, "Situated Knowledges: The Science Question in Feminism and the Privilege of Partial Perspective," *Feminist Studies* 14 (1988): 575–99, doi: 10.2307/3178066.

41. See James Scott, *Domination and the Arts of Resistance* (New Haven, CT: Yale University Press, 1992).

42. See, for example, John A. Neuenschwander, *A Guide to Oral History and the Law* (Oxford: Oxford University Press, 2014); Scott Jaschik, "Oral History, Unprotected U.S. government—Opposing Boston College—Argues Against Researchers' Expectation of Confidentiality," *Inside Higher Ed*, July 5, 2011, https://www.insidehighered.com/news/2011/07/05/federal_government_questions_confidentiality_of_oral_history; and Marta Kurkowska-Budzan and Krzysztof Zamorski, *Oral History: The Challenges of Dialogue* (Philadelphia: John Benjamins, 2009).

43. See Valerie Raleigh Yow, *Recording Oral History: A Guide for the Humanities and Social Sciences* (Walnut Creek, CA: Altamira Press, 2005); and Neuenschwander, *A Guide to Oral History and the Law.*

44. "Principles and Best Practices," Oral History Association, http://www.oralhistory. org/about/principles-and-practices/.

45. See Aaron Hess, "Critical Rhetorical Ethnography: Rethinking the Place and Process of Rhetoric," *Communication Studies* 62, no. 2 (2011): 127–52, doi: 10.1080/10510974.2011.529750.

46. Hess, "Critical Rhetorical Ethnography," 128.

47. Hess, "Critical Rhetorical Ethnography," 129.

48. Sonja Foss, *Rhetorical Criticism: Exploration and Practice* (Long Grove, IL: Waveland Press, 2009).

49. "Frequently Asked Questions," NYC Mayor's Office of Immigrant Affairs, http://www1.nyc.gov/site/immigrants/about/frequently-asked-questions.page.

50. Jeffrey S. Passel, D. Vera Cohn, and Molly Rohal, "Unauthorized Immigrant Totals Rise in 7 States, Fall in 14: Decline in Those from Mexico Fuels Most State Decreases," *Pew Research Center*, November 18, 2014, http://www.pewhispanic.org/files/2014/11/2014-11-18_unauthorized-immigration.pdf.

51. See Daria Arao and Darren Ressler, "Working for a Better Life: A Profile of Immigrants in the New York State Economy," *Fiscal Policy Institute* (2007): 1–115, http://www.fiscalpolicy.org/publications2007/FPI_ImmReport_WorkingforaBetterLife.pdf, and Randolph Capps et al., "How Are Immigrants Faring after Welfare Reform? Preliminary Evidence from Los Angeles and New York City," *Urban Institute* (2002): 11, http://www.urban.org/research/publication/how-are-immigrants-faring-after-welfare-reform/view/full_report.

52. Capps et al., "How Are Immigrants Faring after Welfare Reform?," 1; "Profile of the Unauthorized Population: New York," Migration Policy Institute, http://www.migrationpolicy.org/data/unauthorized-immigrant-population/state/NY.

53. Sylvia Mendoza, "Building False Crisis: The Role of the Media Covering Undocumented Immigrants," *Hispanic Outlook in Higher Education* 25 (2015): 10–12, https://www.hispanicoutlook.com/featured-articles/2015/7/14/building-false-crisis-the-role-of-the-media-covering-undocumented-immigrants.

54. See Seth Holmes and Philippe Bourgois, *Fresh Fruit, Broken Bodies: Migrant Farmworkers in the United States* (Berkeley: University of California Press, 2013).

55. Roberto Gonzales, *Lives in Limbo: Undocumented and Coming of Age in America* (Oakland: University of California Press, 2016).

56. Sarah Mahler, *American Dreaming: Immigrant Life on the Margins* (Princeton, NJ: Princeton University Press, 1995).

57. Leo Chavez, *Shadowed Lives* (Belmont: Cengage Learning, 2013).

58. Joanna Dreby, *Everyday Illegal: When Policies Undermine Immigrant Families* (Oakland: University of California Press, 2015).

59. "Mercer 2015 Cost of Living Rankings," Mercer, https://www.imercer.com/content/2015-cost-of-living-infographic.aspx.

60. Executive Order of January 25, 2017, Border Security and Immigration Enforcement Improvements, *Office of the Press Secretary*, https://www.whitehouse.gov/the-press-office/2017/01/25/executive-order-border-security-and-immigration-enforcement-improvements.

61. See Philip Kasinitz et al., *Inheriting the City: The Children of Immigrants Come of Age* (New York: Russell Sage Foundation, 2008).

62. Mae Ngai, *Impossible Subjects: Illegal Aliens and the Making of Modern America* (Princeton, NJ: Princeton University Press, 2004).

63. Lisa Marie Cacho, *Social Death: Racialized Rightlessness and the Criminalization of the Unprotected* (New York: New York University Press, 2012), 26.

64. For more on intersectionality, see Kimberlé Crenshaw, "Mapping the Margins: Intersectionality, Identity Politics, and Violence Against Women of Color," *Stanford Law Review* 43 (1993): 1241–99, https://chicagounbound.uchicago.edu/cgi/viewcontent.cgi?referer=http://www.law.columbia.edu/pt-br/news/2017/06/kimberle-crenshaw-intersectionality&httpsredir=1&article=1052&context=uclf.

65. Audre Lorde, *Sister Outsider* (Berkeley, CA: Crossing Press, 1984), 138.

66. Karma Chávez, *Queer Migration Politics: Activist Rhetoric and Coalitional Possibilities* (Chicago: University of Illinois Press, 2013), 58–59.

67. Michelle Alexander, *The New Jim Crow: Mass Incarceration in the Age of Colorblindness* (New York: New Press, 2012).

68. United States v. Brignoni-Ponce, 422 U.S. 873 (1975).

69. Nancy Foner and Patrick Simon, eds., *Fear, Anxiety, and National Identity: Immigration and Belonging in North America and Western Europe* (New York: Russell Sage Foundation, 2015), 117, https://www.russellsage.org/sites/all/files/fear-anxiety-and-national-identity.pdf.

70. Foner and Simon, *Fear, Anxiety, and National Identity*, 130.

71. Angy Rivera, interview by Sarah C. Bishop, July 6, 2015, transcript.

72. Piash Ahamed, interview with Sarah C. Bishop, March 31, 2016, transcript.

73. Esther Meroño Baro, interview with Sarah C. Bishop, September 24, 2016, transcript.

74. David Chung, interview with Sarah C. Bishop, July 29, 2016, transcript.

Chapter 1

1. Katherine Chua Almirañez, interview by Sarah C. Bishop, April 14, 2016, transcript.

2. Katherine Chua Almirañez, interview by Sarah C. Bishop, April 14, 2016, transcript.

3. Katherine Chua Almirañez, *Undocumented* (New York: 2011), https://undocumentedtheplay.com/.

4. *Out of the Shadows*, produced by John Howard (2013; Unboxed Voices, 2013), documentary, https://vimeo.com/61496205.

5. Katherine Chua Almirañez, interview by Sarah C. Bishop, April 14, 2016, transcript.

6. Adam Liptak and Michael D. Shear, "Supreme Court Tie Blocks Obama Immigration Plan," *New York Times*, June 23, 2016, http://www.nytimes.com/2016/06/24/us/supreme-court-immigration-obama-dapa.html?_r=0.

7. Gloria Anzaldúa, *The Gloria Anzaldúa Reader* (Durham, NC: Duke University Press, 2009), 30.

8. Alisdair MacIntyre, *After Virtue: A Study in Moral Theory* (Notre Dame, IN: University of Notre Dame Press, 1981), 216.

9. Walter Fisher, *Human Communication as Narration: Toward a Philosophy of Reason, Value, and Action* (Columbia: University of South Carolina Press, 1989), 135.

10. Walter Fisher, "Narration as a Human Communication Paradigm: The Case of Public Moral Argument," *Communication Monographs* 51 (1984): 9, http://nca.tandfonline.com/doi/abs/10.1080/03637758409390180.

11. Walter Fisher, "Narration, Knowledge, and the Possibility of Wisdom," in *Rethinking Knowledge: Reflections across the Disciplines*, ed. Robert Goodman and Walter Fisher (Albany: State University of New York Press, 1995), 170.

12. Robert Rowland, "Mode of Discourse or Paradigm," *Communication Monographs* 54 (1987): 272.

13. Fisher, "Narration as a Human Communication Paradigm," 9.

14. Barbara Warnick, "The Narrative Paradigm, Another Story," *Quarterly Journal of Speech* 73 (1987): 181, https://www.bc.edu/res/gssw-research-home/funding/proposal-development/_jcr_content/content/download_57/file.res/Warnick,%20'The%20Narrative%20Paradigm%20Another%20Story'.pdf.

15. Walter Fisher, "Human Communication as Narration: Toward a Philosophy of Reason, Value, and Action," *Quarterly Journal of Speech* (1988): 349, https://www.bc.edu/res/gssw-research-home/funding/proposal-development/_jcr_content/content/download_38/file.res/Fisher%2C%20'Human%20Communication%20as%20Narration%20Book%20Review%203'.pdf.

16. Fisher, "Narration as a Human Communication Paradigm," 2.

17. Rowland, "Mode of Discourse or Paradigm," 265.

18. Martin Jay, *Songs of Experience: Modern American and European Variations on a Universal Theme* (Berkeley: University of California Press, 2005), 401.

19. Michael Oakeshott, *Experience and Its Modes* (Cambridge: Cambridge University Press, 1986), xxi.

20. James Carey, *Communication as Culture* (Boston: Unwin Hyman, 1989), 20.

21. Raymond Williams, *Keywords: A Vocabulary of Culture and Society* (New York: Oxford University Press, 1976), 127.

22. Williams, *Keywords*, 128.

23. Joan W. Scott, "The Evidence of Experience," *Critical Inquiry* 17, no. 4 (1991): 797.

24. Define American, "Laura Wilkerson Confronts Jose Antonio Vargas on The Kelly File," YouTube Video, July 18, 2016, https://www.youtube.com/watch?v=LzR_A144gbw.

25. Lisa Marie Cacho, *Social Death: Racialized Rightlessness and the Criminalization of the Unprotected* (New York: New York University Press, 2012), 6.

26. Javier Zamora, interview by Sarah C. Bishop, March 21, 2016, interview 12, transcript.

27. Daniel (pseudonym), interview by Sarah C. Bishop, June 15, 2016, transcript.

28. Donna Haraway, "Situated Knowledges: The Science Question in Feminism and the Privilege of Partial Perspective," *Feminist Studies* 14, no. 3 (1988): 581.

29. Haraway, "Situated Knowledges," 584.

30. Donna Haraway, *Simians, Cyborgs, and Women: The Reinvention of Nature* (New York, NY: Routledge, 1991), 184.

31. Jin Park, interview by Sarah C. Bishop, March 14, 2016, interview 8, transcript.

32. Gabriela Quintanilla, interview by Sarah C. Bishop, March 14, 2016, interview 9, transcript.

33. See John L. Austin, *How to Do Things with Words* (Oxford: Clarendon Press, 1962); Erving Goffman, *The Presentation of the Self in Everyday Life* (London: Allen Lane, 1969); Jacques Derrida, *Limited Inc.*, trans. Samuel Weber (Paris: Éditions Galilée, 1990); and Judith Butler, *Excitable Speech: A Politics of the Performative* (New York: Routledge, 1997).

34. James Carey, *Communication as Culture: Essays on Media and Society* (New York, Routledge, 1989), 23.

35. James Scott, *Domination and the Arts of Resistance: Hidden Transcripts* (New Haven, CT: Yale University Press, 1990), xi.

36. Walter J. Nicholls, *The DREAMers: How the Undocumented Youth Movement Transformed the Immigrant Rights Debate* (Redwood City, CA: Stanford University Press, 2013), 50.

37. For more on the myths about undocumented immigration that appear in political and popular US discourse, see the Introduction of this volume.

38. Kent A. Ono and John M. Sloop, *Shifting Borders: Rhetoric, Immigration, and California's Proposition 187* (Philadelphia: Temple University Press, 2002), 23.

39. Ono and Sloop, *Shifting Borders*, 22.

40. Michael Warner, "Publics and Counterpublics," *Public Culture* 14 (2002): 50, https://muse.jhu.edu/article/26277.

41. Butler, *Excitable Speech*, 2.

42. See Gerard A. Hauser, "The Moral Vernacular of Human Rights Discourse," *Philosophy & Rhetoric* 41, no. 4 (2008): 440–66.

43. Hauser, "The Moral Vernacular," 456.

44. Hauser, "The Moral Vernacular," 458.

45. Sonia Espinosa, interview by Sarah C. Bishop, August 18, 2015, transcript.

46. Barbie Zelizer, "Cannibalizing Memory in the Global Flow of News," in *On Media Memory: Collective Memory in a New Media Age,* ed. Motti Nieger et al. (New York: Palgrave Macmillan, 2011), 28, http://link.springer.com/chapter/10.1057%2F9780230307070_2.

47. Zelizer, "Cannibalizing Memory in the Global Flow of News," 23.

48. "Full Text: Donald Trump Announces a Presidential Bid," *Washington Post*, June 16, 2015, https://www.washingtonpost.com/news/post-politics/wp/2015/06/16/full-text-donald-trump-announces-a-presidential-bid/?utm_term=.8daec1ff5eae.

49. See Chapter 3 for more on the "no fault of their own" frame.

50. Cacho, *Social Death*, 44.

51. Radha S. Hegde, *Mediating Migration* (Boston: Polity Press, 2016), 37.

52. Define American, "Share Your Story," Https://defineamerican.com/stories/share/#instructions.

53. "Jose Antonio Vargas," accessed September 9, 2016, http://joseantoniovargas.com/.

54. For more on the divergent goals of reclaimant narratives, see Chapter 5.

55. Daniel, interview by Sarah C. Bishop, transcript.

56. Lina Newton, *Illegal, Alien, or Immigrant: The Politics of Immigration Reform* (New York: New York University Press, 2008), 3.

57. Emma Lazarus, "The New Colossus" (sonnet, New York City, created 1883, engraved on bronze plaque inside the Statue of Liberty 1903).

58. Tanya Somanader, "'We Were Strangers Once, Too': The President Announces New Steps on Immigration," *White House Blog,* last modified November 20, 2014, https://www.whitehouse.gov/blog/2014/11/20/we-were-strangers-once-too-president-announces-new-steps-immigration.

59. See Executive Order 12333, United States Intelligence Activities, December 4, 1981. As amended by Executive Orders 13284 (2003), 13355 (2004) and 13470 (2008), accessed October 25, 2016, https://www.nsa.gov/about/faqs/oversight-faqs.shtml.

60. Fisher, "Narration, Knowledge, and the Possibility of Wisdom," 177.

61. David Schroeder, John Dovidio, Mark Sibicky, Linda Matthews, and Judith Allen, "Empathic Concern and Helping Behavior: Egoism or Altruism?," *Journal of Experimental Social Psychology* 24 (1988): 348, https://doi.org/10.1016/0022-1031(88)90024-8.

62. Karma Chávez, *Queer Migration Politics: Activist Rhetoric and Coalitional Possibilities* (Chicago: University of Illinois Press, 2013), 60.

63. Chávez, *Queer Migration Politics,* 77.

Chapter 2

1. Ximena, interview by Sarah C. Bishop, March 17, 2016, transcript.

2. Ximena, interview by Sarah C. Bishop, March 17, 2016, transcript.

3. Leisy Janet Abrego, "I Can't Go to College Because I Don't Have Papers: Incorporation Patterns of Latino Undocumented Youth," *Latino Studies* 4 (2006): 329, doi: 10.1057/palgrave.lst.8600200.

4. Ximena, interview by Sarah C. Bishop, March 17, 2016, transcript.

5. Ximena, email to Sarah C. Bishop, August 29, 2016.

6. Katherine Chua Almirañez, *Undocumented* (New York: 2011), https://undocumentedtheplay.com/.

7. Alasdair MacIntyre, *After Virtue: A Study in Moral Theory* (Notre Dame, IN: University of Notre Dame Press, 1984), 216.

8. Piash Ahmed, interview by Sarah C. Bishop, March 31, 2016, transcript.

9. Roberto Gonzales, "Learning to Be Illegal: Undocumented Youth and Shifting Legal Contexts in the Transition to Adulthood," *American Sociological Review* 74 (2011): 602–19, doi: 10.1177/0003122411411901.

10. Gonzales, "Learning to Be Illegal," 602.

11. Roberto Gonzales, *Lives in Limbo: Undocumented and Coming of Age in America* (Oakland: University of California Press, 2016), 213.

12. Sam (pseudonym), interview by Sarah C. Bishop, September 16, 2016, transcript.

13. Asylum is protection that is granted by a nation after an individual has arrived in that nation. It is reserved for individuals who are facing persecution in their home countries due to race, religion, nationality, membership in a particular social group, or political opinion. If a person's application for asylum is approved, he or she may become eligible for refugee benefits. For more on asylum, see "Asylum," United States Citizenship and Immigration Services, last modified August 6, 2015, https://www.uscis.gov/humanitarian/refugees-asylum/asylum.

14. Sam (pseudonym), email to Sarah C. Bishop, October 19, 2016.

15. Francisco Barros, interview by Sarah C. Bishop, April 14, 2016, transcript.

16. For more on gratefulness to parents, see Chapter 3.

17. Kattia Minaya, interview by Sarah C. Bishop, October 21, 2016, transcript.

18. Walter J. Nicholls, *The DREAMers: How the Undocumented Youth Movement Transformed the Immigrant Rights Debate* (Redwood City, CA: Stanford University Press, 2013), 128.

19. For more about intergenerational communication between undocumented parents and children, see especially Joanna Dreby, *Everyday Illegal: When Policies Undermine Immigrant Families* (Oakland: University of California Press, 2015).

20. Sonia Espinosa, interview by Sarah C. Bishop, August 18, 2016, transcript.

21. Francisco Barros, interview by Sarah C. Bishop, April 14, 2016, transcript.

22. Roberto Gonzales and Leo Chavez, "'Awakening to a Nightmare': Abjectivity and Illegality in the Lives of Undocumented 1.5 Generation Latino Immigrants in the United States," *Current Anthropology* 53 (2012): 255–81, doi: 10.1086/665414.

23. Omrie (last name removed at the narrator's request), interview by Sarah C. Bishop, June 15, 2016, transcript.

24. M. Brinton Lykes, Kalina Brabeck, and Cristina Hunter, "Exploring Parent–Child Communication in the Context of Threat: Immigrant Families Facing Detention and Deportation in Post-9/11 USA," *Community, Work & Family* 16 (2011):123–46, http://dx.doi.org/10.1080/13668803.2012.752997.

25. Lykesa, Brabeck, and Hunter, "Exploring Parent-Child Communication," 135.

26. Esther Meroño Baro, email message to Sarah C. Bishop, September 26, 2015.

27. Pang (surname withheld at narrator's request), interview by Sarah C. Bishop, May 6, 2015, transcript.

28. Ximena, interview by Sarah C. Bishop, March 17, 2016, transcript.

29. Kattia Minaya, interview by Sarah C. Bishop, October 22, 2016, transcript.

30. Piash (surname withheld at narrator's request), interview by Sarah C. Bishop, March 31, 2016, transcript; INS, or Immigration and Naturalization Services, was the agency responsible for immigration detention and deportation until ICE was created in 2002.

31. Ricardo Aca, interview by Sarah C. Bishop, March 3, 2016, transcript.

32. "Reporting Illegal Activity," United States Customs and Border Protection, accessed October 29, 2016, https://help.cbp.gov/app/answers/detail/a_id/735/~/reporting-illegal-activity.

33. "Yearbook of Immigration Statistics: 2014 Enforcement Actions," United States Department of Homeland Security (2016): 91, accessed September 23, 2016, https://www.dhs.gov/sites/default/files/publications/ois_yb_2014.pdf.

34. Jennifer Medina, "Too Scared to Report Sexual Abuse. The Fear: Deportation," *New York Times,* April 30, 2017, https://www.nytimes.com/2017/04/30/us/immigrants-deportation-sexual-abuse.html.

35. "Fear of Deportation Spurs 4 Women to Drop Domestic Abuse Cases in Denver," *NPR*, March 21, 2017, http://www.npr.org/2017/03/21/520841332/fear-of-deportation-spurs-4-women-to-drop-domestic-abuse-cases-in-denver.

36. "Fear of Deportation Spurs 4 Women to Drop Domestic Abuse Cases in Denver."

37. Katie Mettler, "'This Is Really Unprecedented': ICE Detains Woman Seeking Domestic Abuse Protection at Texas Courthouse," *Washington Post,* February 16, 2017, https://www.washingtonpost.com/news/morning-mix/wp/2017/02/16/

this-is-really-unprecedented-ice-detains-woman-seeking-domestic-abuse-protection-at-texas-courthouse/?utm_term=.c10c48f190fb.

38. Jenny (Pseudonym), interview by Sarah C. Bishop, June 15, 2016, transcript.

39. Gonzales and Chavez, " 'Awakening to a Nightmare,' " 264.

40. Samantha Sabo and Alison Elizabeth Lee, "The Spillover of US Immigration Policy on Citizens and Permanent Residents of Mexican Descent: How Internalizing "Illegality" Impacts Public Health in the Borderlands," *Frontiers in Public Health* 3 (2015): 155, https://www.ncbi.nlm.nih.gov/pmc/articles/PMC4464055/; see also Sharon McGuire and Jane Georges, "Undocumentedness and Liminality as Health Variables," *Advances in Nursing Science* 26 (2003): 185–95, http://citeseerx.ist.psu.edu/viewdoc/download?doi=10.1.1.501.8479&rep=rep1&type=pdf.

41. For more on vulnerable immigrants' avoidance of support services, see Marissa Raymond-Flesch et al., " 'There Is No Help Out There and if There Is, It's Really Hard to Find': A Qualitative Study of the Health Concerns and Health Care Access of Latino 'Dreamers,' " *Journal of Adolescent Health* 55 (2014): S18–S19, doi: 10.1016/j.jadohealth.2013.10.051.

42. Javier (surname withheld at narrator's request), interview by Sarah C. Bishop, March 21, 2016, transcript.

43. Katherine Chua Almirañez, interview by Sarah C. Bishop, April 14, 2016, transcript.

44. Sonia Espinosa, interview by Sarah C. Bishop, August 18, 2015, transcript.

45. Pang (surname withheld at narrator's request), interview by Sarah C. Bishop, May 6, 2015, transcript.

46. Piash (surname withheld at narrator's request), interview by Sarah C. Bishop, March 31, 2016, transcript.

47. Because of these travel restrictions, several of the narrators I interviewed reporting missing the deaths and funerals of family members living in their birth nations.

48. See Arnold Van Gennep, *The Rites of Passage* (London: Routledge, 1960).

49. Roberto Gonzales, *Lives in Limbo: Undocumented and Coming of Age in America* (Oakland: University of California Press, 2016).

50. See Ulf Hannerz, "Cosmopolitans and Locals in World Culture," *Theory, Culture, Society* 7 (1990): 237–51, doi:10.1177/026327690007002014; Matt Bai, "The Way We Live Now: 10-28-01: Encounter; Hyphenated Americans," *New York Times Magazine*, October 28, 2001, http://www.nytimes.com/2001/10/28/magazine/the-way-we-live-now-10-28-01-encounter-hyphenated-americans.html; Linda Trinh Moser and Kathryn West, *American Multicultural Identity* (Ipswich, MA: Salem Press, 2014); Chay Yew, David Roman, and Craig Lucas, *The Hyphenated American: Four Plays: Red, Scissors, A Beautiful Country, and Wonderland* (New York: Grove Press, 2002).

51. Gabriela Quintanilla, interview by Sarah C. Bishop, March 14, 2016, transcript.

52. Elaine Burroughs, "Discursive Representations of 'Illegal Immigration' in the Irish Newsprint Media: The Domination and Multiple Facets of the 'Control' Argumentation," *Discourse & Society* 26 (2015): 165–83, doi: 10.1177/0957926514556029; Michael Breen, Eoin Devereux, and Amanda Haynes, "Fear, Framing and Foreigners: The Othering of Immigrants in the Irish Print Media," *International Journal of Critical Psychology* 16 (2006):100–121, http://hdl.handle.net/10395/1350; Sean Hier and Joshua Greenberg, "Constructing a Discursive Crisis: Risk, Problematization and Illegal

Chinese in Canada," *Ethnic and Racial Studies* 25 (2002): 490–513, http://dx.doi.org/10.1080/01419870020036701; Teun Van Dijk, "Ideologies, Racism, Discourse: Debates on Immigration and Ethnic Issues," in *Comparative Perspectives on Racism (Research in Migration and Ethnic Relations)*, ed. Jessika Ter Wal and Maykel Verkuyten (Farnham: Ashgate, 2000), 91–115.

53. California, Texas, Florida, New York, New Jersey, and Illinois house approximately 60 percent of undocumented immigrants living in the United States. Krogstad and Passel, "5 Facts about Illegal Immigration," http://www.pewresearch.org/fact-tank/2015/11/19/5-facts-about-illegal-immigration-in-the-u-s/.

54. Ximena, interview by Sarah C. Bishop, March 17, 2016, transcript.

55. Irene Bloemraad, Els de Graauw, and Rebecca Hamlin, "Immigrants in the Media: Civic Visibility in the United States and Canada," *Journal of Ethnic and Migration Studies* 41 (2015): 874–96, http://dx.doi.org/10.1080/1369183X.2014.1002198.

56. Jon (surname withheld at narrator's request), interview by Sarah C. Bishop, March 21, 2016, transcript.

57. Jon (surname withheld at narrator's request), interview by Sarah C. Bishop, March 21, 2016, transcript.

58. Ximena, interview by Sarah C. Bishop, March 17, 2016, transcript.

59. Josue Guerrero, interview by Sarah C. Bishop, April 19, 2016, transcript.

60. Omrie (surname withheld at narrator's request), interview by Sarah C. Bishop, June 15, 2016, transcript.

61. Robert Teranishi, Carola Suárez-Orozco, and Marcelo Suárez-Orozco, "In the Shadows of the Ivory Tower: Undocumented Undergraduates and the Liminal State of Immigration Reform," *Institute for Immigration, Globalization, & Education* (2015): 1–32, http://undocuscholars.org/assets/undocuscholarsreport2015.pdf

62. Natalia (surname withheld at narrator's request), interview by Sarah C. Bishop, June 27, 2016, transcript.

63. Karina Horsti, "Global Mobility and the Media: Presenting Asylum Seekers as a Threat," *Nordic Research on Media & Communication* 24 (2003): 51, August 19, 2016, http://www.nordicom.gu.se/sites/default/files/kapitel-pdf/23_041-054.pdf.

64. Linda Alcoff, "The Problem of Speaking for Others," *Cultural Critique* 20 (1992): 9, August 19, 2016, doi 10.2307/1354221, emphasis added.

65. "UWD Newsroom," United We Dream, https://unitedwedream.org/news/; "Media: NYIC in the News," New York Immigration Coalition, http://www.thenyic.org/news.

66. Angy Rivera, interview by Sarah C. Bishop, July 6, 2015, transcript.

67. In my own project, I have attempted to mitigate this concern by speaking with undocumented activists at each stage of the work, circulating drafts of the writing to the narrators whose experiences I include and adapting the prose according to these narrators' suggestions and recommendations.

68. David Chung, interview by Sarah C. Bishop, July 29, 2016, transcript.

69. David Chung, interview by Sarah C. Bishop, July 29, 2016, transcript.

70. "United We Dream Condemns Rep. Goodlatte's Comments Opposing Citizenship for DREAMers and Families," United We Dream, accessed October 30, 2016, http://unitedwedream.org/press-releases/united-we-dream-condemns-rep-goodlattes-comments-opposing-citizenship-for-dreamers-and-families/.

71. United We Dream, "United We Dream Condemns Rep. Goodlatte's Comments."

72. Kattia Minaya, interview by Sarah C. Bishop, October 21, 2016, transcript.

73. Adam (surname removed at the narrator's request), interview by Sarah C. Bishop, June 15, 2016, transcript.

74. Jin Park, interview by Sarah C. Bishop, March 14, 2016, transcript.

75. "Meet the Undocumented Immigrant Who Works in a Trump Hotel," YouTube Video, 2:43, posted by "NewLeftMedia," August 17, 2015, https://www.youtube.com/watch?v=e-r9E5n5FnM.

76. Ricardo Aca, interview by Sarah C. Bishop, March 3, 2016, transcript.

77. Piash (surname withheld at narrator's request), interview by Sarah C. Bishop, March 31, 2016, transcript.

78. Ximena, interview by Sarah C. Bishop, March 17, 2016, transcript.

79. See Benedict Anderson, *Imagined Communities: Reflections on the Origin and Spread of Nationalism* (New York: Verso, 2006).

80. Kathryn Abrams, "Performative Citizenship in the Civil Rights and Immigrant Rights Movements" in *A Nation of Widening Opportunities: The Civil Rights Act at Fifty,* ed. Ellen D. Katz and Samuel R. Bagenstos (Ann Arbor: University of Michigan Press, 2015), http://quod.lib.umich.edu/m/maize/13855464.0001.001/1:3/--nation-of-widening-opportunities?rgn=div1;view=fulltext.

81. Daniel (last name removed at the narrator's request), interview by Sarah C. Bishop, June 27, 2016, transcript.

82. Adela Licona, *Zines in Third Space: Radical Cooperation and Borderlands Rhetoric* (Albany: State University of New York Press, 2012), 13.

83. Licona, *Zines in Third Space: Radical Cooperation and Borderlands Rhetoric*, 13.

84. Licona, *Zines in Third Space: Radical Cooperation and Borderlands Rhetoric*, 12–13.

85. Gina Diaz, "While Undocumented," *My Undocumented Life,* September 4, 2015, https://mydocumentedlife.org/2015/09/04/while-undocumented/.

86. Julio Salgado, "I Exist," Julio Salgado Art, June 24, 2011, http://juliosalgadoart.com/post/6892057848/lets-do-this.

87. Alcoff, "The Problem of Speaking for Others," 10.

88. Gonzales and Chavez, " 'Awakening to a Nightmare,' " 262.

Chapter 3

1. Daniel (surname withheld at the narrator's request), interview by Sarah C. Bishop, June 15, 2016, transcript.

2. Daniel (surname withheld at the narrator's request), interview by Sarah C. Bishop, June 15, 2016, transcript.

3. Daniel (surname withheld at the narrator's request), interview by Sarah C. Bishop, June 15, 2016, transcript.

4. For a relevant history, see Walter J. Nicholls, *The DREAMers: How the Undocumented Youth Movement Transformed the Immigrant Rights Debate* (Stanford, CA: Stanford University Press, 2013).

5. Linda Alcoff, "The Problem of Speaking for Others," *Cultural Critique* 20 (1991): 5–32, accessed August 9, 2016, doi 10.2307/1354221.

6. Magdalena Bobowik, Nekane Basabe, and Dario Paez, "'Heroes of Adjustment': Immigrant's Stigma and Identity," *International Journal of Intercultural Relations* 41 (2014): 112–24, accessed August 9, 2016, doi: 0.1016/j.ijintrel.2014.04.002.

7. See, for example, Erving Goffman, *Frame Analysis: An Essay on the Organization of Experience* (New York: Harper & Row, 1974); Gail Fairhurst and Robert Sarr, *The Art of Framing* (San Francisco: Jossey-Bass, 1996); Dietram A. Scheufele, "Framing as a Theory of Media Effects," *Journal of Communication* 49 (1999): 103–22, doi: 10.1111/j.1460-2466.1999.tb02784.x.

8. Walter Fisher, *Human Communication as Narration: Toward a Philosophy of Reason, Value, and Action* (Columbia: University of South Carolina Press, 1989), 18.

9. Favianna Rodriguez, quoted in Paul Kuttner, "Interview with Cultural Organizer Favianna Rodriguez," *Cultural Organizing*, February 18, 2013, http://culturalorganizing.org/tag/culturestrike/.

10. "How Do I Talk to the Community about What the President Has Announced?" United We Dream, accessed July 15, 2016, https://docs.google.com/file/d/0B2H_VZDWC2OzZDB4UGx3Qi1NbkU/edit.

11. Michel Foucault, "What Is an Author?" in *Foucault Reader 1984*, ed. Paul Rabinow (New York: Knopf Doubleday, 1984), 120.

12. Foucault, "What Is an Author?" 109.

13. Alcoff, "The Problem of Speaking for Others," 7.

14. Unnamed artist, interview by Walter J. Nicholls, *The DREAMers*, 2013.

15. Daniel (surname withheld at the narrator's request), interview by Sarah C. Bishop, June 15, 2016, transcript.

16. Alcoff, "The Problem of Speaking for Others," 20.

17. Lauren M. Ellis and Eric C. Chen, "Negotiating Identity Development among Undocumented Immigrant College Students: A Grounded Theory Study," *Journal of Counseling Psychology* 60 (2013): 258, accessed August 9, 2016, doi: 10.1037/a0031350.

18. Ellis and Chen, "Negotiating Identity Development," 258.

19. Stephanie Valencia, "President Obama on Obstruction of the DREAM Act: 'Maybe My Biggest Disappointment' of Last Weeks," *White House Blog*, December 23, 2010, https://whitehouse.gov/blog/2010/12/23/president-obama-obstruction-dream-act-maybe-my-biggest-disappointment-last-weeks.

20. "Mayors Representing over 1 Million NJ Residents Call on Legislature to Pass Tuition Equity & State Aid Bill for Undocumented Students," United We Dream, accessed July 1, 2016, http://unitedwedream.org/press-releases/mayors-representing-1-million-nj-residents-call-legislature-pass-tuition-equity-state-aid-bill-undocumented-students/.

21. https://twitter.com/realDonaldTrump/status/908278070611779585.

22. "No Fault of Their Own," Define American, last modified June 22, 2011, https://defineamerican.com/blog/no-fault-of-their-own/.

23. "The DREAM Act," American Immigration Council, last modified May 18, 2011, http://immigrationpolicy.org/just-facts/dream-act.

24. Jung Rae Jang, interview by Sarah C. Bishop, June 15, 2016, transcript.

25. Jung Rae Jang, interview by Sarah C. Bishop, June 15, 2016, transcript.

26. Daniel (surname withheld at the narrator's request), interview by Sarah C. Bishop, June 15, 2016, transcript.

27. Nicholls, *The DREAMers*, 127.

28. Jenny (Pseudonym), interview by Sarah C. Bishop, June 15, 2016, transcript.

29. See, for example, "Causes and Impacts Relating to Forced and Voluntary Migration," *BBC*, accessed August 31, 2016, http://www.bbc.co.uk/education/guides/z8g334j/revision/1; Jonathan W. Moses, "The American Century? Migration and the Voluntary Social Contract," *Politics & Society* 37 (2009): 454–76, accessed September 1, 2016, doi: 10.1177/0032329209338928; Aivar Jürgenson, "Voluntary and Forced Migration Dichotomy on the Background of Migration Macro and Micro Theories," *Acta Historica Tallinnensia* 13 (2008): 92–117, accessed September 1, 2016, http://www.kirj.ee/public/Acta_hist/2008/issue_2/Acta-2008-13-92-117.pdf; Hannah Bradby, Rachel Humphris, Dave Newall, and Jenny Phillimore, "Public Health Aspects of Migrant Health: A Review of the Evidence on Health Status for Refugees and Asylum Seekers in the European Region," *Health Evidence Network* 44 (2015): 1–33, accessed September 1, 2016, http://www.epgencms.europarl.europa.eu/cmsdata/upload/3a3f00c0-9a75-4c84-94ad-06e4bd2ce412/WHO-HEN-Report-A5-2-Refugees_FINAL_EN.pdf.

30. Felix Rivera, interview by Sarah C. Bishop, May 5, 2016, transcript.

31. Daniel (surname withheld at the narrator's request), interview by Sarah C. Bishop, June 15, 2016, transcript.

32. Josue Guerrero, interview by Sarah C. Bishop, April 19, 2016, transcript.

33. Lisette Candia, "Undocumented at Harvard: The Real American Heroes," *Huffington Post*, April 1, 2015, http://huffingtonpost.com/lisette-candia/undocumented-at-harvard-real-american-heroes_b_6984788.html.

34. We Are Mitú, "What My Undocumented Parents Sacrificed for Me," YouTube video, 01:06, posted [October 2015], https://youtube.com/watch?v=RtgK1tjSfSk.

35. Sometimes DAPA is referred to as Deferred Action for Parental Accountability.

36. Unnamed former director, quoted in Nicholls, *The DREAMers*, 52.

37. Karma Chávez, *Queer Migration Politics: Activist Rhetoric and Coalitional Possibilities* (Chicago: University of Illinois Press, 2013), 10.

38. James C. Scott, *Domination and the Arts of Resistance* (New Haven, CT: Yale University Press, 1992), xii.

39. Nicholls, *The DREAMers*, 52.

40. Lisa M. Cacho, *Social Death: Racialized Rightlessness and the Criminalization of the Unprotected* (New York: New York University Press, 2012), 129.

41. Daniel (surname withheld at the narrator's request), interview by Sarah C. Bishop, June 15, 2016, transcript.

42. Daniel (surname withheld at the narrator's request), interview by Sarah C. Bishop, June 15, 2016, transcript.

43. Sonia Espinosa, interview by Sarah C. Bishop, August 18, 2015, transcript.

44. Pang T. (full surname withheld at narrator's request), interview by Sarah C. Bishop, May 6, 2015, transcript.

45. David, interview by Sarah C. Bishop, July 29, 2016, transcript.

46. Nicholls, *The DREAMers*, 12–13.

47. "Jose Antonio Vargas," accessed September 9, 2016, http://joseantoniovargas.com/.

48. U.S. Committee on the Judiciary, Senate, *Comprehensive Immigration Reform: Hearings Before the United States Senate Committee on the Judiciary*, 113th Congress, February 13, 2013, statement of Jose Antonio Vargas, Founder, Define

American, https://www.judiciary.senate.gov/imo/media/doc/2-13-13VargasTestimony. pdf.

49. See, for example, J. David Cisneros, "Contaminated Communities: The Metaphor of 'Immigrant as Pollutant' in Media Representations of Immigration," *Rhetoric & Public Affairs* 1 (2008): 569–601, doi: 10.1353/rap.0.0068; Joachim Trebbe and Philomen Schoenhagen, "Ethnic Minorities in the Mass Media: Always the Same and Always Negative," presentation, Annual Meeting of the International Communication Association, Montreal, Quebec, Canada, May 21, 2008; Cacho, *Social Death.*

50. In the next chapter, I interrogate more closely the power and limitations of digital communication for the movement.

51. See, for example, Penelope Lockwood, "'Someone Like Me Can Be Successful': Do College Students Need Same-Gender Role Models?" *Psychology of Women Quarterly* 30 (2006): 36–46, doi: 10.1111/j.1471-6402.2006.00260.x; Edward C. Halperin, "Do Medical Students Choose Historical Role Models Who "Look Like Me"?" *Connecticut Medicine* 79 (2015): 291–93.

52. Nicholls, *The DREAMers*, 4.

53. Joshua Meyrowitz, *No Sense of Place: The Impact of Electronic Media on Social Behavior* (London: Oxford University Press, 1985), 103.

54. Meyrowitz, *No Sense of Place,* 103.

55. For more on fear of immigrants, see Nancy Foner and Patrick Simon, eds., *Fear, Anxiety, and National Identity: Immigration and Belonging in North America and Western Europe* (New York: Russell Sage Foundation, 2015).

56. Esther Meroño Baro, interview by Sarah C. Bishop, September 24, 2015, transcript.

57. Sonia Espinosa, interview by Sarah C. Bishop, August 18 2015, transcript.

58. For more on radical contextualization, see Lawrence Grossberg, *Cultural Studies in the Future Tense* (Durham, NC: Duke University Press, 2010).

59. See Marissa Raymond-Flesch, Rachel Siemons, Nadereh Pourat, Ken Jacobs, and Claire Brindis, "'There Is No Help Out There and if There Is, It's Really Hard to Find': A Qualitative Study of the Health Concerns and Health Care Access of Latino 'Dreamers,'" *Journal of Adolescent Health* 55 (2014): 323–28. http://dx.doi.org/10.1016/j.jadohealth.2014.05.012; "The Great Immigration Panic," *New York Times*, June 3, 2008, http://www.nytimes.com/2008/06/03/opinion/03tue1.html; Nomi Dave and Leslye Orloff, "Identifying Barriers: Survey of Immigrant Women and Domestic Violence in the D.C. Metropolitan Area," *Poverty and Race* 6 (1997): 9–12.

60. Sonia Espinosa, interview by Sarah C. Bishop, August 18 2015, transcript.

61. Kimberlé Crenshaw, "Demarginalizing the Intersection of Race and Sex: A Black Feminist Critique of Antidiscrimination Doctrine, Feminist Theory and Antiracist Politics," *University of Chicago Legal Forum* 1989 (1989): 139–67, August 19, 2015, http://chicagounbound.uchicago.edu/cgi/viewcontent.cgi?article=1052&context=uclf.

62. Chávez, *Queer Migration Politics*, 58–59.

63. Daniel (surname withheld at the narrator's request), interview by Sarah C. Bishop, June 15, 2016, transcript.

64. Citation withheld for privacy.

65. Citation withheld for privacy.

66. AskAngy, "Dating While Undocumented," YouTube video, 05:11, posted October 10, 2011, https://youtube.com/watch?v=71ydyce-Hjg.

67. The anti-immigrant posts read (1) You have no right to be here, much less date here. I don't blame you for wanting to be in the u.s. but do it legally. (2) No, the roads aren't paved with gold, but we're still better off than a lot of other countries. Rather than improve their own countries, they come here to take what they consider "their share" of our success. That's what Americans get upset about. Now, tell me, why do you "look over your shoulder" in MX? As to Juarez, Juarez and Tijuana could be poster children for the chaos Mexico brings. . . or the firebombing of Border Patrol offices, or the sniping of El Paso Sheriff. . . . So go back to your country. (3) It's the same as dating any other criminal. In any nation with laws, criminals have to look over their shoulder, knowing that they MIGHT get arrested and MIGHT even get punished! If illegals were really as "enlightened" as they want to believe themselves, then when caught, instead of pretending to be martyrs, they would say, "Had a good run, now time to Pay the Price!" (4) Why don't you stop trying to class it up? You're not "undocumented." You're an illegal alien. Further, little good for the American public will result from your exploration of romance in a country in which you have no business residing, because the odds are you'll just drop an anchor baby that citizen taxpayers will be required to financially subsidize. (5) GO BACK TO YOUR COUNTRY! COME BACK LEGALLY WE DO NOT WANT YOU EVEN IF YOU HAVE A VAGINA. GO HOME. (6) Take a hint. Go home! "Undocumented"???? The correct term is ***ILLEGAL***!!! Get it right! (7) Dirty cockroach! go back to mexshithole and get a job in a donkey show.

68. Angy Rivera, interview by Sarah C. Bishop, July 6, 2015, transcript.

69. Alcoff, "The Problem of Speaking for Others," 7–8.

70. Alcoff, "The Problem of Speaking for Others," 8.

71. AskAngy, "8 Black Immigrant Organizers You Should Follow on Twitter," Tumblr, accessed July 15, 2016, http://askangy.tumblr.com/post/147406700975/8-black-immigrant-organizers-you-should-follow-on.

72. Olga Kuchinskaya, *The Politics of Invisibility: Public Knowledge about Radiation Health Effects after Chernobyl* (Cambridge, MA: MIT Press, 2014), 8–9.

73. Nicholls, *The DREAMers*, 49.

CHAPTER 4

1. See Radha S. Hegde, *Mediating Migration* (Boston: Polity Press, 2016); Kathryn Abrams, "Performative Citizenship in the Civil Rights and Immigrant Rights Movements," in *A Nation of Widening Opportunities: The Civil Rights Act at Fifty*, ed. Ellen D. Katz and Samuel R. Bagenstos (Ann Arbor: University of Michigan Press, 2015), http://quod.lib.umich.edu/m/maize/13855464.0001.001/1:3/--nation-of-widening-opportunities?rgn=div1;view=fulltext.

2. Citation withheld for the narrator's privacy.

3. See Alvin Toffler, *The Third Wave: The Classic Study of Tomorrow* (New York: Bantam, 1980).

4. See Charles Leadbeater and Paul Miller, *The Pro-Am Revolution: How Enthusiasts Are Changing Our Economy and Society* (London: Demos, 2004), http://www.demos.co.uk/files/proamrevolutionfinal.pdf.

5. See, for example, Katie Davis, "Friendship 2.0: Adolescents' Experiences of Belonging and Self-Disclosure Online," *Journal of Adolescence* 35 (2012): 1527–36, doi: 10.1016/j.adolescence.2012.02.013; Pavica Sheldon, "Profiling the Non-Users: Examination of Life-Position Indicators, Sensation Seeking, Shyness, and Loneliness among Users and Non-Users of Social Network Sites," *Computers in Human Behavior* 28 (2012): 1960–65, doi:10.1016/j.chb.2012.05.016; and Sabine Trepte and Leonard Reinecke, eds., *Privacy Online: Perspectives on Privacy and Self-Disclosure in the Social Web* (New York: Springer-Verlag, 2011).

6. See Kimberly Kahn, Katherine Spencer, and Jack Glaser, "Online Prejudice and Discrimination: From Dating to Hating," in *The Social Net: Understanding Our Online Behavior*, ed. Yair Amichai-Hamburger (Oxford: Oxford University Press, 2013), doi: 10.1093/acprof:oso/9780199639540.001.0001.

7. Readers who may wish to contribute to Piash's medical costs can do so at https://www.gofundme.com/zk9s6cg.

8. Barack Obama announced the DAPA program in 2014, but an injunction was filed against it the following year during *Texas vs. the United States*. I interviewed Katherine in April 2015. Two months later, on June 23, the Supreme Court upheld the injunction, to the disappointment of undocumented activists across the United States.

9. See Manuel Castells, *The Rise of the Network Society*, vol. 1 of his trilogy, *The Information Age: Economy, Society, and Culture* (Malden, MA: Blackwell, 1996).

10. See, for example, Rosa Ramirez, "Mexican Immigrants Less Educated, Lowest Paid," *NationalJournal.com*, December 7, 2012, http://news.yahoo.com/mexican-immigrants-less-educated-lowest-paid-163116545--politics.html; and Rebecca Smith, "Immigrants' Right to Workers' Comp: Undocumented Foreign-Born Workers Are Often Hired for the Most Dangerous and Lowest Paid Jobs. They Deserve Workers' Compensation Protections—but Don't Always Get Them," *Trial*, April 1, 2004, http://www.highbeam.com/doc/1G1-115693626.html.

11. See Lois Ann Lorentzen, ed., *Hidden Lives and Human Rights in the United States: Understanding the Controversies and Tragedies of Undocumented Immigration* (Santa Barbara, CA: Praeger, 2014).

12. Abraham Maslow, "A Theory of Human Motivation," *Psychological Review* 50 (1943): 381, doi: 10.1037/h0054346. Emphasis in original.

13. Linda Alcoff, "The Problem of Speaking for Others," *Cultural Critique* 20 (1991): 5–32, 21, accessed August 9, 2016, doi 10.2307/1354221.

14. Juana María Rodríguez, *Queer Latinidad: Identity Practices, Discursive Spaces* (New York, NY: New York University Press, 2003), 6.

15. Judith Butler, *Excitable Speech: A Politics of the Performative* (New York: Routledge, 1997), 142.

16. Renee Lyons et al., "Coping as a Communal Process," *Journal of Social and Personal Relationships* 15 (1998): 579, doi: 10.1177/0265407598155001.

17. Nicolas Carr, "Digital Sharecropping," *Rough Type Blog*, December 19, 2006, http://www.roughtype.com/?p=634.

18. See Chris Anderson, *The Long Tail: Why the Future of Business Is Selling Less of More* (New York: Hyperion, 2008).

19. Adrian Athique, *Digital Media and Society: An Introduction* (Cambridge: Polity, 2013), 171.

20. See Stop Notario Fraud, "Who Is Authorized to Help Immigrants with Their Legal Matters?" http://www.stopnotariofraud.org/faq.php; Elise Foley, "Advocates Warn Immigrants to Watch Out for Scammers," *Huffington Post*, November 26, 2014, http://www.huffingtonpost.com/2014/11/26/immigration-scammers_n_6225946.html; and "Top 4 Most Common Immigration Fraud . . . ," Law Office of Peter Duong, http://peterduonglaw.com/top-4-common-immigration-fraud-scams/.

21. See "Common Scams," United States Citizenship and Immigration Services, last modified August, 15, 2016, https://www.uscis.gov/avoid-scams/common-scams.

22. See, for example, Reinis Udris, "Cyberbullying among High School Students in Japan: Development and Validation of the Online Disinhibition Scale," *Computers in Human Behavior* 41 (2014): 253–61, doi: 10.1016/j.chb.2014.09.036.

23. See Otto Santa Ana, "'Like an Animal I was Treated': Anti-Immigrant Metaphor in U.S. Public Discourse," *Discourse and Society* 10 (1999): 191–224, doi: 10.1177/0957926599010002004; Santa Ana, *Brown Tide Rising: Metaphors of Latinos in Contemporary American Public Discourse* (Austin: University of Texas Press, 2002).

24. Marco Gemignani and Yolanda Hernandez-Albujar, "Hate Groups Targeting Unauthorized Immigrants in the US: Discourses, Narratives and Subjectivation Practices on Their Websites," *Ethnic and Racial Studies* 38, no. 15 (2015): 2754–70.

25. Bernadette Nadya Jaworsky, *The Boundaries of Belonging: Online Work of Immigration-Related Social Movement Organizations* (New York: Palgrave Macmillan), 11.

26. See, for example, Silvia Knobloch-Westerwick et al., "Political Online Information Searching in Germany and the United States: Confirmation Bias, Source Credibility, and Attitude Impacts," *Journal of Communication* 65 (2015): 489–511, doi: 10.1111/jcom.12154.

27. Pablo Barberá et al., "Tweeting from Left to Right: Is Online Political Communication More Than an Echo Chamber?" *Psychological Science* 26 (2015): 1531, doi: 10.1177/0956797615594620.

28. Seth Flaxman, Sharad Goel, and Justin Rao, "Filter Bubbles, Echo Chambers, and Online News Consumption," *Public Opinion Quarterly* 80 (2016): 311–12, doi: 10.1093/poq/nfw006.

29. Flaxman et al., "Filter Bubbles," 317.

30. Paul F. Lazarsfeld and Robert K. Merton, "Mass Communication, Popular Taste and Organized Social Action" in *Media Studies: A Reader*, 2nd ed., ed. Paul Marris and Sue Thornham (New York, NY: New York University Press, 2002), 18–20, 22, 23. Emphasis in original

31. Lazarsfeld and Merton, "Mass Communication," 23.

32. Walter Fisher, "The Narrative Paradigm: In the Beginning," *Journal of Communication* 35, no. 4 (1985): 87, https://www.bc.edu/res/gssw-research-home/funding/proposal-development/_jcr_content/content/download_40/file.res/Fisher%2C%20'The%20Narrative%20Paradigm%20in%20the%20Beginning'.pdf.

33. Fisher, "The Narrative Paradigm," 86.

34. For more on invitational rhetoric and its potential, see Sonja K. Foss and Cindy L. Griffin, "Beyond Persuasion: A Proposal for Invitational Rhetoric" *Communication Monographs* 62, no. 1 (1995): 2–18.

35. bell hooks, *Black Looks: Race and Representation* New York, NY: Routledge, 1992), 26.

CHAPTER 5

1. Javier Zamora, "Let Me Try Again," *Kenyon Review* (July/Aug 2016), http://www.kenyonreview.org/journal/julyaug-2016/selections/javier-zamora/.

2. Javier Zamora, interview by Sarah C. Bishop, March 21, 2016, transcript.

3. Javier Zamora, interview by Sarah C. Bishop, March 21, 2016, transcript.

4. Javier Zamora, "Looking at a Coyote," *Poetry Foundation*, last modified November 2015, https://www.poetryfoundation.org/poetrymagazine/poems/detail/58468.

5. Javier Zamora, interview by Sarah C. Bishop, March 21, 2016, transcript.

6. See Greg Philo, "Active Audiences and the Construction of Public Knowledge," *Journalism Studies* 9 (2008): 535–44, accessed August 9, 2016, http://dx.doi.org/10.1080/14616700802114217; Angela Lee, Seth Lewis, and Matthew Powers, "Audience Clicks and News Placement: A Study of Time-Lagged Influence in Online Journalism," *Communication Research* 41 (2012): 505–30, accessed August 9, 2016, doi:10.1177/0093650212467031; Guilherme Pires and John Stanton, *Ethnic Marketing: Culturally Sensitive Theory and Practice* (New York: Routledge, 2015), 288–311; Richard Pace, "Television's Interpellation: Heeding, Missing, Ignoring, and Resisting the Call for Pan-National Identity in the Brazilian Amazon," *American Anthropologist* 111 (2009): 407–19, accessed August 9, 2016, doi: 10.1111/j.1548-1433.2009.01151.x.

7. Ximena, interview by Sarah C. Bishop, March 17, 2016, transcript.

8. Javier Zamora, interview by Sarah C. Bishop, March 21, 2016, transcript.

9. Jon (surname withheld at narrator's request), interview by Sarah C. Bishop, March 21, 2016, transcript.

10. Daniel (pseudonym), interview by Sarah C. Bishop, June 27, 2016, transcript.

11. Katherine Chua Almiranez, interview by Sarah C. Bishop, April 14, 2016, transcript.

12. Omrie (surname withheld at narrator's request), interview by Sarah C. Bishop, June 15, 2016, transcript.

13. Esther Meroño Baro, interview by Sarah C. Bishop, September 24, 2015, transcript.

14. Esther Meroño Baro, e-mail message to Sarah C. Bishop, September 29, 2015.

15. Jenny (Pseudonym), interview by Sarah C. Bishop, June 15, 2016, transcript.

16. Ben (surname withheld at narrator's request), interview by Sarah C. Bishop, April 21, 2016, transcript.

17. Jin Park, interview by Sarah C. Bishop, March 14, 2016, transcript.

18. Ahram Kim, e-mail message to Sarah C. Bishop, May 15, 2016.

19. Mitasha Palha, interview by Sarah C. Bishop, April 14, 2016, transcript.

20. Leo Chavez, *Covering Immigration: Popular Images and the Politics of the Nation* (Berkeley: University of California Press, 2001); Leo Chavez, *The Latino Threat: Constructing Citizens, Immigrants, and the Nation* (Stanford, CA: Stanford University Press, 2013); Erik Bleich, Irene Bloemraad, and Els de Graauw, "Migrants, Minorities and the Media: Information, Representations and Participation in the Public Sphere," *Journal of Ethnic and Migration Studies* 41 (2015): 857–73, http://dx.doi.org/10.1080/1369183X.2014.1002197; Irene Bloemraad, Els de Graauw, and Rebecca

Hamlin, "Immigrants in the Media: Civic Visibility in the United States and Canada," *Journal of Ethnic and Migration Studies* 41(2015): 874–96, http://dx.doi.org/10.1080/1369183X.2014.1002198; Regina P. Branton and Johanna Dunaway, "Spatial Proximity to the U.S.-Mexico Border and Newspaper Coverage of Immigration Issues," *Political Research Quarterly* 62 (2009): 289–302, doi: 10.1177/1065912908319252l; Christine Du Bois and Sidney Mintz, *Images of West Indian Immigrants in Mass Media: The Struggle for a Positive Ethnic Reputation* (New York: LFB Scholarly Publishing, 2004); Edmund Hamann and Jenelle Reeves, "ICE Raids, Children, Media, and Making Sense of Latino Newcomers in Flyover Country," *Anthropology & Education Quarterly* 43 (2012): 24–40, doi: 10.1111/j.1548-1492.2011.01155.x; Youna Kim, *Transnational Migration, Media and Identity of Asian Women: Diasporic Daughters* (New York: Routledge, 2011); Jennifer Merolla, S. Karthick Ramakrishnan, and Chris Haynes, "'Illegal,' 'Undocumented,' or 'Unauthorized': Equivalency Frames, Issues Frames, and Public Opinion on Immigration," *Perspectives on Politics* 11 (2013): 789–807, doi:10.1017/S1537592713002077; Otto Santa Ana, "'Like an Animal I was Treated': Anti-Immigrant Metaphor in U.S. Public Discourse," *Discourse and Society* 10 (1999): 191–224, doi: 10.1177/0957926599010002004; Otto Santa Ana, *Brown Tide Rising: Metaphors of Latinos in Contemporary American Public Discourse* (Austin: University of Texas Press, 2002).

21. See Branton and Dunaway, "Spatial Proximity to the U.S.-Mexico Border and Newspaper Coverage of Immigration Issues."

22. See Leo Chavez, *The Latino Threat: Constructing Citizens, Immigrants, and the Nation* (Stanford, CA: Stanford University Press, 2013); Irene Bloemraad, Els de Graauw, and Rebecca Hamlin, "Immigrants in the Media: Civic Visibility in the United States and Canada," *Journal of Ethnic and Migration Studies* 41 (2015): 874–96, http://dx.doi.org/10.1080/1369183X.2014.1002198.

23. Gerald V. O'Brien, "Indigestible Food, Conquering Hordes, and Waste Materials: Metaphors of Immigrants and the Early Immigration Restriction Debate in the United States," *Metaphor and Symbol* 18 (2003): 33, doi: 10.1207/S15327868MS1801_3.

24. J. David Cisneros, "Contaminated Communities: The Metaphor of 'Immigrant as Pollutant' in Media Representations of Immigration," *Rhetoric & Public Affairs* 11 (2008): 569–601, doi: 10.1353/rap.0.0068.

25. Jonathan Xavier Inda, "Foreign Bodies: Migrants, Parasites, and the Pathological Nation," *Discourse: Journal for Theoretical Studies in Media and Culture* 22 (2000): 46–62, doi: 10.1353/dis.2000.0006, 47.

26. Sheila Lakshmi Steinberg, "Undocumented Immigrants or Illegal Aliens? Southwestern Media Portrayals of Latino Immigrants," *Humboldt Journal of Social Relations* 28 (2004): 109–33.

27. Sylvia Mendoza, "Building False Crisis: The Role of the Media Covering Undocumented Immigrants," *Hispanic Outlook in Higher Education* 25 (2015): 10–12, http://www.hispanicoutlook.com/featured-articles/2015/7/14/building-false-crisis-the-role-of-the-media-covering-undocumented-immigrants.

28. *Killing Us Softly IV*, directed by Jean Kilbourne and Sut Jhally (2010: Media Education Foundation, 2010), DVD.

29. Angy Rivera, interview by Sarah C. Bishop, July 6, 2015, transcript.

30. Kendall King and Gemma Punti, "On the Margins: Undocumented Students' Narrated Experiences of (II)legality," *Linguistics and Education* (2012): 235–49, August 19, 2016, http://dx.doi.org/10.1016/j.linged.2012.05.002.

31. Thomas Faist and Christian Ulbricht, "Constituting National Identity through Transnationality: Categorizations of Inequalities in German Integration Debates," in *Fear, Anxiety, and National Identity: Immigration and Belonging in North America and Western Europe*, ed. Nancy Foner and Patrick Simon (New York: Russell Sage Foundation, 2015), 192.

32. Jaeho Cho et al., "Cue Convergence: Associative Effects on Social Intolerance," *Communication Research* 33 (2006): 136–54, https://www.journalism.wisc.edu/~dshah/CR2006.pdf.

33. Cisneros, "Contaminated Communities," 581.

34. Cho et al., "Cue Convergence,"136–54.

35. Tatyana S. Thweatt, "Attitudes Towards New Americans in the Local Press: A Critical Discourse Analysis," *North Dakota Journal of Speech and Theatre* 18 (2005): 26.

36. Stuart Hall et al., *Culture, Media, Language: Working Paper in Cultural Studies (1972–1979)* (New York: Unwin Hyman, 2003), 121.

37. Cho et al., "Cue Convergence,"138.

38. Elaine Burroughs, "Discursive Representations of 'Illegal Immigration' in the Irish Newsprint Media: The Domination and Multiple Facets of the 'Control' Argumentation," *Discourse & Society* 26 (2015): 165–83, doi: 10.1177/0957926514556029; Stuart Hall, "Culture, the Media and the Ideological Effect," in *Mass Communication and Society*, ed. James Curran, Michael Gurevitch, and Janet Woollacott (London: Open University Press, 1977), 315–48; Teun Van Dijk, *Racism and the Press* (London: Routledge, 1991).

39. Pang (surname withheld at narrator's request), interview by Sarah C. Bishop, May 6, 2015, transcript.

40. Jens M. Krogstad and Jeffrey S. Passel, "5 Facts about Illegal Immigration in the U.S.," *Pew Research Center,* November 19, 2015, http://www.pewresearch.org/fact-tank/2015/11/19/5-facts-about-illegal-immigration-in-the-u-s/.

41. Chris (surname withheld at narrator's request), interview by Sarah C. Bishop, June 9, 2015, transcript.

42. Chris (surname withheld at narrator's request), interview by Sarah C. Bishop, June 9, 2015, transcript, 877.

43. Pang T. (full surname withheld at narrator's request), interview by Sarah C. Bishop, May 6, 2015, transcript.

44. Sonia Espinosa, interview by Sarah C. Bishop, August 18, 2015, transcript.

45. Leo Chavez, *The Latino Threat* (Stanford, CA: Stanford University Press, 2008), 47.

46. Javier (surname withheld at narrator's request), interview by Sarah C. Bishop, March 21, 2016, transcript.

47. Ricardo (surname withheld at narrator's request), interview by Sarah C. Bishop, March 3, 2016, transcript.

48. Freddy (surname withheld at narrator's request), interview by Sarah C. Bishop, March 15, 2016, transcript.

49. Rubén Rumbaut and Walter Ewing, "The Myth of Immigrant Criminality and the Paradox of Assimilation: Incarceration Rates among Native and Foreign-Born Men,"

Immigration Policy Center (2007): 1–20, 1, https://www.americanimmigrationcouncil.org/sites/default/files/research/Imm%20Criminality%20%28IPC%29.pdf.

50. David Chung, interview by Sarah C. Bishop, July 29, 2016, transcript.

51. Jin Park, interview by Sarah C. Bishop, March 14, 2016, transcript.

52. Jung Rae, interview by Sarah C. Bishop, June 15, 2016, transcript.

53. James Jeong, interview by Sarah C. Bishop, May 26, 2016, transcript.

54. Gloria Anzaldua, *Borderlands* (San Francisco: Aunt Lutes Books, 1999), 107.

55. Sonia Espinosa, interview by Sarah C. Bishop, August 18, 2015, transcript.

56. For more about the program and its relationship to undocumented immigration, see Mae Ngai, *Impossible Subjects: Illegal Aliens and the Making of Modern America* (Princeton, NJ: Princeton University Press, 2004).

57. "Undocumented Immigrants' State and Local Tax Contributions," *Institution on Taxation and Economic Policy*, February 24, 2016, http://www.itep.org/immigration/.

58. Angy Rivera, interview by Sarah C. Bishop, July 6, 2015, transcript.

59. See "Public Tunes Out Recent News," *Times Mirror Center for the Public and the Press*, May 19, 1994, accessed August 9, 2016, http://www.people-press.org/1994/05/19/public-tunes-out-recent-news/; Alec Gallup and Lydia Saad, "Americans Know Little about European Union," *Gallup*, June 16, 2004, accessed August 9, 2016, http://www.gallup.com/poll/12043/americans-know-little-about-european-union.aspx; James Curran, Shanto Iyengar, Anker Brink Lund, and Inka Salovaara-Moring, "Media System, Public Knowledge and Democracy: A Comparative Study," *European Journal of Communication* 24 (2009): 5–26, accessed August 10, 2016, doi: 10.1177/0267323108098943.

60. Emily Ryo, "Deciding to Cross Norms and Economics of Unauthorized Migration," *American Sociological Review* 78 (2013): 574–603, accessed August 10, 2016, http://asr.sagepub.com/content/78/4/574.abstract.

61. Jenny (pseudonym), interview by Sarah C. Bishop, June 15, 2016, transcript.

62. Javier Zamora, interview by Sarah C. Bishop, March 21, 2016, transcript.

63. Javier Zamora, interview by Sarah C. Bishop, March 21, 2016, transcript.

64. Francisco Barros, interview by Sarah C. Bishop, April 14, 2016, transcript.

65. *Jus soli* means "right of the soil," or, birthright citizenship.

66. United States Citizenship and Immigration Services, "What Are Benefits and Responsibilities of Citizenship?" in *A Guide to Naturalization* (Washington, DC: USCIS, 2012), accessed August 1, 2016, https://www.uscis.gov/sites/default/files/files/article/chapter2.pdf.

67. See Peggy McIntosh, "White Privilege: Unpacking the Invisible Backpack," excerpt from Working Paper 189 (1989), http://www.deanza.edu/faculty/lewisjulie/White%20Priviledge%20Unpacking%20the%20Invisible%20Knapsack.pdf; Allan Johnson, *Privilege, Power, Difference* (New York: McGraw Hill, 2006).

68. Javier Zamora, interview by Sarah C. Bishop, March 21, 2016, transcript.

69. Freddy (surname withheld at narrator's request), interview by Sarah C. Bishop, March 15, 2016, transcript.

70. Omrie (surname withheld at narrator's request), interview by Sarah C. Bishop, June 15, 2016, transcript.

71. Adam (surname withheld at narrator's request), interview by Sarah C. Bishop, June 15, 2016, transcript.

72. Johnson, *Privilege, Power, Difference*, 698.

Conclusion

1. Walter R. Fisher, *Human Communication as Narration: Toward a Philosophy of Reason, Value, and Action* (Columbia: University of South Carolina Press: 1987), 68.

2. Steven Hseih, "Living Undocumented: A Conversation with Jose Antonio Vargas," *Nation,* May 1, 2014, https://www.thenation.com/article/living-undocumented-conversation-jose-antonio-vargas/.

3. Jose Antonio Vargas, *Documented: A Film by an Undocumented American,* Documentary, 2013, http://documentedthefilm.com/.

4. "Immigration," *Gallup.*

5. Charles W. Mills, "White Ignorance and Hermeneutical Injustice: A Comment on Medina and Fricker," *Social Epistemology Review and Reply Collective* 3 (2013): 38–43.

6. Linda M. Alcoff, "The Problem of Speaking for Others," *Cultural Critique* 20 (Winter 1991–1992), 24, http://www.jstor.org/stable/1354221.

7. Charles Goodwin, "Professional Vision," *American Anthropologist* 96 (1994): 606–33; Shannon Sullivan and Nancy Tuana, "White Ignorance and Colonial Oppression," in *Race and Epistemologies of Ignorance*, ed. Shannon Sullivan and Nancy Tuana (Albany: State University of New York Press, 2007), 154.

8. Javier Zamora, interview by Sarah C. Bishop, March 21, 2016, transcript.

9. "Immigration," *Gallup.*

10. http://www.gallup.com/poll/184577/favor-path-citizenship-illegal-immigrants.aspx; http://ap-gfkpoll.com/uncategorized/our-latest-poll-findings-21; Robert P. Jones, Daniel Cox, Betsy Cooper, and Rachel Lienesch, "How Americans View Immigrants and What They Want from Immigration Reform: Findings from the 2015 American Values Atlas," *PRRI,* 2016, http://www.prri.org/research/poll-immigration-reform-views-on-immigrants/.

11. Robert P. Jones, Daniel Cox, E. J. Dionne Jr., William A. Galston, Betsy Cooper, and Rachel Lienesch, "How Immigration and Concerns about Cultural Changes Are Shaping the 2016 Election: Findings from the 2016 PRRI/Brookings Immigration Survey," *PRRI,* June 23, 2016, https://www.prri.org/wp-content/uploads/2016/06/PRRI-Brookings-2016-Immigration-survey-report.pdf.

12. Jones et al., "How Immigration and Concerns about Cultural Changes Are Shaping the 2016 Election," 3.

13. Joana Dreby, *Everyday Illegal* (Berkeley: University of California Press, 2015), 49–50.

14. "Helping Undocumented Students Achieve Higher Education," Higher Dreams, accessed October 29th, 2016, http://higherdreams.org.

15. Joshua Meyrowitz, *No Sense of Place* (London: Oxford University Press, 1985), 101.

16. Evelyn Glenn, "Citizenship and Identity," in *Race and Ethnicity in Society: The Changing Landscape*, ed. Elizabeth Higginbotham and Margaret L. Andersen (Belmont, CA: Thomson/Wadsworth, 2006), 158.

17. Joachim Trebbe and Philomen Schoenhagen, "Ethnic Minorities in the Mass Media: Always the Same and Always Negative," paper presented at the annual meeting

of the International Communication Association, Montreal, Quebec, Canada, May 21, 2008, 1.

18. Edward Said, *Orientalism* (London: Penguin, 2003).

19. See Leo Chavez, *The Latino Threat: Constructing Immigrants, Citizens, and the Nation* (Stanford, CA: Stanford University Press, 2008).

20. Jan Nederveen Pieterse, *Globalization & Culture: Global Melange* (Lanham, MD: Rowman & Littlefield, 2004), 94.

21. Otto Santa Ana, "'Like an Animal I was Treated': Anti-Immigrant Metaphor in US Public Discourse," *Discourse & Society* 10 (1999): 192, doi: 10.1177/0957926599010002004.

22. See, for example, Susan Dunn, "Trump's 'America First' Has Ugly Echoes from U.S. History," *CNN*, last modified April 28, 2016, http://www.cnn.com/2016/04/27/opinions/trump-america-first-ugly-echoes-dunn/.

23. Dunn, "Trump's 'America First' Has Ugly Echoes from U.S. History."

24. See also Thomas A. Aleinikoff, "Citizens, Aliens, Membership, and the Constitution," *Constitutional Commentary* 7, no. 1 (1990); Steven A. Epstein and Hector Carrillo, "Immigrant Sexual Citizenship: Intersectional Templates among Mexican Gay Immigrants to the United States," *Citizenship Studies* 18, no. 3–4 (2014): 259–276; Erika Lee, "A Nation of Immigrants and a Gatekeeping Nation: American Immigration Law and Policy," in *A Companion to American Immigration*, ed. Reed Ueda (Urbana: University of Illinois Press, 2011), 1–35, doi: 10.1002/9780470997116.ch2; Eithne Luibhéid, *Entry Denied: Controlling Sexuality at the Border* (Minneapolis: University of Minnesota Press, 2002); Juan F. Perea, "Am I American or Not? Reflections on Citizenship, Americanization, and Race," in *Immigration and Citizenship*, ed. Noah M. J. Pickus (Lanham: Rowman & Littlefield, 1998), 49–76, doi: 10.1111/j.1467-923X.2007.00864.x.

25. See Mike Featherstone, "Global Culture: An Introduction," *Global Theory, Culture, and Society* 7 (1990): 1–14, doi: 10.1177/026327690007002001; David Harvey, *The Condition of Postmodernity* (Oxford: Blackwell, 1989).

26. See Benedict Anderson, *Imagined Communities: Reflections on the Origin and Spread of Nationalism* (New York: Verso, 2006); and Arjun Appadurai, "Grassroots Globalization and the Research Imagination," *Public Culture* 12 (2000): 1–19, doi: doi:10.1215/08992363-12-1-1.

27. Madan Sarup, *Identity, Culture, and the Postmodern World* (Edinburgh: Edinburgh University Press, 1996), 3.

28. See, for example, Nancy Foner and Patrick Simon, eds., *Fear, Anxiety, and National Identity: Immigration and Belonging in North America and Western Europe* (New York: Russell Sage Foundation, 2015), https://www.russellsage.org/publications/fear-anxiety-and-national-identity.

29. Jonathan Xavier Inda, "Foreign Bodies: Migrants, Parasites, and the Pathological Nation," *Discourse: Journal for Theoretical Studies in Media and Culture* 22 (2000): 46–47, doi: 10.1353/dis.2000.0006.

30. Aviva Chomsky, *Undocumented: How Immigration Became Illegal* (Boston: Beacon Press, 2014), 19.

31. Esther Meroño Baro, email message to Sarah C. Bishop, September 26, 2015.

32. Walter Nicholls, *The DREAMers: How the Undocumented Youth Movement Transformed the Immigrant Rights Debate* (Stanford, CA: Stanford University Press, 2013), 171.

33. Michalinos Zembylas, "Agamben's Theory of Biopower and Immigrants/ Refugees/Asylum Seekers: Discourses of Citizenship and the Implications," *Journal of Curriculum Theorizing* 26 (2010): 33.

34. Ximena, interview by Sarah C. Bishop, March 17, 2016, transcript.

35. Jenny (Pseudonym), interview by Sarah C. Bishop on June 15, 2016, transcript.

36. For more on the inequality of citizenship, see Robert Courtney Smith, *Mexican New York: Transnational Lives of New Immigrants* (Berkeley: University of California Press: 2006), 65.

37. "Grounds for Revocation of Naturalization," U.S. Citizenship and Immigration Services, last modified August 3, 2016, https://www.uscis.gov/policymanual/HTML/ PolicyManual-Volume12-PartL-Chapter2.html.

38. For more about "Nothing about Us without Us," see James I. Charlton, *Nothing about Us without Us: Disability Oppression and Empowerment* (Berkeley: University of California Press, 1998); Culture Strike, CultureStrike, http://culturestrike.tumblr. com/ (blog), August 23, 2014, http://culturestrike.tumblr.com/post/95607552312/ image-by-cesar-maxit-via-ndlon-ma%C3%B1ana-inicia.

39. Linda Alcoff, "The Problem of Speaking for Others," *Cultural Critique* 20 (1991–1992): 20, doi 10.2307/1354221.

40. Paul Lazarsfeld and Robert King Merton, *Mass Communication, Popular Taste, and Organized Social Action* (Indianapolis: Bobbs-Merrill, 1957), 19.

41. For more on the danger of infallible actors, see Bruno Latour, *The Pasteurization of France* (Cambridge: Harvard University Press, 1988), 53

42. Ben (surname withheld at narrator's request), interview by Sarah C. Bishop, April 21, 2016, transcript.

43. Esther Meroño Baro, interview by Sarah C. Bishop, September 24, 2015, transcript.

44. See, for example, J. David Cisneros, "(Re)Bordering the Civic Imaginary: Rhetoric, Hybridity, and Citizenship in La Gran Marcha," *Quarterly Journal of Speech*, 97 (2011): 26–49, doi: 10.1080/00335630.2010.536564; J. David Cisneros, "A Nation of Immigrants and a Nation of Laws: Race, Multiculturalism, and Neoliberal Exception in Barack Obama's Immigration Discourse," *Communication, Culture, & Critique* 8 (2015): 356–75, doi: 10.1111/cccr.12088; Radha S. Hegde, *Mediating Migration* (Boston: Polity Press, 2016); Raka Shome and Radha Hedge, "Postcolonial Approaches to Communication: Charting the Terrain, Engaging the Intersections," *Communication Theory*, 12 (2002): 249–270, doi: 10.1111/j.1468-2885.2002.tb00269.x; Kent A. Ono and John M. Sloop, *Shifting Borders: Rhetoric, Immigration, and California's Proposition 187* (Philadelphia: Temple University Press, 2002).

45. Lisa Bosniak, *The Citizen and the Alien: Dilemmas of Contemporary Membership* (Princeton, NJ: Princeton University Press, 2008).

46. Chhunny Chhean and Chia-Chi Li, "In Brief: Linda Bosniak's The Citizen and the Alien," *Asian American Law Journal* 14 (2009): 247, http://dx.doi.org/https://doi.org/ 10.15779/Z38SG5B.

47. Sofya Aptekar, *The Road to Citizenship: What Naturalization Means for Immigrants and the United States* (New Brunswick, NJ: Rutgers University Press, 2015), 129.

48. Aptekar, *The Road to Citizenship,* 13.

49. Alvin I. Goldman, *Knowledge in a Social World* (Oxford: Oxford University Press, 1990).

50. Daniel (pseudonym), interview by Sarah C. Bishop, June 27, 2016, transcript.

51. Kattia Minaya, interview by Sarah C. Bishop, October 21, 2016, transcript.

52. Fisher, *Human Communication as Narration*, 65.

BIBLIOGRAPHY

Abrams, Kathryn R. "Performative Citizenship in the Civil Rights and Immigrant Rights Movements." In *A Nation of Widening Opportunities: The Civil Rights Act at Fifty,* edited by Ellen D. Katz and Samuel R. Bagenstos. Ann Arbor: University of Michigan Press, 2015. http://quod.lib.umich.edu/m/maize/13855464.0001.001/1:3/--nation-of-widening-opportunities?rgn=div1;view=fulltext.

Abrego, Leisy Janet. "I Can't Go to College Because I Don't Have Papers: Incorporation Patterns of Latino Undocumented Youth." *Latino Studies* 4 (2006): 212–23. doi: 10.1057/palgrave.lst.8600200.

Alcoff, Linda. "The Problem of Speaking for Others." *Cultural Critique* 20 (1991): 5–32. Accessed August 9, 2016. doi 10.2307/1354221.

Aleinikoff, Thomas A. "Citizens, Aliens, Membership, and the Constitution." *Constitutional Commentary* 7, no. 1 (1990): 9–34

Alexander, Michelle. *The New Jim Crow: Mass Incarceration in the Age of Colorblindness.* New York: New Press, 2012.

Almirañez, Katherine C. *Undocumented.* New York, 2011. https://undocumentedtheplay.com/.

Amaya, Hector. *Citizenship Excess: Latino/as, Media, and the Nation.* New York: New York University Press, 2013.

American Immigration Council. "The DREAM Act." Last modified May 18, 2011. http://immigrationpolicy.org/just-facts/dream-act.

Anderson, Benedict. *Imagined Communities: Reflections on the Origin and Spread of Nationalism.* New York: Verso, 2006.

Anderson, Chris. *The Long Tail: Why the Future of Business Is Selling Less of More.* New York: Hyperion, 2008.

Anzaldúa, Gloria. *Borderlands.* San Francisco: Aunt Lutes Books, 1999.

———. *The Gloria Anzaldúa Reader.* Durham, NC: Duke University Press, 2009.

Appadurai, Arjun. "Grassroots Globalization and the Research Imagination." *Public Culture* 12 (2000): 1–19. doi: doi:10.1215/08992363-12-1-1.

Aptekar, Sofya. The Road to Citizenship: What Naturalization Means for Immigrants and the United States. New Brunswick, NJ: Rutgers University Press, 2015

Arao, Daria, and Darren Ressler. "Working for a Better Life: A Profile of Immigrants in the New York State Economy." *Fiscal Policy Institute* (2007): 1–115. http://www.fiscalpolicy.org/publications2007/FPI_ImmReport_WorkingforaBetterLife.pdf.

AskAngy. "8 Black Immigrant Organizers You Should Follow on Twitter." Tumblr. Accessed July 15, 2016. http://askangy.tumblr.com/post/147406700975/8-black-immigrant-organizers-you-should-follow-on

AskAngy. "Dating While Undocumented." YouTube video, 05:11. Posted October 10, 2011. https://youtube.com/watch?v=71ydyce-Hjg.

Athique, Adrian. *Digital Media and Society: An Introduction.* Cambridge: Polity, 2013.

Austin, John L. *How to Do Things with Words.* Oxford: Clarendon Press, 1962.

Bai, Matt. "The Way We Live Now: 10–28–01: Encounter; Hyphenated Americans." *New York Times Magazine*, October 28, 2001. http://www.nytimes.com/2001/10/28/magazine/the-way-we-live-now-10-28-01-encounter-hyphenated-americans.html.

Bailey, Olga, Myria Georgiou, and Ramaswami Harindranath. *Transnational Lives and the Media: Re-Imagining Diaspora.* New York: Palgrave Macmillan, 2007.

Barberá, Pablo, John T. Jost, Jonathan Nagler, Joshua A. Tucker, and Richard Bonneau. "Tweeting from Left to Right: Is Online Political Communication More Than an Echo Chamber?" *Psychological Science* 26 (2015): 1531–542. doi: 10.1177/0956797615594620.

Barthes, Roland. *Mythologies.* Translated by Annette Lavers. New York: Farrar, Straus and Giroux, 1972.

Berger, Dan, Peter Funke, and Todd Wolfson. "Communications Networks, Movements and the Neoliberal City: The Media Mobilizing Project in Philadelphia." *Transforming Anthropology* 19 (2011): 187–201. doi: 10.1111/J.1548-7466.2011.01128.X.

Bishop, Sarah. "Welcome Home: Examining Power and Representation in the United States Citizenship and Immigration Services' Guide for New Immigrants." *Journal of Intercultural Communication Research* 42 (2013): 155–71. doi: 10.1080/17475759.2012.756423.

Bleich, Erik, Irene Bloemraad, and Els de Graauw. "Migrants, Minorities and the Media: Information, Representations and Participation in the Public Sphere." *Journal of Ethnic and Migration Studies* 41 (2015): 857–73. http://dx.doi.org/10.1080/1369183X.2014.1002197

Bloemraad, Irene, Els de Graauw, and Rebecca Hamlin. "Immigrants in the Media: Civic Visibility in the United States and Canada." *Journal of Ethnic and Migration Studies* 41 (2015): 874–96. http://dx.doi.org/10.1080/1369183X.2014.1002198.

Bobowik, Magdalena, Nekane Basabe, and Dario Paez. "'Heroes' of Adjustment: Immigrant's Stigma and Identity Management." *International Journal of Intercultural Relations* 41 (2014): 112–24. doi: 10.1016/j.ijintrel.2014.04.002.

Bozdağ, Çiğdem. "Policies of Media and Cultural Integration in Germany: From Guestworker Programmes to a More Integrative Framework." *Global Media and Communication* 10 (2014): 289–301.

Bradby, Hannah, Rachel Humphris, Dave Newall, and Jenny Phillimore. "Public Health Aspects of Migrant Health: A Review of the Evidence on Health Status for Refugees and Asylum Seekers in the European Region." *Health Evidence Network* 44 (2015): 1–33. Accessed September 1, 2016. http://www.epgencms.europarl.europa.

eu/cmsdata/upload/3a3f00c0-9a75-4c84-94ad-06e4bd2ce412/WHO-HEN-Report-A5-2-Refugees_FINAL_EN.pdf.

Branton, Regina, and Johanna Dunaway. "Spatial Proximity to the U.S.—Mexico Border and Newspaper Coverage of Immigration Issues." *Political Research Quarterly* 62 (2009): 289–302. doi: 10.1177/1065912908319252l.

Breen, Michael, Eoin Devereux, and Amanda Haynes. "Fear, Framing and Foreigners: The Othering of Immigrants in the Irish Print Media." *International Journal of Critical Psychology* 16 (2006): 100–121. http://hdl.handle.net/10395/1350

Burroughs, Elaine. "Discursive Representations of 'Illegal Immigration' in the Irish Newsprint Media: The Domination and Multiple Facets of the 'Control' Argumentation." *Discourse & Society* 26 (2015): 165–83. doi: 10.1177/0957926514556029.

Butler, Judith. *Excitable Speech: A Politics of the Performative.* New York: Routledge, 1997.

Byrd, Samuel. "'The Collective Circle': Latino Immigrant Musicians and Politics in Charlotte, North Carolina." *American Ethnologist* 41 (2014): 246–60. doi: 10.1111/amet.12073.

Cacho, Lisa Marie. *Social Death: Racialized Rightlessness and the Criminalization of the Unprotected.* New York: New York University Press, 2012.

Candia, Lisette. "Undocumented at Harvard: The Real American Heroes." *Huffington Post*, April 1, 2015. http://huffingtonpost.com/lisette-candia/undocumented-at-harvard-real-american-heroes_b_6984788.html.

Carey, James. *Communication as Culture.* Boston: Unwin Hyman, 1989.

Carr, Nicolas. "Digital Sharecropping." *Rough Type Blog*, December 19, 2006. http://www.roughtype.com/?p=634.

Castells, Manuel. *The Rise of the Network Society: The Information Age*, vol. 1: *Economy, Society, and Culture*. Malden, MA: Blackwell, 1996.

"Causes and Impacts Relating to Forced and Voluntary Migration." *BBC*. Accessed August 31, 2016. http://www.bbc.co.uk/education/guides/z8g334j/revision/1.

Charlton, James I. *Nothing about Us without Us: Disability Oppression and Empowerment.* Berkeley: University of California Press, 1998.

Chávez, Karma R. *Queer Migration Politics: Activist Rhetoric and Coalitional Possibilities.* Chicago: University of Illinois Press, 2013.

Chavez, Leo. *Covering Immigration: Popular Images and the Politics of the Nation.* Berkeley: University of California Press, 2001.

———. *The Latino Threat.* Stanford, CA: Stanford University Press, 2008.

———. *The Latino Threat: Constructing Citizens, Immigrants, and the Nation.* Stanford, CA: Stanford University Press, 2013.

———. "The Power of the Imagined Community: The Settlement of Undocumented Mexicans and Central Americans in the United States." *American Anthropologist* 96 (1994): 52–73. doi: 10.1525/aa.1994.96.1.02a00030.

———. *Shadowed Lives.* Belmont: Cengage Learning, 2013.

Chhean Chhunny, and Chia-Chi Li. "In Brief: Linda Bosniak's The Citizen and the Alien." *Asian American Law Journal* 14 (2009): 247. http://dx.doi.org/https://doi.org/10.15779/Z38SG5B.

Cho, Jaeho, et al. "Cue Convergence: Associative Effects on Social Intolerance." *Communication Research* 33 (2006): 136–54. https://www.journalism.wisc.edu/~dshah/CR2006.pdf.

Chomsky, Aviva. *Undocumented: How Immigration Became Illegal.* Boston: Beacon Press, 2014.

Chua Almiranez, Katherine. *Undocumented.* New York: 2011. https://undocumentedtheplay.com.

Cisneros, David J. "Contaminated Communities: The Metaphor of 'Immigrant as Pollutant' in Media Representations of Immigration." *Rhetoric & Public Affairs* 1 (2008): 569–601. doi: 10.1353/rap.0.0068.

———. "A Nation of Immigrants and a Nation of Laws: Race, Multiculturalism, and Neoliberal Exception in Barack Obama's Immigration Discourse." *Communication, Culture, & Critique* 8 (2015): 356–75, doi: 10.1111/cccr.12088.

———. "(Re)Bordering the Civic Imaginary: Rhetoric, Hybridity, and Citizenship in La Gran Marcha." *Quarterly Journal of Speech* 97 (2011): 26–49. doi: 10.1080/00335630.2010.536564

Cisneros, Josue. *The Border Crossed Us: Rhetorics of Borders, Citizenship, and Latina/o Identity.* Tuscaloosa: University of Alabama Press, 2014.

Cohen, Tom. "Obama Administration to Stop Deporting Some Young Illegal Immigrants." *CNN*, June 16, 2012. http://cnn.com/2012/06/15/politics/immigration/.

Cornelius, Wayne. "Interviewing Undocumented Immigrants: Methodological Reflections Based on Fieldwork in Mexico and the U.S." *International Migration Review* 16 (1982): 378–411. doi: 10.2307/2545104.

Crenshaw, Kimberlé. "Demarginalizing the Intersection of Race and Sex: A Black Feminist Critique of Antidiscrimination Doctrine, Feminist Theory and Antiracist Politics." *University of Chicago Legal Forum* 1989 (1989): 139–67. August 19, 2016. http://chicagounbound.uchicago.edu/cgi/viewcontent.cgi?article=1052&context=uclf.

———. "Mapping the Margins: Intersectionality, Identity Politics, and Violence against Women of Color." *Stanford Law Review* 43 (1993): 1241–99. http://socialdifference.columbia.edu/files/socialdiff/projects/Article__Mapping_the_Margins_by_Kimblere_Crenshaw.pdf.

CultureStrike Blog, August 23, 2014. http://culturestrike.tumblr.com/post/95607552312/image-by-cesar-maxit-via-ndlon-ma%C3%B1ana-inicia.

Curran, James, Shanto Iyengar, Anker Brink Lund, and Inka Salovaara-Moring. "Media System, Public Knowledge and Democracy: A Comparative Study." *European Journal of Communication* 24 (2009): 5–26. Accessed August 10, 2016. doi: 10.1177/0267323108098943.

Dave, Nomi, and Leslye Orloff. "Identifying Barriers: Survey of Immigrant Women and Domestic Violence in the D.C. Metropolitan Area." *Poverty and Race* 6 (1997): 9–12.

Davis, Katie. "Friendship 2.0: Adolescents' Experiences of Belonging and Self-Disclosure Online." *Journal of Adolescence* 35 (2012): 1527–36. doi: 10.1016/j.adolescence.2012.02.013.

Define American. "No Fault of Their Own." Last modified June 22, 2011. https://defineamerican.com/blog/no-fault-of-their-own/.

———. "Share Your Story." https://defineamerican.com/stories/share/#instructions.

DeJaeghere, Joan, and Kate McCleary. "The Making of Mexican Migrant Youth Civic Identities: Transnational Spaces and Imaginaries." *Anthropology & Education Quarterly* 41 (2010): 228–44. doi: 10.1111/J.1548-1492.2010.01085.X.

Derrida, Jacques. *Limited Inc.* Translated by Samuel Weber. Paris: Éditions Galilée, 1990.

Diaz, Gina. "While Undocumented." *My Undocumented Life*, September 4, 2015. https://mydocumentedlife.org/2015/09/04/while-undocumented/.

Dick, Hillary. "Making Immigrants Illegal in Small-Town USA." *Journal of Linguistic Anthropology* 21 (2011): E35–E55. doi: 10.1111/J.1548-1395.2011.01096.X.

Dreby, Joanna. *Everyday Illegal: When Policies Undermine Immigrant Families*. Oakland: University of California Press, 2015.

Du Bois, Christine, and Sidney Mintz. *Images of West Indian Immigrants in Mass Media: The Struggle for a Positive Ethnic Reputation*. New York: LFB Scholarly Publishing LLC, 2004.

Dunn, Susan. "Trump's 'America First' Has Ugly Echoes from U.S. History." *CNN*, last modified April 28, 2016. http://www.cnn.com/2016/04/27/opinions/trump-america-first-ugly-echoes-dunn/.

Durham, Meenakshi. "Constructing the 'New Ethnicities': Media, Sexuality, and Diaspora Identity in the Lives of South Asian Immigrant Girls." *Critical Studies in Media Communication* 21 (2004): 140–61. http://www.csun.edu/~vcspc00g/301/newethnicities-csmc.pdf.

Ellis, Lauren M., and Eric C. Chen. "Negotiating Identity Development among Undocumented Immigrant College Students: A Grounded Theory Study." *Journal of Counseling Psychology* 60 (2013): 258. Accessed August 19, 2016. doi: 10.1037/a0031350.

Epstein, Steven A., and Hector Carrillo. "Immigrant Sexual Citizenship: Intersectional Templates among Mexican Gay Immigrants to the United States." *Citizenship Studies* 18, no. 3–4 (2014): 259–276.

Executive Order of January 25, 2017, Border Security and Immigration Enforcement Improvements. *Office of the Press Secretary*, https://www.whitehouse.gov/the-press-office/2017/01/25/executive-order-border-security-and-immigration-enforcement-improvements.

Executive Order 12333, United States Intelligence Activities, December 4, 1981.

Fairhurst, Gail, and Robert Sarr. *The Art of Framing*. San Francisco: Jossey-Bass, 1996.

Faist, Thomas, and Christian Ulbricht. "Constituting National Identity through Transnationality: Categorizations of Inequalities in German Integration Debates." In *Fear, Anxiety, and National Identity: Immigration and Belonging in North America and Western Europe*, edited by Nancy Foner and Patrick Simon, 189–212. New York: Russell Sage Foundation, 2015.

"Fear of Deportation Spurs 4 Women to Drop Domestic Abuse Cases in Denver." NPR, March 21, 2017. http://www.npr.org/2017/03/21/520841332/fear-of-deportation-spurs-4-women-to-drop-domestic-abuse-cases-in-denver.

Featherstone, Mike. "Global Culture: An Introduction." *Global Theory, Culture, and Society* 7 (1990): 1–14. doi: 10.1177/026327690007002001.

Fisher, Walter. *Human Communication as Narration: Toward a Philosophy of Reason, Value, and Action*. Columbia: University of South Carolina Press, 1989.

———. "Human Communication as Narration: Toward a Philosophy of Reason, Value, and Action." *Quarterly Journal of Speech* (1988): 347–49. https://www.bc.edu/res/gssw-research-home/funding/proposal-development/_jcr_content/content/download_38/file.res/Fisher%2C%20'Human%20Communication%20as%20Narration%20Book%20Review%203'.pdf.

———. "Narration as a Human Communication Paradigm: The Case of Public Moral Argument." In *Contemporary Rhetorical Theory: A Reader*, edited by Mark J. Porrovecchio and Celeste Michelle Condit, 265–187. New York: Guilford Press, 1999.

———. "Narration, Knowledge, and the Possibility of Wisdom." In *Rethinking Knowledge: Reflections across the Disciplines*, edited by Robert Goodman and Walter Fisher, 169–94. Albany: State University of New York Press, 1995.

———. "The Narrative Paradigm: In the Beginning." *Journal of Communication* 35, no. 4 (1985): 74–90. https://www.bc.edu/res/gssw-research-home/funding/proposal-development/_jcr_content/content/download_40/file.res/Fisher%2C%20'The%20Narrative%20Paradigm%20in%20the%20Beginning'.pdf.

Flaxman, Seth, Sharad Goel, and Justin Rao. "Filter Bubbles, Echo Chambers, and Online News Consumption." *Public Opinion Quarterly* 80 (2016): 298–320. doi: 10.1093/poq/nfw006.

Flores, Lisa. "Constructing Rhetorical Borders: Peons, Illegal Aliens, and Competing Narratives of Immigration." *Critical Studies in Media Communication* 20 (2003): 362–87. doi: 10.1080/0739318032000142025.

Foley, Elise. "Advocates Warn Immigrants to Watch Out for Scammers." *Huffington Post*, November 26, 2014. http://www.huffingtonpost.com/2014/11/26/immigration-scammers_n_6225946.html.

Foner, Nancy, and Patrick Simon, eds. *Fear, Anxiety, and National Identity: Immigration and Belonging in North America and Western Europe*. New York: Russell Sage Foundation, 2015. https://www.russellsage.org/sites/all/files/fear-anxiety-and-national-identity.pdf.

Foss, Sonja. *Rhetorical Criticism: Exploration and Practice*. Long Grove: Waveland Press, 2009.

Foss, Sonja K., and Cindy L. Griffin. "Beyond Persuasion: A Proposal for Invitational Rhetoric." *Communication Monographs* 62, no. 1 (1995): 2–18.

Foucault, Michel. "What Is an Author?" In *The Foucault Reader 1984*, edited by Paul Rabinow, 101–20. New York: Knopf Doubleday, 1984.

"Full Text: Donald Trump Announces a Presidential Bid." *Washington Post*, June 16, 2015. https://www.washingtonpost.com/news/post-politics/wp/2015/06/16/full-text-donald-trump-announces-a-presidential-bid/?utm_term=.8daec1ff5eae.

Gallup, Alec, and Lydia Saad. "Americans Know Little about European Union." *Gallup*, June 16, 2004. Accessed August 9, 2016. http://www.gallup.com/poll/12043/americans-know-little-about-european-union.aspx.

Galvez, Alyshia. *Guadalupe in New York: Devotion and the Struggle for Citizenship Rights among Mexican Immigrants*. New York: New York University Press, 2009.

Gemignani, Marco, and Yolanda Hernandez-Albujar. "Hate Groups Targeting Unauthorized Immigrants in the US: Discourses, Narratives and Subjectivation Practices on Their Websites." *Ethnic and Racial Studies* 38, no. 15 (2015): 2754–70.

Glenn, Evelyn. "Citizenship and Identity." In *Race and Ethnicity in Society: The Changing Landscape*, edited by Elizabeth Higginbotham and Margaret L. Andersen, 158–65. Belmont, CA: Thomson/Wadsworth, 2006.

Goffman, Erving. *Frame Analysis: An Essay on the Organization of Experience*. New York: Harper & Row, 1974.

———. *The Presentation of the Self in Everyday Life*. London: Allen Lane, 1969.

Goldman, Alvin I. *Knowledge in a Social* World. Oxford: Oxford University Press, 1990.

Gonzales, Roberto. "Learning to Be Illegal: Undocumented Youth and Shifting Legal Contexts in the Transition to Adulthood." *American Sociological Review* 74 (2011): 602–19. doi: 10.1177/0003122411411901.

———. *Lives in Limbo: Undocumented and Coming of Age in America.* Oakland: University of California Press, 2016.

Gonzales, Roberto, and Leo Chavez. "'Awakening to a Nightmare': Abjectivity and Illegality in the Lives of Undocumented 1.5 Generation Latino Immigrants in the United States." *Current Anthropology* 53 (2012): 255–81. doi: 10.1086/665414.

Goodman, H. A. "Illegal Immigrants Benefit the U.S. Economy." *The Hill.* http://thehill.com/blogs/congress-blog/foreign-policy/203984-illegal-immigrants-benefit-the-us-economy.

Goodwin, Charles. "Professional Vision." *American Anthropologist* 96 (1994): 606–33.

"The Great Immigration Panic." *New York Times*, June 3, 2008. http://www.nytimes.com/2008/06/03/opinion/03tue1.html.

Grossberg, Lawrence. *Cultural Studies in the Future Tense.* Durham, NC: Duke University Press, 2010.

Habermas, Jürgen. "Reflections on the Linguistic Foundations of Sociology: The Christian Gauss Lectures (Princeton University, February–March 1971)." In *On the Pragmatics of Social Interaction. Preliminary Studies in the Theory of Communicative Action*, translated by B. Fultner, 1–103. Cambridge, MA: MIT Press, 1971.

Hall, Stuart. "Culture, the Media and the Ideological Effect." In *Mass Communication and Society*, edited by James Curran, Michael Gurevitch, and Janet Woollacott, 315–48. London: Open University Press, 1977.

———. *Representation: Cultural Representations and Signifying Practices.* Thousand Oaks, CA: SAGE, 1997.

Hall, Stuart, Doothy Hobson, Andrew Lowe, and Paul Willis. *Culture, Media, Language: Working Paper in Cultural Studies (1972–1979).* New York: Unwin Hyman, 2003.

Halperin, Edward C. "Do Medical Students Choose Historical Role Models Who "Look Like Me"?" *Connecticut Medicine* 79 (2015): 291–93.

Hamann, Edmund, and Jenelle Reeves. "ICE Raids, Children, Media, and Making Sense of Latino Newcomers in Flyover Country." *Anthropology & Education Quarterly* 43 (2012): 24–40. doi: 10.1111/j.1548-1492.2011.01155.x.

Hanisch, Carol. "The Personal Is Political." CarolHanisch.org, 2009. http://www.carolhanisch.org/CHwritings/PIP.html.

Hannerz, Ulf. "Cosmopolitans and Locals in World Culture." In *Global Culture: Nationalism, Globalization and Modernity*, edited by Mike Featherstone, 237–52. Thousand Oaks: SAGE, 2004.

———. "Cosmopolitans and Locals in World Culture." *Theory, Culture, Society* 7 (1990): 237–51. doi:10.1177/026327690007002014.

Haraway, Donna. *Simians, Cyborgs, and Women: The Reinvention of Nature.* New York, NY: Routledge, 1991.

———. "Situated Knowledges: The Science Question in Feminism and the Privilege of Partial Perspective." *Feminist Studies* 14 (1988): 575–99. doi: 10.2307/3178066.

Harvey, David. *The Condition of Postmodernity.* Oxford: Blackwell, 1989.

Hauser, Gerard A. "The Moral Vernacular of Human Rights Discourse." *Philosophy & Rhetoric* 41, no. 4 (2008): 440–66.

Hegde, Radha S. *Mediating Migration*. Boston: Polity Press, 2016.

Hess, Aaron. "Critical Rhetorical Ethnography: Rethinking the Place and Process of Rhetoric." *Communication Studies* 62, no. 2 (2011): 127–52.

Hier, Sean, and Joshua Greenberg. "Constructing a Discursive Crisis: Risk, Problematization and Illegal Chinese in Canada." *Ethnic and Racial Studies* 25 (2002): 490–513. http://dx.doi.org/10.1080/01419870020036701.

Higher Dreams. "Helping Undocumented Students Achieve Higher Education." Accessed August 10, 2016. http://higherdreams.org.

Holmes, Seth, and Philippe Bourgois. *Fresh Fruit, Broken Bodies: Migrant Farmworkers in the United States*. Berkeley: University of California Press, 2013.

hooks, bell. *Black Looks: Race and Representation*. New York: Routledge, 1992.

Horsti, Karina. "Global Mobility and the Media: Presenting Asylum Seekers as a Threat." *Nordic Research on Media & Communication* 24 (2003): 51, August 19, 2016. http://www.nordicom.gu.se/sites/default/files/kapitel-pdf/23_041-054.pdf.

Hseih, Steven. "Living Undocumented: A Conversation with Jose Antonio Vargas." *Nation*, May 1, 2014. https://www.thenation.com/article/living-undocumented-conversation-jose-antonio-vargas/.

"Immigration." *Gallup*. Accessed August 1, 2016. http://www.gallup.com/poll/1660/immigration.aspx.

Inda, Jonathan Xavier. "Foreign Bodies: Migrants, Parasites, and the Pathological Nation." *Discourse: Journal for Theoretical Studies in Media and Culture* 22 (2000): 46–62. doi: 10.1353/dis.2000.0006.

Institute on Taxation and Economic Policy. "Undocumented Immigrants' State and Local Tax Contributions." Last modified February 24, 2016. http://www.itep.org/immigration/.

Jaschik, Scott. "Oral History, Unprotected U.S. Government—Opposing Boston College—Argues against Researchers' Expectation of Confidentiality." *Inside Higher Ed*, July 5, 2011. https://www.insidehighered.com/news/2011/07/05/federal_government_questions_confidentiality_of_oral_history.

Jaworsky, Bernadette Nadya. *The Boundaries of Belonging: Online Work of Immigration-Related Social Movement Organizations*. New York: Palgrave Macmillan.

Jay, Martin. *Songs of Experience: Modern American and European Variations on a Universal Theme*. Berkeley: University of California Press, 2005.

Johnson, Allan. *Privilege, Power, Difference*. New York: McGraw Hill, 2006.

Jones, Bradley. "Americans' Views of Immigrants Marked by Widening Partisan, Generational Divides." *Pew Research Center*, April 15, 2016. http://www.pewresearch.org/fact-tank/2016/04/15/americans-views-of-immigrants-marked-by-widening-partisan-generational-divides/.

Jones, Jeffrey. "One in Five Voters Say Immigration Stance Critical to Vote." *Gallup*, September 9, 2015. http://www.gallup.com/poll/185381/one-five-voters-say-immigration-stance-critical-vote.aspx.

Jones, Robert P., Daniel Cox, Betsy Cooper, and Rachel Lienesch. "How Americans View Immigrants and What They Want from Immigration Reform: Findings from the 2015 American Values Atlas." *PRRI*, 2016. http://www.prri.org/research/poll-immigration-reform-views-on-immigrants/.

Jones, Robert P., Daniel Cox, E. J. Dionne Jr., William A. Galston, Betsy Cooper, and Rachel Lienesch. "How Immigration and Concerns about Cultural Changes Are Shaping the 2016 Election: Findings from the 2016 PRRI/Brookings Immigration Survey." *PRRI*, June 23, 2016. https://www.prri.org/wp-content/uploads/2016/06/PRRI-Brookings-2016-Immigration-survey-report.pdf.

"Jose Antonio Vargas." Accessed September 9, 2016. http://joseantoniovargas.com/.

Jurgens, Jeffrey. Review of *Migrant Media: Turkish Broadcasting and Multicultural Politics in Berlin*, by Kira Kosnick. *American Ethnologist* 37 (2010): 844–45. doi: 10.1111/j.1548 1425.2010.01287_14.x.

Jürgenson, Aviar. "Voluntary and Forced Migration Dichotomy on the Background of Migration Macro and Micro Theories." *Acta Historica Tallinnensia* 13 (2008): 92–117. Accessed September 1, 2016. http://www.kirj.ee/public/Acta_hist/2008/issue_2/Acta-2008-13-92-117.pdf.

Kahn, Kimberly, Katherine Spencer, and Jack Glaser. "Online Prejudice and Discrimination: From Dating to Hating." In *The Social Net: Understanding Our Online Behavior*, edited by Yair Amichai-Hamburger. Oxford: Oxford University Press, 2013. doi: 10.1093/acprof:oso/9780199639540.001.0001.

Kasinitz, Philip, John Mollenkopf, Mary Waters, and Jennifer Holdaway. *Inheriting the City: The Children of Immigrants Come of Age*. New York: Russell Sage Foundation, 2008.

KhosraviNik, Majid. "The Representation of Refugees, Asylum Seekers and Immigrants in British Newspapers: A Critical Discourse Analysis." *Journal of Language and Politics* 9 (2010): 1–28.

Killing Us Softly IV, special ed. DVD. Directed by Jean Kilbourne and Sut Jhally. Media Education Foundation, 2010.

Kim, Youna. *Transnational Migration, Media and Identity of Asian Women: Diasporic Daughters*. New York: Routledge, 2011.

King, Kendall, and Gemma Punti. "On the Margins: Undocumented Students' Narrated Experiences of (Il)legality." *Linguistics and Education* (2012): 235–49, August 19, 2016. http://dx.doi.org/10.1016/j.linged.2012.05.002.

Knobloch-Westerwick, Silvia, Cornelia Mothes, Benjamin Johnson, Axel Westerwick, and Wolfgang Donsbach. "Political Online Information Searching in Germany and the United States: Confirmation Bias, Source Credibility, and Attitude Impacts." *Journal of Communication* 65 (2015): 489–511. doi: 10.1111/jcom.12154.

Krogstad, Jens M., and Jeffrey S. Passel. "5 Facts about Illegal Immigration in the U.S." *Pew Research Center*, November 19, 2015. http://www.pewresearch.org/fact-tank/2015/11/19/5-facts-about-illegal-immigration-in-the-u-s/

Kuchinskaya, Olga. *The Politics of Invisibility: Public Knowledge about Radiation Health Effects after Chernobyl*. Cambridge, MA: MIT Press, 2014.

Kurkowska-Budzan, Marta, and Krzysztof Zamorski. *Oral History: The Challenges of Dialogue*. Philadelphia: John Benjamins, 2009.

Kuttner, Paul. "Interview with Cultural Organizer Favianna Rodriguez." *Cultural Organizing*. February 18, 2013. http://culturalorganizing.org/tag/culturestrike/.

Langellier, Kristin M. "Personal Narrative, Performance, Performativity: Two or Three Things I Know for Sure." *Text and Performance Quarterly* 19, no. 2 (1999): 125–44.

Latour, Bruno. *The Pasteurization of France*. Cambridge: Harvard University Press, 1988.

"Laura Wilkerson Confronts Jose Antonio Vargas on The Kelly File." https://www.you-tube.com/watch?v=LzR_A144gbw.

Law Office of Peter Duong. "Top 4 Most Common Immigration Fraud . . ." http://peterduonglaw.com/top-4-common-immigration-fraud-scams/.

Lazarsfeld, Paul F., and Robert K. Merton. *Mass Communication, Popular Taste, and Organized Social Action*. Indianapolis: Bobbs-Merrill, 1957.

———. "Mass Communication, Popular Taste and Organized Social Action." In *Media Studies: A Reader*, 2nd ed., edited by Paul Marris and Sue Thornham, 18–20, 22, 23. New York, NY: New York University Press, 2002.

Leadbeater, Charles, and Paul Miller. *The Pro-Am Revolution: How Enthusiasts Are Changing Our Economy and Society*. London: Demos, 2004. http://www.demos.co.uk/files/proamrevolutionfinal.pdf.

Lee, Angela, Seth Lewis, and Matthew Powers. "Audience Clicks and News Placement: A Study of Time-Lagged Influence in Online Journalism." *Communication Research* 41 (2012): 505–30. Accessed August 9, 2016. doi:10.1177/0093650212467031.

Lee, Erika. "A Nation of Immigrants and a Gatekeeping Nation: American Immigration Law and Policy." In *A Companion to American Immigration*, edited by Reed Ueda, 1–35. Urbana: University of Illinois Press, 2011. doi: 10.1002/9780470997116.ch2.

Licona, Adela. *Zines in Third Space: Radical Cooperation and Borderlands Rhetoric*. Albany: State University of New York Press, 2012.

Liptak, Adam, and Michael D. Shear. "Supreme Court Tie Blocks Obama Immigration Plan." *New York Times*, June 23, 2016. http://www.nytimes.com/2016/06/24/us/supreme-court-immigration-obama-dapa.html?_r=0.

Lockwood, Penelope. "'Someone Like Me Can Be Successful': Do College Students Need Same-Gender Role Models?" *Psychology of Women Quarterly* 30 (2006): 36–46. doi: 10.1111/j.1471-6402.2006.00260.x.

Lorde, Audre. *Sister Outsider*. Berkeley: Crossing Press, 1984.

Lorentzen, Lois Ann, ed. *Hidden Lives and Human Rights in the United States: Understanding the Controversies and Tragedies of Undocumented Immigration*. Santa Barbara, CA: Praeger, 2014.

Luibhéid, Eithne. *Entry Denied: Controlling Sexuality at the Border*. Minneapolis: University of Minnesota Press, 2002.

Lykes, M. Brinton, Kalina M. Brabeck, and Cristina J. Hunter. "Exploring Parent-Child Communication in the Context of Threat: Immigrant Families Facing Detention and Deportation in Post-9/11 USA." *Community, Work & Family* 16 (2013): 123–46. http://dx.doi.org/10.1080/13668803.2012.752997.

Lyons, Renee, Kristi Mickelson, Michael Sullivan, and James Coyne. "Coping as a Communal Process." *Journal of Social and Personal Relationships* 15 (1998): 579–605. doi: 10.1177/0265407598155001.

MacIntyre, Alasdair. *After Virtue: A Study in Moral Theory*. Notre Dame, IN: University of Notre Dame Press, 1984.

Mahler, Sarah. *American Dreaming: Immigrant Life on the Margins*. Princeton, NJ: Princeton University Press, 1995.

Marcus, George, and Michael Fischer. *Anthropology as Cultural Critique: An Experimental Moment in the Human Sciences*. Chicago: University of Chicago Press, 1986.

Martínez, Konane. "Thirty Cans of Beef Stew and a Thong: Anthropologist as Academic, Administrator, and Activist in the U.S.–Mexico Border Region." *Annals of Anthropological Practice* 31 (2009): 100–113. doi: 10.1111/j.1556-4797.2009.01021.x.

Marx, Karl. *Capital: A Critique of Political Economy*, vol. 1, *Book One: The Process of Production of Capital*. Translated by Samuel Moore and Edward Aveling, edited by Frederick Engels. Moscow: Progress, 1887.

Mascaro, Lisa. "Trump Promises Relief for 'Dreamers,' but Immigrant Advocates Are Taking No Chances." *Los Angeles Times*, February 1, 2017. http://www.latimes.com/nation/politics/trailguide/la-na-trailguide-updates-1481150209-htmlstory.html.

Maslow, Abraham. "A Theory of Human Motivation." *Psychological Review* 50 (1943): 370–96. doi: 10.1037/h0054346.

McGuire, Sharon, and Jane Georges. "Undocumentedness and Liminality as Health Variables." *Advances in Nursing Science* 26 (2003): 185–95. http://citeseerx.ist.psu.edu/viewdoc/download?doi=10.1.1.501.8479&rep=rep1&type=pdf.

McIntosh, Peggy. "White Privilege: Unpacking the Invisible Backpack." Excerpt from Working Paper 189 (1989). http://www.deanza.edu/faculty/lewisjulie/White%20Priviledge%20Unpacking%20the%20Invisible%20Knapsack.pdf.

Medina, Jennifer. "Too Scared to Report Sexual Abuse. The Fear: Deportation." *New York Times*, April 30, 2017. https://www.nytimes.com/2017/04/30/us/immigrants-deportation-sexual-abuse.html.

"Meet the Undocumented Immigrant Who Works in a Trump Hotel." YouTube Video, 2:43. Posted by "NewLeftMedia," August 17, 2015. https://www.youtube.com/watch?v=e-r9E5n5FnM.

Mendoza, Sylvia. "Building False Crisis: The Role of the Media Covering Undocumented Immigrants." *Hispanic Outlook in Higher Education* 25 (2015): 10–12. http://www.hispanicoutlook.com/featured-articles/2015/7/14/building-false-crisis-the-role-of-the-media-covering-undocumented-immigrants.

Mercer. "Mercer 2015 Cost of Living Rankings." https://www.imercer.com/content/2015-cost-of-living-infographic.aspx.

Merolla, Jennifer, S. Karthick Ramakrishnan, and Chris Haynes. "'Illegal,' 'Undocumented,' or 'Unauthorized': Equivalency Frames, Issues Frames, and Public Opinion on Immigration." *Perspectives on Politics* 11 (2013): 789–807. doi:10.1017/S1537592713002077

Mettler, Katie. "'This Is Really Unprecedented': ICE Detains Woman Seeking Domestic Abuse Protection at Texas Courthouse." *Washington Post*, February 16, 2017. https://www.washingtonpost.com/news/morning-mix/wp/2017/02/16/this-is-really-unprecedented-ice-detains-woman-seeking-domestic-abuse-protection-at-texas-courthouse/?utm_term=.c10c48f190fb.

Meyrowitz, Joshua. *No Sense of Place: The Impact of Electronic Media on Social Behavior.* London: Oxford University Press, 1985.

Migration Policy Institute. "Profile of the Unauthorized Population: New York." http://www.migrationpolicy.org/data/unauthorized-immigrant-population/state/NY.

Mills, Charles. "White Ignorance and Hermeneutical Injustice: A Comment on Medina and Fricker." *Social Epistemology Review and Reply Collective* 3 (2013): 38–43.

Moser, Linda Trinh, and Kathryn West. *American Multicultural Identity.* Ipswich, MA: Salem Press, 2014.

Moses, Jonathan W. "The American Century? Migration and the Voluntary Social Contract." *Politics & Society* 37 (2009): 454–76. Accessed September 1, 2016. doi: 10.1177/0032329209338928.

Neuenschwander, John A. *A Guide to Oral History and the Law*. Oxford: Oxford University Press, 2014.

Newton, Lina. *Illegal, Alien, or Immigrant: The Politics of Immigration Reform*. New York: New York University Press, 2008.

New York City Mayor's Office of Immigrant Affairs. "Frequently Asked Questions." http://www1.nyc.gov/site/immigrants/about/frequently-asked-questions.page.

New York Immigration Coalition. "Media: NYIC in the News." http://www.thenyic.org/news.

Ngai, Mae. *Impossible Subjects: Illegal Aliens and the Making of Modern America*. Princeton, NJ: Princeton University Press, 2004.

Nicholls, Walter J. *The DREAMers: How the Undocumented Youth Movement Transformed the Immigrant Rights Debate*. Redwood City, CA: Stanford University Press, 2013.

Noguerón-Liu, Silvia. "Usted Va al Capitolio También?: Adult Immigrants' Positioning in Response to News and Digital Media about Immigration Policy." *Anthropology & Education Quarterly* 47 (2016): 113–29. doi: 10.1111/aeq.12144.

Oakeshott, Michael. *Experience and Its Modes*. Cambridge: Cambridge University Press, 1986.

O'Brien, Gerald V. "Indigestible Food, Conquering Hordes, and Waste Materials: Metaphors of Immigrants and the Early Immigration Restriction Debate in the United States." *Metaphor and Symbol* 18 (2003): 33. doi: 10.1207/S15327868MS1801_3.

Ono, Kent, and John Sloop. *Shifting Borders: Rhetoric, Immigration, and California's Proposition 187*. Philadelphia: Temple University Press, 2002.

Oral History Association. "Principles and Best Practices." http://www.oralhistory.org/about/principles-and-practices/.

Out of the Shadows. Produced by John Howard. 2013. Unboxed Voices, 2013. Documentary.

Pace, Richard. "Television's Interpellation: Heeding, Missing, Ignoring, and Resisting the Call for Pan-National Identity in the Brazilian Amazon." *American Anthropologist* 111 (2009): 407–19. Accessed August 9, 2016. doi: 10.1111/j.1548-1433.2009.01151.x.

Passel, Jeffrey S., and D'Vera Cohn. "As Mexican Share Declined, U.S. Unauthorized Immigrant Population Fell in 2015 Below Recession Level." *Pew Research Center*, April 25, 2017. http://www.pewresearch.org/fact-tank/2017/04/25/as-mexican-share-declined-u-s-unauthorized-immigrant-population-fell-in-2015-below-recession-level/.

———. "Overall Number of U.S. Unauthorized Immigrants Holds Steady since 2009." *Pew Research Center*, September 20, 2016. http://www.pewhispanic.org/2016/09/20/overall-number-of-u-s-unauthorized-immigrants-holds-steady-since-2009/.

Passel, Jeffrey S., D'Vera Cohn, Jens M. Krogstad, and Ana Gonzalez-Barrera. "As Growth Stalls, Unauthorized Immigrant Population Becomes More Settled." *Pew Research Center*. Last modified September 3, 2014. http://www.pewhispanic.org/2014/09/03/as-growth-stalls-unauthorized-immigrant-population-becomes-more-settled/#fn-20779-4.

Passel, Jeffrey S., D'Vera Cohn, and Molly Rohal. "Unauthorized Immigrant Totals Rise in 7 States, Fall in 14: Decline in Those from Mexico Fuels Most State Decreases." *Pew Research Center*, November 18, 2014. http://www.pewhispanic.org/files/2014/11/2014-11-18_unauthorized-immigration.pdf.

Perea, Juan F. "Am I American or Not? Reflections on Citizenship, Americanization, and Race." In *Immigration and Citizenship*, edited by Noah M. J. Pickus, 49–76. Lanham: Rowman & Littlefield, 1998. doi: 10.1111/j.1467-923X.2007.00864.x.

Philo, Greg. "Active Audiences and the Construction of Public Knowledge." *Journalism Studies* 9 (2008): 535–44. Accessed August 9, 2016. http://dx.doi.org/10.1080/14616700802114217.

Pieterse, Jan Nederveen. *Globalization & Culture: Global Melange*. Lanham, MD: Rowman & Littlefield, 2004.

Pires, Guilherme, and John Stanton. *Ethnic Marketing: Culturally Sensitive Theory and Practice*. New York: Routledge, 2015.

Pribilsky, Jason. *La Chulla Vida: Gender, Migration, and the Family in Andean Ecuador and New York City*. Syracuse: Syracuse University Press, 2007.

Proctor, Robert. "Agnotology: A Missing Term to Describe the Cultural Production of Ignorance." In *Agnotology: The Making and Unmaking of Ignorance*, edited by Robert Proctor and Londa Schiebinger. Stanford, CA: Stanford University Press, 2008.

"Public Tunes Out Recent News." *Times Mirror Center for the Public and the Press*, May 19, 1994. Accessed August 9, 2016. http://www.people-press.org/1994/05/19/public-tunes-out-recent-news/.

Quesada, James, Sonya Arreola, Alex Kral, Sahar Khoury, Kurt Organista, and Paula Worby. "'As Good as It Gets': Undocumented Latino Day Laborers Negotiating Discrimination in San Francisco and Berkeley, California, USA." *City and Society* 26 (2014): 29–50. doi: 10.1111/ciso.12033.

Raine, Lee, and Mary Madden. "Americans' Views on Government Surveillance Programs." *Pew Research Center*, March 16, 2015. http://www.pewinternet.org/2015/03/16/americans-views-on-government-surveillance-programs/.

Ramirez, Rosa. "Mexican Immigrants Less Educated, Lowest Paid." *NationalJournal.com*, December 7, 2012. http://news.yahoo.com/mexican-immigrants-less-educated-lowest-paid-163116545--politics.html.

Randolph Capps, Leighton Ku, Michael E. Fix, Chris Furgiuele, Jeffrey S. Passel, Rajeev Ramchand, Scott McNiven, and Dan Perez-Lopez. "How Are Immigrants Faring after Welfare Reform? Preliminary Evidence from Los Angeles and New York City." *Urban Institute* (2002): 1–99. http://www.urban.org/research/publication/how-are-immigrants-faring-after-welfare-reform/view/full_report.

Raymond-Flesch, Marissa, Rachel Siemons, Nadereh Pourat, Ken Jacobs, and Claire Brindis. "'There Is No Help Out There and if There Is, It's Really Hard to Find': A Qualitative Study of the Health Concerns and Health Care Access of Latino 'Dreamers.'" *Journal of Adolescent Health* 55 (2014): S18–S19. doi: 10.1016/j.jadohealth.2013.10.051.

Rodríguez, Juana María. *Queer Latinidad: Identity Practices, Discursive Spaces*. New York, NY: New York University Press, 2003.

Rowland, Robert. "Mode of Discourse or Paradigm." *Communication Monographs* 54 (1987): 264–75.

Rumbaut, Rubén, and Walter Ewing. "The Myth of Immigrant Criminality and the Paradox of Assimilation: Incarceration Rates among Native and Foreign-Born Men." *Immigration Policy Center* (2007): 1–20. https://www.americanimmigrationcouncil. org/sites/default/files/research/Imm%20Criminality%20%28IPC%29.pdf

Ryo, Emily. "Deciding to Cross Norms and Economics of Unauthorized Migration." *American Sociological Review* 78 (2013): 574–603. Accessed August 10, 2016. http://asr.sagepub.com/content/78/4/574.abstract.

Sabo, Samantha, and Alison Elizabeth Lee. "The Spillover of US Immigration Policy on Citizens and Permanent Residents of Mexican Descent: How Internalizing "Illegality" Impacts Public Health in the Borderlands." *Frontiers in Public Health* 3 (2015): 155. https://www.ncbi.nlm.nih.gov/pmc/articles/PMC4464055/.

Saghaye-Biria, Hakima. "American Muslims as Radicals? A Critical Discourse Analysis of the U.S. Congressional Hearing on 'The Extent of Radicalization in the American Muslim Community and That Community's Response.'" *Discourse & Society* 25 (2012): 508–24.

Said, Edward. *Orientalism*. London: Penguin, 2003.

Salgado, Julio. "I Exist." Julio Saldago Art. June 24, 2011. http://juliosalgadoart.com/post/6892057848/lets-do-this.

Santa Ana, Otto. *Brown Tide Rising: Metaphors of Latinos in Contemporary American Public Discourse*. Austin: University of Texas Press, 2002.

———. "'Like an Animal I was Treated': Anti-Immigrant Metaphor in U.S. Public Discourse." *Discourse and Society* 10 (1999): 191–224. doi: 10.1177/0957926599010002004.

Sargent, Greg. "The First Big Political War of Trump's Presidency Will Be Explosive." *Washington Post*, November 10, 2016. https://www.washingtonpost.com/blogs/plum-line/wp/2016/11/10/the-first-big-political-war-of-trumps-presidency-will-be-explosive/?utm_term=.6fac25981514.

Sarup, Madan. *Identity, Culture, and the Postmodern World*. Edinburgh: Edinburgh University Press, 1996.

Sassen, Saskia. "Spatialities and Temporalities of the Global: Elements for a Theorization." *Public Culture* 12 (2000): 215–32. doi:10.1215/08992363-12-1-215.

Scheufele, Dietram A. "Framing as a Theory of Media Effects." *Journal of Communication* 49 (1999): 103–22. doi: 10.1111/j.1460-2466.1999.tb02784.x.

Schroeder, David, John Dovidio, Mark Sibicky, Linda Matthews, and Judith Allen. "Empathic Concern and Helping Behavior: Egoism or Altruism?" *Journal of Experimental Social Psychology* 24 (1988): 333–53. https://doi.org/10.1016/0022-1031(88)90024-8.

Scott, James. *Domination and the Arts of Resistance: Hidden Transcripts*. New Haven, CT: Yale University Press, 1992.

Scott, Joan W. "The Evidence of Experience," *Critical Inquiry* 17, no. 4 (1991): 797.

Sheldon, Pavica. "Profiling the Non-Users: Examination of Life-Position Indicators, Sensation Seeking, Shyness, and Loneliness among Users and Non-Users of Social Network Sites." *Computers in Human Behavior* 28 (2012): 1960–965. doi: 10.1016/j.chb.2012.05.016.

Shome, Raka, and Radha Hedge. "Postcolonial Approaches to Communication: Charting the Terrain, Engaging the Intersections." *Communication Theory* 12 (2002): 249–70. doi: 10.1111/j.1468-2885.2002.tb00269.x.

Shwer, Mikaela. *No Le Digas A Nadie (Don't Tell Anyone)*. Film. Portret Films. 2015.

Simon, Rita. *Public Opinion and the Immigrant: Print Media Coverage, 1880–1980*. Lexington, KY: Lexington Books, 1985.

Smith, Rebecca. "Immigrants' Right to Workers' Comp: Undocumented Foreign-Born Workers Are Often Hired for the Most Dangerous and Lowest Paid Jobs. They Deserve Workers' Compensation Protections—But Don't Always Get Them." *Trial*, April 1, 2004. http://www.highbeam.com/doc/1G1-115693626.html.

Smith, Robert. *Mexican New York: Transnational Lives of New Immigrants*. Berkeley: University of California Press, 2006.

Somanader, Tanya. "'We Were Strangers Once, Too': The President Announces New Steps on Immigration." *White House Blog*, last modified November 20, 2014. https://www.whitehouse.gov/blog/2014/11/20/we-were-strangers-once-too-president-announces-new-steps-immigration.

Steinberg, Sheila Lakshmi. "Undocumented Immigrants or Illegal Aliens? Southwestern Media Portrayals of Latino Immigrants." *Humboldt Journal of Social Relations* 28 (2004): 109–33.

Stop Notario Fraud. "Who Is Authorized to Help Immigrants with Their Legal Matters?" http://www.stopnotariofraud.org/faq.php.

Sullivan, Shannon, and Nancy Tuana. "White Ignorance and Colonial Oppression: Or, Why I Know So Little about Puerto Rico." In *Race and Epistemologies of Ignorance*, edited by Shannon Sullivan and Nancy Tuana. New York: State University of New York Press, 2007.

Teranishi, Robert, Carola Suárez-Orozco, and Marcelo Suárez-Orozco. "In the Shadows of the Ivory Tower: Undocumented Undergraduates and the Liminal State of Immigration Reform." *Institute for Immigration, Globalization, & Education* (2015): 1–32. http://undocuscholars.org/assets/undocuscholarsreport2015.pdf

Thweatt, Tatyana S. "Attitudes towards New Americans in the Local Press: A Critical Discourse Analysis." *North Dakota Journal of Speech and Theatre* 18 (2005): 25–43.

Toffler, Alvin. *The Third Wave: The Classic Study of Tomorrow*. New York: Bantam, 1980.

Trebbe, Joachim, and Philomen Schoenhagen. "Ethnic Minorities in the Mass Media: Always the Same and Always Negative." Presentation, Annual Meeting of the International Communication Association, Montreal, Quebec, Canada. May 21, 2008.

Trepte, Sabine, and Leonard Reinecke, eds. *Privacy Online Perspectives on Privacy and Self-Disclosure in the Social Web*. New York: Springer-Verlag, 2011.

Tuana, Nancy. "Conceptualizing Moral Literacy." *Journal of Educational Administration* 45 (2007): 364–78, http://dx.doi.org/10.1108/09578230710762409.

Turner, William. *Libellus de re herbaria novus*. London: Priv. Print, 1877. LYRASIS Members and Sloan Foundation. https://archive.org/details/libellusdereherb00turn.

Udris, Reinis. "Cyberbullying among High School Students in Japan: Development and Validation of the Online Disinhibition Scale." *Computers in Human Behavior* 41 (2014): 253–61. doi: 10.1016/j.chb.2014.09.036.

United States Citizenship and Immigration Services. "Asylum." Last modified August 6, 2015. https://www.uscis.gov/humanitarian/refugees-asylum/asylum.

———. "Common Scams." Last modified August, 15, 2016. https://www.uscis.gov/avoid-scams/common-scams.

———. "Grounds for Revocation of Naturalization." Last modified August 3, 2016. https://www.uscis.gov/policymanual/HTML/PolicyManual-Volume12-PartL-Chapter2.html.

———. "Number of I-821D, Consideration of Deferred Action for Childhood Arrivals by Fiscal Year, Quarter, Intake, Biometrics and Case Status: 2012–2016 (March 31)." https://www.uscis.gov/sites/default/files/USCIS/Resources/Reports%20and%20Studies/Immigration%20Forms%20Data/All%20Form%20Types/DACA/I821d_performancedata_fy2016_qtr2.pdf.

———. "What Are the Benefits and Responsibilities of Citizenship?" In *A Guide to Naturalization*. Washington, DC: USCIS, 2012. Accessed August 1, 2016. https://www.uscis.gov/sites/default/files/files/article/chapter2.pdf.

United States Committee on the Judiciary. Senate. *Comprehensive Immigration Reform: Hearings before the United States Senate Committee on the Judiciary*. 113th Cong. February 13, 2013. https://www.judiciary.senate.gov/imo/media/doc/2-13-13VargasTestimony.pdf.

United States Customs and Border Protection. "Reporting Illegal Activity." Accessed October 29, 2016. https://help.cbp.gov/app/answers/detail/a_id/735/~/reporting-illegal-activity.

United States Department of Homeland Security. "Yearbook of Immigration Statistics: 2014 Enforcement Actions." *U.S. Department of Homeland Security* (2016): 1–122. Accessed September 23, 2016. https://www.dhs.gov/sites/default/files/publications/ois_yb_2014.pdf.

United States Immigration and Customs Enforcement. "ICE Overview 2016." Accessed October 29, 2016. https://www.ice.gov/overview-2016.

United States v. Brignoni-Ponce, 422 U.S. 873 (1975).

United We Dream. "How Do I Talk to the Community about What the President Has Announced?" Accessed July 15, 2016. https://docs.google.com/file/d/0B2H_VZDWC2OzZDB4UGx3Qi1NbkU/edit.

———. "Mayors Representing over 1 Million NJ Residents Call on Legislature to Pass Tuition Equity & State Aid Bill for Undocumented Students." Accessed July 1, 2016. http://unitedwedream.org/press-releases/mayors-representing-1-million-nj-residents-call-legislature-pass-tuition-equity-state-aid-bill-undocumented-students/.

———. "United We Dream Condemns Rep. Goodlatte's Comments Opposing Citizenship for DREAMers and Families." Accessed October 30, 2016. http://unitedwedream.org/press-releases/united-we-dream-condemns-rep-goodlattes-comments-opposing-citizenship-for-dreamers-and-families/.

———. "UWD Newsroom." https://unitedwedream.org/news/

Valencia, Stephanie. "President Obama on Obstruction of the DREAM Act: "Maybe My Biggest Disappointment" of Last Weeks." *White House Blog*, December 23, 2010. https://whitehouse.gov/blog/2010/12/23/president-obama-obstruction-dream-act-maybe-my-biggest-disappointment-last-weeks.

Van Dijk, Teun A. "Ideologies, Racism, Discourse: Debates on Immigration and Ethnic Issues." In *Comparative Perspectives on Racism*, edited by Jessika ter Wal and Maykel Verkuyten, 91–116. Aldershot: Ashgate, 2000.

———. *Racism and the Press*. London: Routledge, 1991.

Van Gennep, Arnold. *The Rites of Passage*. London: Routledge, 1960.

Vargas, Jose Antonio. *Documented: A Film by an Undocumented American*. Documentary.

Walzter, Luke. "On Supporting Undocumented Students at CUNY." City University of New York. https://tlc.commons.gc.cuny.edu/2017/01/25/on-supporting-undocumented-students-at-cuny/.

Warner, Michael. "Publics and Counterpublics." *Public Culture* 14 (2002): 49–90. https://muse.jhu.edu/article/26277.

Warnick, Barbara. "The Narrative Paradigm, Another Story." *Quarterly Journal of Speech* 73 (1987): 172–82. https://www.bc.edu/res/gssw-research-home/funding/proposal-development/_jcr_content/content/download_57/file.res/Warnick,%20'The%20Narrative%20Paradigm%20Another%20Story'.pdf.

We Are Mitú. "What My Undocumented Parents Sacrificed for Me." YouTube video, 01:06. Posted [October 2015]. https://youtube.com/watch?v=RtgK1tjSfSk.

"What's Next for Ethnic Media?" *Pew Research Center*, August 21, 2006. http://www.journalism.org/2006/08/21/whats-next-for-the-ethnic-media/.

Williams, Raymond. *Culture & Society 1780–1950*. New York: Columbia University Press, 1963.

———. *Keywords: A Vocabulary of Culture and Society*. New York: Oxford University Press, 1976.

Willink, Kate. *Bringing Desegregation Home: Memories of the Struggle toward School Integration in Rural North Carolina*. New York: Palgrave-Macmillan, 2009.

Wodak, Ruth. "The Genesis of Racist Discourse in Austria since 1989." In *Texts and Practices: Readings in Critical Discourse Analysis*, edited by Carmen Rosa Caldas-Coulthard and Malcolm Coulthard, 107–28. New York: Routledge, 1996.

Ye Hee Lee, Michelle. "Clinton's Inaccurate Claim That Immigrant Detention Facilities Have a Legal Requirement to Fill Beds." *Washington Post*, May 15, 2015. https://www.washingtonpost.com/news/fact-checker/wp/2015/05/15/clintons-inaccurate-claim-that-immigrant-detention-facilities-have-a-legal-requirement-to-fill-beds/.

Yew, Chay, David Roman, and Craig Lucas. *The Hyphenated American: Four Plays: Red, Scissors, A Beautiful Country, and Wonderland*. New York: Grove Press, 2002.

Yow, Valerie Raleigh. *Recording Oral History: A Guide for the Humanities and Social Sciences*. Walnut Creek, CA: Altamira Press, 2005.

Zamora, Javier. "Let me Try Again." In *Kenyon Review: July/August 2016*. Edited by David H. Lynn. Gambler: Kenyon Review, 2016. http://www.kenyonreview.org/journal/julyaug-2016/selections/javier-zamora/.

———. "Looking at a Coyote." *Poetry Foundation*. Last modified November 2015. https://www.poetryfoundation.org/poetrymagazine/poems/detail/58468.

Zelizer, Barbie. "Cannibalizing Memory in the Global Flow of News." In *On Media Memory: Collective Memory in a New Media Age*, edited by Motti Nieger, Oren Meyers, and Eyal Zandberg, 27–36. New York: Palgrave Macmillan, 2011. http://link.springer.com/chapter/10.1057%2F9780230307070_2.

Zembylas, Michalinos. "Agamben's Theory of Biopower and Immigrants/Refugees/Asylum Seekers: Discourses of Citizenship and the Implications." *Journal of Curriculum Theorizing* 26 (2010): 33.

INDEX

Abrams, Kathryn 77, 78
cultural citizenship 109
Abrego, Leisy Janey 56
Aca, Ricardo 65, 76, 77, 111, 143
*Meet the Undocumented Immigrant
Who Works in a Trump
Hotel* 76, 111
academic research on migration 98, 165
avenues of future study 165–8
communication studies in 9
intersectionality, as it relates to 22
role of nationalism in anti-immigrant
sentiment 10
underrepresented perspectives 4,
8, 9, 12
activism
online 26
storytelling as strategy of 2, 3, 22,
28 (*see also* Chávez, Karma;
interactionality)
Adam 75, 150
Africa 69
immigration on the rise from 9, 20
Ahram 138
Albania 9, 50
Alcoff, Linda 86, 103, 154, 163
"The Problem of Speaking for
Others" 79, 84, 86, 87, 118
Alexander, Michelle 22. *See also*
intersectionality; *New Jim
Crow, The*

Allen, Judith
"egoistic response" 53
Almirañez, Katherine Chua 27–30, 31,
32, 33, 34, 47, 68, 115, 136
amateur professionalism 110, 116, 123
America. *See* United States
American audiences 152
American Immigration Council 88
Americans (US-born citizens) 116, 136,
137, 138, 145, 146, 148, 150, 151,
153, 155, 158, 162, 167
Anderson, Chris
"The Long Tail" 122, 123
See also digital activism, themes of
Angy 23, 72, 73, 95, 102, 103, 104, 112,
113, 115, 118, 124, 125, 140, 141,
147, 148, 155
anti-immigrant sentiment
Bracero program 146, 147
"celebration" *vs.* "degradation"
portrayal 29
"One-note" narrative 99
portrayal in media 3
stereotypes 3
United States v. Brignoni-Ponce 22
See also Kelly, Megyn; Republican
National Convention;
villainization
Anzaldúa, Gloria 30
Borderlands/La Frontera 79, 146
See also reclaimant narrative

217

CPSIA information can be obtained
at www.ICGtesting.com
Printed in the USA
BVHW031343090120
569012BV00003B/12/P

9 780190 917166